P9-DCJ-900

DISCARD

382
D44w

Phillips Library
Bethany College
Bethany, W. Va. 26032

DISCARD

U.S.-CHINESE TRADE NEGOTIATIONS

U.S.-CHINESE TRADE NEGOTIATIONS

John W. De Pauw

PRAEGER

PRAEGER SPECIAL STUDIES • PRAEGER SCIENTIFIC

Library of Congress Cataloging in Publication Data

De Pauw, John Whylen, 1937–
    U.S.-Chinese trade negotiations.

    (Praeger scientific)
    Bibliography: p.
    Includes index.
    1. United States--Commercial treaties. 2. China--
Commercial treaties. 3. United States--Commerce--China.
4. China--Commerce--United States. I. Title.
HF1732.C5D4 1981   382'.0951'073   80-27254
ISBN 0-03-056688-6

Published in 1981 by Praeger Publishers
CBS Educational and Professional Publishing
A Division of CBS, Inc.
521 Fifth Avenue, New York, New York 10175 U.S.A.

© 1981 by Praeger Publishers

All rights reserved

123456789   145   987654321

Printed in the United States of America

To the memory of my parents,

Victor and Hazel De Pauw

382
D44u

FOREWORD
by Catherine Bedell

The decade-long U.S.-Chinese efforts toward diplomatic and economic normalization culminated in the passage by Congress on January 24, 1980, of the U.S.-China trade agreement. This agreement, so very important to the future of U.S.-China trade, had been reached in July 1979 and was forwarded to Congress in October. President Carter, in his request for approval of the agreement, stated:

> Conclusion of this agreement is the most important step we can take to provide greater economic benefits to both countries from this relationship. It will also give further impetus to the progress we have made in our overall relationship since normalization of our diplomatic relations earlier this year.

The two countries have then in a relatively short period of time made much progress in the normalization of relations, particularly in the area of trade. Indeed, trade between the United States and China has increased dramatically, to the point where total trade turnover between the two countries in 1980 will possibly approach $4.0 billion.

Although such increased trade has to some extent demystified trading procedures and standardized U.S. approaches to the China market, actual commercial practices have not changed much. Yet paradoxically, in the words of one U.S. scholar writing in 1977, "we woefully lack information about the actual across-the-table negotiations and the specific authority vested in Chinese officials to make decisions." In order to help fill this informational void, the author of this book, Dr. John W. De Pauw, has done a thorough job of examining the process of business negotiations with the People's Republic of China. He has carefully analyzed the governmental and nongovernmental impediments—both U.S. and Chinese—faced by U.S. firms undertaking commercial negotiations with the Chinese government. I commend this book as valuable reading for all interested in U.S.-Chinese relations—academician, businessman, and government decision maker alike.

Chairman,
U.S. International Trade Commission

FOREWORD
by Jon Holstine

The resurgence of U.S. trade with China in the years since
1971 had its origins in the events surrounding the Nixon administration's early search for political rapprochement with China. President
Jimmy Carter's historic announcement in mid-December 1978 that the
United States would formally recognize the People's Republic of China
as of January 1, 1979, brought to fruition the process initiated by
President Richard Nixon some years earlier. Leaving aside debates
about strategic benefits, which rest on common U.S. and Chinese
perceptions of dangers represented by the Soviet Union, and disgruntle-
ment in some quarters at the precipitate manner in which the move
was accomplished, there was no doubt that the United States would return to a market that virtually had been closed to it for some 30 years.
It is this aspect of the new situation that occasions this book.

Dr. De Pauw has written this book for the thoughtful businessman, scholar, or government official who is interested in prospects
of trade with the People's Republic of China (PRC). Such a book is
necessary, because trade with China is not quite like trade with any
other country. China has been through a number of revolutions since
the turn of the century, some of the most violent of which have occurred since the 1949 take-over by the Communists. It has embraced
an alien ideology, communism; allied itself with its Communist neigh-
bors; and then fallen out with them, especially the Soviet Union and
Vietnam. It has sought to develop its agriculture and industry with
sparse outside assistance and plentiful domestic labor, mainly making
its way alone. Most recently the PRC has resolved to follow ways it
earlier shunned, electing to obtain capital and technical expertise
from the Western nations, thus creating a market for the businessman who can provide what China needs on the right terms.

As the reader will discover from Dr. De Pauw's analysis, each
of China's turns over the last three or four decades has left its mark
on the way the Chinese operate. Today the U.S. businessman con-
fronts a nation of almost a billion people who use both traditional and
modern approaches to industry, agriculture, and commerce. The
pursuit of mutually rewarding transactions will be a hazardous, difficult, and often baffling operation. This volume offers the reader,
whether an actual or a prospective China trader, an analyst of Chinese affairs, or a student of East-West trade, an appreciation of the
many obstacles, pitfalls, and frustrations that mark U.S.-Chinese
commercial negotiations.

Dr. De Pauw's description of trade with the PRC is structural in approach. Socialist states seem to thrive on bureaucracy, rivaled in such efforts only by their trade apparatus and perhaps by that of the U.S. government. For that reason this account is a highly useful introduction to the officialdom that governs the PRC's trade and, where appropriate, U.S. trade administration.

At the same time Dr. De Pauw writes about actual business experience, drawing on case studies provided by questionnaire material and in-depth interviews. The case studies are useful in that they exemplify the operation of the institutions that Dr. De Pauw describes. There is no substitute for experience, however, and China can provide the new trader with much of that, in abundant measure, in a relatively short time.

Dr. De Pauw's combination of institutional analysis and case study experience provides the reader with useful insights into the dynamics of the Chinese trading apparatus, but he does not neglect the larger considerations surrounding these operations. Historical tendencies are not overcome in a decade or even a century, despite mobilization of very capable social controls. For that reason trading with China will never operate entirely according to purely commercial imperatives. Failure to remain aware of the larger context of Sino-American trade relations, including political and diplomatic departures that occur suddenly, can permit the unwary to take a disastrous course.

If trade with the Soviet Union is fraught with political twists and turns, so will trade with China be fraught with political uncertainties. While the same sort of political difficulties now seem less likely in the case of China, trade with that country offers, along with a tremendous prospect for success, a great opportunity for frustration. Dr. De Pauw's analysis has the advantage of having seen the political difficulties and frustrations that have warped trade opportunities with the Soviet Union. Trading with China offers a significant opportunity. Yet it should be explored with foresight, and Dr. De Pauw's study can assist the reader in looking clearly at the prospects offered by the resurgent China market.

Staff Consultant,
House Foreign Affairs Committee
Asian and Pacific Affairs

ACKNOWLEDGMENTS

This study owes much to the assistance and encouragement of many people. I accept full responsibility for all conclusions reached, but wish to acknowledge and express my gratitude and appreciation to those who have helped: to Hugh Donaghue and Patty Garrett of the Control Data Corporation for their beneficial assistance and support; to John Phillip Emerson, Jon Holstine, and Jeanette Pinard, who helped me avoid many scholarly pitfalls and failings; to Catherine Bedell, former Chairman and Commissioner at the U.S. International Trade Commission, for her unfailing encouragement and friendship; to Dorothy Berkowitz and Pat Greer of the U.S. International Trade Commission for their bibliographical aid; to J. Dale Pafenberg, William Carr, Mike Uretsky, William Snow, Harold Taylor, Stan Garil, John MacHatton, C. Ross Cunningham, and Col. William Little, who continually reminded me that it could be done; to Donna Grigsby, who poured much effort into the typing and proofing of the manuscript; and finally to my wife Barbara, daughter Jolie, and son Benjamin, without whom this study probably would never have been completed.

CONTENTS

LIST OF FIGURES AND TABLES

U.S.-CHINESE TRADE NEGOTIATIONS

1

INTRODUCTION

The Chinese, with a documented history of almost 4,000 years, have been trading with the Western world for a considerable part of that time. Silk, for example, was a Chinese secret and monopoly until the silkworm, smuggled into Europe about A.D. 550, was traded for thoroughbred horses, colored glass, myrrh, wool, and linen. [1] Marco Polo's tales of travel and adventure gave the thirteenth-century Western world one of its glimpses of the fabled "Middle Kingdom."* His account of the great court of the Mongol Kublai Khan and China's peoples was the first detailed record of China by a European. At that time Chinese achievements in literature, philosophy, art, and craftsmanship were among the highest in the world. Christopher Columbus, perhaps lured by fabulous tales of unparalleled wealth and untold riches, sailed for the Middle Kingdom but found America. Legions of explorers and merchants dreaming of a direct route to the treasures of the Orient followed Columbus.

Just as Western trade with China has a long history, so do U.S. commercial contacts with China. In fact, the China trade proved to be something of a godsend for the United States in the first years following independence. Barred from the rich "sugar triangle" trade with the British Caribbean islands, the merchants of the big eastern seaboard cities found the China trade, particularly tea from Canton, to be at least a partial replacement for the lost West Indies trade. [2] Among the Chinese the Americans were regarded as the "new people." Of interest is the journal of a U.S. merchant that records the following observations on the subject of price "negotiations" with the Chinese.

---

*The Chinese name for China, Chung Kuo, means "Middle Kingdom."

1

"You are not Englishman?" said he. "No." "But you
speak English word, and when you first come, I no can
tell difference; but now I understand very well. When I
speak Englishman his price, he say, 'So much,—take it,
—let alone.' I tell him, 'No, my friend, I give you so
much.' He look at me,—'Go to hell, you damned rascal;
what! you come here,—set a price my goods?' Truly,
Massa Typan, I see very well you no hap Englishman.
All Chinaman very much love your country."

He further observed:

Thus far, it may be supposed, the fellow's remarks
pleased me. Justice obliges me to add his [the Chinese
merchant's] conclusion: "All men come first time China
very good gentleman, all same you. I think two three
time more you come Canton you make all same Englishman too."[3]

This perception by the Chinese merchant, so important in interpersonal relations (as will be pointed out in Chapter 3), could, if typical,
explain the Chinese penchant for dealing with "old friends," and the
time and patience required to prove friendship in commercial negotiations.

Americans have long dreamed of penetrating the Chinese market. The "kerosene sellers" of yesterday perhaps have their counterparts in the soft drink salesmen of today. All are transfixed by the
thought of hundreds of millions of Chinese customers. A Guaranty
Trust Company of New York pamphlet, Trading with China: Methods
Found Successful in Dealing with the Chinese, written in 1919, suggested that China "is a vast field of opportunity that has hardly been
scratched—a field that will yield a rich harvest to the American who
cultivates it with intelligence and understanding."[4] This observation
perhaps has relevance for today's U.S. businessman interested in
China trade.

Such optimism concerning the China market must be tempered
with the observation that the U.S. salesman's dream of millions of
Chinese customers are forgotten when he realizes that the millions
of Chinese customers are not necessarily consumers with money to
pay for foreign goods. A deputy minister of foreign trade, Chen Jie,
echoed this point in May 1979, at the initialing of the U.S.-China
Trade Agreement, when he hailed the agreement as "a major step
toward full normalization" of Chinese-American economic relations,
but indicated that trade between China and the United States will develop slowly. Specifically, according to Mr. Chen, "The borrowing

[to finance trade] from our side is based on our ability to pay. We still stick to self-reliance and hard work. . . . If I cannot pay, I will not borrow.''[5]

The resurgence of U.S. trade with China in the years since 1971 had its origins in the events surrounding the Nixon administration's search for political rapprochement with China beginning in January 1969.[6] President Nixon's trip to China in February 1972 was but the culmination of a U.S. initiative begun in 1969 to resume U.S.-Chinese commercial relations.[7] Parenthetically, it is interesting that the gradual restoration of U.S. diplomatic relations with China is similar to the efforts described in Chapter 3 of many U.S. companies to establish contacts with the appropriate foreign trade organizations and end users.

The efforts to establish the normalization of diplomatic relations with China did not, of course, happen overnight. In March 1969, for example, according to Henry Kissinger, "Chinese-American relations seemed essentially frozen in the same hostility of mutual incomprehension and distrust that had characterized them for twenty years.''[8] Such relations had been interrupted in 1950 by the Korean War, a war in which U.S. and Chinese soldiers had fought ferociously against each other. Although numerous bilateral talks between the two countries had taken place since 1954 in both Geneva and Warsaw, nothing more than an accord on repatriation of some nationals had been reached.

On March 28, 1969, in a directive calling for a review of restrictions on trade with Communist countries, Kissinger specifically requested a reexamination of the U.S. embargo on trade with "Asian Communist countries." As a result of this reassessment, in June the U.S. government decided, "on broad foreign policy grounds," to modify trade controls against China. These "modifications" took the form of permitting U.S. tourists to purchase up to $100 of Chinese-made noncommercial goods and eliminating the ban on travel to the People's Republic of China (PRC). Thus, a small step ultimately (but tortuously) yielded a somewhat rosier political climate that was more conducive to bilateral talks on resuming diplomatic and economic relations.*

It is interesting to note that the Chinese also were reassessing their policies vis-à-vis the United States. One Chinese observer noted, for example, that "the foreign policy of any state is bound to become readjusted in accordance with the changes it faces in the do-

---

*The growing Soviet bellicosity, particularly the Ussuri River clashes in March 1969, may also have contributed to Chinese reassessment of relations with the United States.

mestic and international situation."[9] In particular, among the changes perceived by the Chinese was the fact that "the Soviet Union, as a hegemonistic power, has become aggressively assertive everywhere." Moreover, the United States in the conduct of world affairs, as perceived by the Chinese leadership, has pursued policies "very different from those pursued in the 1950's and 1960's. . . . This has made a pro-American orientation possible."[10]

President Nixon's historic visit to China in February 1972 and the resulting Shanghai Communiqué established some basic guidelines for U.S. policy toward China. Specifically, with regard to commercial relations the communiqué stated:

> Both sides view bilateral trade as another area from which mutual benefit can be derived, and agreed that economic relations based on equality and mutual benefit are in the interest of the peoples of the two countries. They agree to facilitate the progressive development of trade between their two countries.[11]

President Jimmy Carter in February 1977 stated that the new administration's policy toward China "will be guided by the Shanghai Communiqué and normalization is its goal."[12] Vice-President Walter Mondale, in a speech in Peking two years later, went even further by suggesting that in trade, U.S. interests are served by China's expanding exports of natural resources and industrial products, and imports financed through these exports.[13]

A capstone in this decade-long U.S.-Chinese effort toward diplomatic and economic normalization was the passage by Congress on January 24, 1980, of the U.S.-China Trade Agreement granting most-favored-nation status to Chinese exports to the United States.[14] The agreement had been reached in July 1979 and was sent to Congress in October. In his request for approval of this agreement with the Chinese, President Carter stated:

> Conclusion of this agreement is the most important step we can take to provide greater economic benefits to both countries from this relationship. It will also give further impetus to the progress we have made in our overall relationship since normalization of our diplomatic relations earlier this year.[15]

In short, the two countries had come a long way toward political rapprochement since the early 1970s, especially in trade relations.

Table 1.1 shows that trade between the United States and China has increased dramatically since the historic visit of President Nixon

TABLE 1.1

United States-People's Republic of China Trade, 1970-79
(million U.S. dollars)

Year	Total Trade	U.S. Exports	U.S. Imports	Imbalance
1970	—	—	—	—
1971	5.0	—	5.0	−5.0
1972	95.9	63.5	32.4	+31.1
1973	805.1	740.2	64.9	+675.3
1974	933.8	819.1	114.7	+704.4
1975	461.9	303.6	158.3	+145.3
1976	337.3	135.4	201.9	−66.5
1977	374.5	171.5	203.0	−31.5
1978	1,188.2	864.6	323.6	+541.0
1979	2,318.0	1,723.8	594.2	+1,129.6
January-June 1980	1,940.4	1,487.0	453.4	+1,033.6

Source: U.S., Department of Commerce, Highlights of Exports
and Imports, FT-990 series (Washington, D.C.: Government Printing Office, 1970-80).

in 1972, to the point where total trade turnover between the two countries is approaching $3 billion. Although such increased trade has to
some extent demystified trading procedures and standardized U.S.
approaches to the China market, actual commercial practices have
not changed much, according to many observers.[16] In particular,
"Foreign trade in China," in the opinion of one well-qualified U.S. observer, "is carried on by experts. They know their products and objectives. Given the opportunity, they have proved themselves to be
just as shrewd, realistic, canny and enterprising as any businessman
in this country."[17] Echoing this sentiment, another long-time U.S.
trader suggests that negotiating with the PRC officials is like playing
a game of chess.[18] They are superb negotiators and skillful psychologists who are reputed to be even harder bargainers than the Soviets.
Yet despite this there is relatively little available published data on
the subject. In fact, I. W. Zwartman, writing in 1977, noted that
"we woefully lack information about the actual, across-the-table negotiations and the specific authority vested in Chinese officials to
make decisions."[19]

Assuming the difficulty of negotiating with the Chinese and the lack of information, this study seeks to provide a perspective from which to view U.S.-Chinese commercial negotiations. Although much has been written about the history and activity surrounding U.S.-Chinese trade, little has been published about the process of negotiating with Chinese trade officialdom. The objective of the study will be to determine what impediments—governmental or nongovernmental, U.S. or Chinese—are faced by U.S. firms undertaking commercial negotiations with the Chinese government. Such "hindrances and impediments" are defined in this study as any unwarranted delays or obstructions standing in the way of progress toward a completed U.S.-Chinese commercial transaction. U.S. and Chinese political and economic relations, while not overlooked, are not discussed in detail, except to provide an overview to the actual commercial negotiations discussed.

This study is part of a growing body of literature on the processes of negotiation. In 1960, beginning with T. C. Schelling,[20] negotiation emerged as a discipline, albeit with advocates of different approaches. In examining U.S.-Chinese commercial negotiations no attempt is made to suggest that one approach works better than another. In fact, the myriad U.S.-Chinese commercial transactions and their concomitant negotiations may defy classification. However, if one approach were considered among the competing approaches, it might be the one that views most commercial negotiations at a basic micro level of analysis as a set of personal and interpersonal dynamics that results in outcomes of varying acceptability to the participants. At this basic level, according to this type of analysis, the resolution of a commercial transaction through negotiation may be motivated by the following factors:[21]

The individual personality needs of negotiators;
The personality compatibility among negotiators representing opposing parties;
Negotiator perceptions and expectations of the opponent—strengths and weaknesses, intentions and goals, and commitments to positions; and
Persuasive mechanisms employed to modify the bargaining positions and values of the opponent to achieve a more favorable convergence of interests.

Although this study does not treat these factors independently, Chapter 3, in discussing the difficulties encountered in U.S. commercial negotiations, particularly interpersonal relations as an obstacle in negotiation, does focus on the personal and interpersonal dynamics affecting U.S.-Chinese commercial negotiations.

SOURCES OF DATA

Data were collected primarily from four sources: a mail questionnaire sent to 192 U.S. companies accounting for a large percentage of all annual U.S.-Chinese trade volume for 1970-79; personal interviews or correspondence with U.S. business executives, lawyers,
and government officials familiar with U.S.-Chinese commercial negotiations; basic source documents obtained from the Control Data
Corporation (CDC) bearing on the company's negotiations for the sale
of computers to the Chinese; and the results of other surveys of U.S.
companies relating to U.S.-China trade.[22]
    The paucity of published data on the process and outcome of
U.S.-Chinese commercial negotiations in general, and the almost
total lack of published information on the procedural aspects of U.S.-
Chinese commercial negotiations in particular, pointed up the necessity of seeking primary source information through questionnaires,
personal interviews, and company documents and papers.
    The primary research effort consisted of obtaining information
from selected companies that had undertaken negotiations with the
PRC. From company responses to the questionnaire, as well as from
other primary and secondary materials, the study focused on eliciting
a pattern of successful business negotiations with the PRC for the sale
of products and services. In particular the research was directed at
identifying the procedural aspects of U.S. companies' negotiations,
as well as their assessment of the hindrances and impediments to negotiations and their regard for the commonality-of-interest factor in
U.S.-Chinese commercial negotiations. Effort was addressed to examining those factors that contribute to success or failure of such negotiations, as well as to describing the mechanics of U.S.-Chinese
business negotiations. Perhaps the most useful part of the study is
the utilization of the CDC experience as a case study and juxtaposition
of this experience with the information learned from company responses to the basic questionnaire.
    The basic questionnaire was constructed after consultation with
numerous experts both within and outside the U.S. government. The
author's experience in the construction of over 30 different questionnaires during the course of various investigations for the U.S. International Trade Commission also facilitated the development of the
preliminary research instrument. In addition to the author's questionnaire, results from other recent surveys of U.S. companies doing
business were used, as well as personal diary notes kept by the vice-
president of one large U.S. firm during his participation in commercial negotiations with the Chinese.
    CDC allowed the author access to its files on commercial nego-
tiations with the Chinese government for 1971-79 and the first six

months of 1980. In addition, the company allowed the author to use copies of documents and unpublished papers pertinent to these negotiations, with the proviso that there be no attribution of individual names mentioned during the negotiations. The importance of these company documents to this study cannot be overemphasized because they provided valuable insights into the nature of the process of U.S.-Chinese commercial negotiations. Also, during the course of the investigation, it became apparent that a more detailed questionnaire for CDC was necessary, since executives of this corporation indicated a willingness to be interviewed at length. Consequently, with the basic questionnaire as a guide, a personal interview questionnaire was devised and used during interviews in the fall of 1979.

THE RESPONDENTS

The basic questionnaire was sent to 192 U.S. companies engaged in a wide variety of commerce and business activity with the PRC. There were 112 usable questionnaire responses, including telephone follow-ups to firms not responding within the specified time period. There also were 12 in-depth, detailed follow-up questionnaire responses, which included additional telephone contacts and further written questionnaire responses, from a cross section of U.S. companies. In detailing the results of my research below, all of the responses, both preliminary and in-depth, are included. Together these companies accounted for an estimated 50 percent to 80 percent of all annual U.S.-Chinese trade volume for 1972-79. Moreover, by class of goods traded with China, some of the companies selected in a given year may have accounted for nearly all of the trade in a particular commodity class. CDC, with its $6.8 million sale of two Cyber 172 computer systems to China in 1973 and its $69 million sale of a similar system in 1978, accounted for virtually all of U.S. sales of computers for these years. Besides choosing firms that had significant commercial experience with the Chinese government, another rationale for the selection of these companies was to choose U.S. firms that had undertaken (or, in the case of one firm, was currently undertaking) a variety of commercial negotiations with the PRC.

Additional sources included official U.S. and Chinese agreements, regulations, and decrees, as well as personal interviews with company executives, lawyers, and U.S. government officials who have had extensive negotiating experience with the Chinese government. A list of these sources is in the bibliography.

NOTES

1. U.S., Congress, Senate, "The China Trade," by K. H. J. Clarke, Congressional Record, December 20, 1973, p. S.23471. This is a good summation of early Chinese trade with the West.

2. William Burke, The China Trade (San Francisco: Federal Reserve, 1972), p. 5.

3. Quoted in Foster Rhea Dulles, The Old China Trade (New York: AMS Press, 1930), pp. 10-11.

4. Guaranty Trust Company of New York, Trading with China: Methods Found Successful in Dealing with the Chinese (New York: Guaranty Trust Company, 1919), p. 5. See also the very popular book written by advertising and marketing manager, Carl Crow, 400 Million Chinese Customers (New York: Harcourt Brace, 1973). Further information is in the China Business Review, July-August 1980, p. 13, which also echoes this theme. "The People's Republic of China has a market of over 1 billion potential customers. Capitalize on it . . . by placing advertising in Chinese network television, Beijing local television, airport billboards."

5. "U.S.-China Trade Pact Is Initiated," New York Times, May 15, 1979, p. C-1.

6. U.S., Congress, Joint Economic Committee, China: A Reassessment of the Economy, 94th Cong., 1st sess., July 10, 1975, p. 551.

7. U.S., Congress, Joint Economic Committee, Chinese Economy Post-Mao, vol. 1, Policy and Performance (Washington, D.C.: U.S. Government Printing Office, November 9, 1978), pp. 742-44.

8. Henry Kissinger, White House Years (Boston: Little, Brown, 1979), p. 171. In all, between 1954 and 1968, 134 bilateral meetings were held.

9. U.S., Joint Publications Research, "The United States Is a Paradise of Democracy," by Jie Jun, JPRS no. 73987 (Washington, D.C.: Foreign Broadcast Information Service, August 23, 1979), p. 73.

10. Ibid. The writer of this article makes a very interesting point about perceptions:

> The United States and us have been insulated from each other for nearly 30 years. There has been a lack of mutual understanding. Up to the 1960's, the Chinese in the minds of the Americans still dragged along in a pair of baggy long pants. Similarly, what has been an American like in our minds? America was but a slum area of poor people; it had to do only with car accidents, hold-ups, murders, social crimes, violence of the blacks and strikes staged by the workers;

and it thus cut an image of a setting sun in the west with
hardly any life left, something "ready for the museum,"
and of corruption and decline that consisted in the very
aforesaid things. This apparently is also a twisted image.
But conciliation is the trend today, and the common desire
of the people of both countries.

11. "U.S.-China Agreement, Shanghai Communiqué" (Los Angeles: U.S.-China People's Friendship Association, May 1975), p. 4.
12. U.S., Congress, Joint Economic Committee, Chinese Economy Post-Mao, p. 746.
13. "Excerpts from a Speech Mondale Made in Peking," New
York Times, August 28, 1979, p. 17.
14. U.S., Congress, House, Concurrent Resolution 204, 96th
Cong., 20th sess., January 24, 1980.
15. "Chinese Trade Pact Is Sent to Congress," New York Times,
October 24, 1979, p. A-1.
16. U.S., Congress, Joint Economic Committee, Chinese Economy Post-Mao, p. 755.
17. "Counsel from an Old China Hand," Fortune, March 26,
1979, p. 66.
18. "In Search of Roots," East-West Markets, July 24, 1978,
p. 22.
19. Donald W. Klein, "The Foreign Trade Apparatus," in Law
and Politics in China's Foreign Trade, ed. Victor H. Li (Seattle:
University of Washington Press, 1977), p. 319.
20. T. C. Schelling, The Strategy of Conflict (Cambridge,
Mass.: Harvard University Press, 1960).
21. I. William Zartman, The Negotiation Process, Theories
and Application (Beverly Hills, Calif.: Sage, 1978), pp. 55-56.
22. James A. Brunner, "Frequency Distributions: U.S.-Peo-
ple's Republic of China Trade Survey" (Toledo, Ohio: Department of
Marketing, University of Toledo, 1975); and Rosalie L. Tung, "Summary of Findings of U.S.-China Trade Negotiations Study" (Eugene:
Graduate School of Management, University of Oregon, February
1980).

2
THE ORGANIZATIONS
RESPONSIBLE FOR NEGOTIATING
BUSINESS CONTRACTS

The importance of the Chinese organizational structure for the conduct of foreign trade to the U.S. firm undertaking negotiations cannot be overemphasized. In fact, Jeffrey Schultz noted that "a particularly frustrating aspect of trading with China has been not knowing how China's foreign trade structure is organized or who one's Chinese trade counterparts are."[1] The purpose of this chapter is to highlight and discuss the principal Chinese organizations responsible for negotiating business contracts and to describe the bureaucratic features of the Chinese foreign trade system.

With the establishment of the People's Republic of China (PRC) in 1949, a foreign trade structure was created to conduct trade activities with other countries as a part of the overall plan of economic reform. During the early years of their economic development, the Chinese leadership imitated the Soviet foreign trade system. According to one Chinese observer,

> After liberation, in line with Comrade Mao Zedong's instructions and study of the experience of the Soviet Union at the time, we established a foreign trade system which was highly centralized and state-monopolized.[2]

Since 1949 the Chinese foreign trade system has basically remained a copy of the Soviet model, emphasizing monopoly, centralized control, and high concentration.[3] In fact, both the foreign trade systems and the Soviet and Chinese economies still resemble each other. The economies are characterized by central planning as well as by a tendency to focus on physical output as a criterion for evaluating performance. It is noteworthy that even today Chinese specialists in Soviet affairs, while critical of Soviet international policy, openly praise

11

Soviet domestic policy, citing improved living conditions in the Soviet Union. [4]

Although there are similarities, one should not forget that the Chinese economy is somewhat more decentralized, and that there have been conscious attempts, particularly in 1979-80, to rethink basic economic premises germane to the Chinese model of economic development. [5] The result of these internal "dialogues" is not yet known, but they could mean further economic decentralization. This still does not mean, however, that there is not now, or would not continue to be, strong direction from the center, especially in the administration of foreign trade. As stated above, China's foreign trade is centrally controlled; imports and exports are under the leadership of the Ministry of Foreign Trade, which provides strong centralized direction to China's foreign trade. [6]

Before considering in some detail the centralized aspect of the Chinese trade system, it is important first to examine the Chinese foreign trade system, particularly the Ministry of Foreign Trade and its branches. Unless U.S. commercial negotiators understand the organizational structure of the Chinese foreign trade system, and above all its centralized bureaucratic character, any specific U.S.-Chinese commercial undertaking can fail.

THE CHINESE FOREIGN TRADE SYSTEM

All foreign and domestic trade in China is under the policy direction of the State Council as enunciated by the Chinese Communist party. This all-embracing control of the state over foreign trade is explicitly spelled out in the Provisional Norms, promulgated in 1950, which are still in effect. [7]

> All foreign dealers and agents of foreign trade organizations who carry out foreign trade in China and are subject to the action of Chinese laws . . . must apply for registration in the local administration for supervision over foreign trade. [8]

The State Council consists of the premier, 12 vice-premiers, and a number of specialized ministries, commissions, bureaus, and other special agencies. Figure 2.1 shows the organization of the central government of the PRC. As can be seen from the figure, as of March 1980 the Ministry of Foreign Trade is just one of 39 ministries of the State Council. The State Council, in effect China's cabinet, interprets Communist party policy and directs the work of the government.

Most high government officials are also members of the Politburo of the Central Committee of the Communist party, while most ministers, including Li Chiang, minister of foreign trade, are members of the Central Committee. The agencies and ministries concerned with foreign trade are shown in Figure 2.2, which depicts the "bureaucratic maze" that constitutes China's foreign trade system. In fact, Donald W. Klein has even referred to the system as the "foreign trade labyrinth."[9]

The Chinese foreign trade system, as mentioned above, has many of the elements found in the Soviet system. In fact, Soviet writers describing the Chinese foreign trade organization specifically refer to it as a "system."[10] In the Soviet as well as the Chinese context, the "system" means a monolithic grouping of foreign trade bodies that conduct virtually all of that country's foreign trade.[11] Such a monolithic grouping facilitates state control. As Figure 2.2 shows, the Chinese foreign trade system is a vast, complex state organization centered on the Ministry of Foreign Trade and assisted by the China Council for the Promotion of International Trade (CCPIT) and a number of other government agencies, banks, and insurance companies. These organizations in turn work under the direct supervision of the State Council and its Staff Office of Finance and Trade. Coordination is accomplished by the Department of Finance and Trade Work of the Central Committee of the Chinese Communist party. Vice-Premier Li Hsien-nien, the country's most senior authority on trade and economic matters, heads both the staff office and the department. Li Chiang is currently minister of foreign trade.

Chinese officials in the past have suggested that a foreign trade system under centralized state control is necessary in order to do the following:

1. Safeguard the absolute leadership of the Communist party in foreign trade,

2. Consolidate the independence of China's foreign trade, and

3. Guarantee the planned development of foreign trade under the policy and guidance of the Communist party.[12]

Doubtless, Communist party control over foreign trade is desired, but recent developments emphasizing increased trade with the West, particularly with the United States, in high-technology products, have made the second item questionable. This is particularly true because China faces the dilemma of being able to maintain strict economic independence while basing its economic development, particularly the search for oil, on Western technology.

The first and third items have relevance in that China's foreign trade system is an extension of the political system. Thus, it is the Communist party that is supposed to inform "system" personnel of current political and economic objectives and to ensure that they are carried out.

FIGURE 2.1

Organizational Chart of the Government Structure of the People's Republic of China

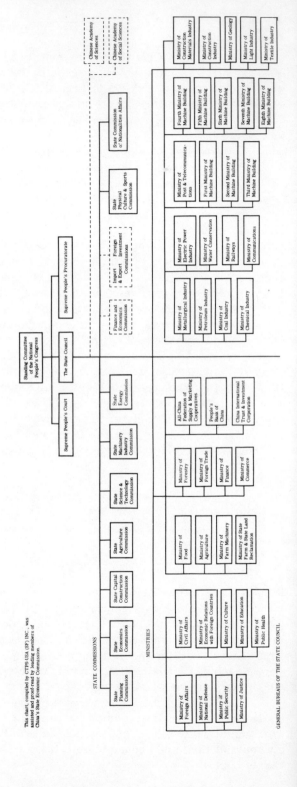

This chart, compiled by CTPS-USA (SF) INC., was assisted and proof-read by leading members of China's State Economic Commission.

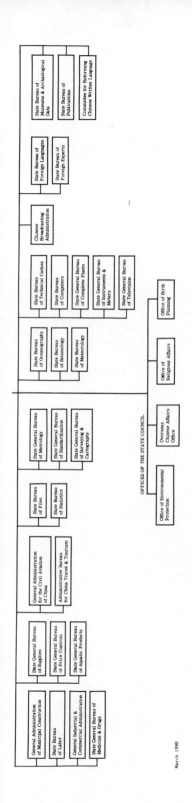

March 1980

OFFICES OF THE STATE COUNCIL

Source: Liu Chaojin and Wang Linsheng, China's Foreign Trade: Its Policy and Practice (San Francisco: CTPS-USA, June 1980).

15

FIGURE 2.2

Chinese Foreign Trade Organization, April 1979

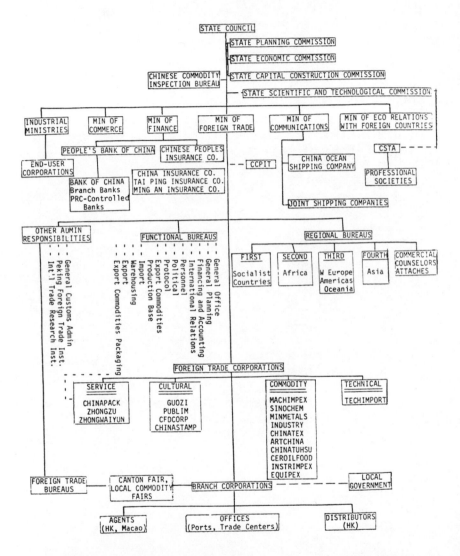

Sources: China Trade Quarterly, vol. 1, no 1 (1979); Gene Hsaio, The Foreign Trade of China: Policy, Law and Practice (Berkeley: University of California Press, 1977); and Jeffrey Schultz, China's Foreign Trade Corporations . . . Organizations and Personnel (Washington, D.C.: National Council for U.S.-China Trade, April 1979).

Although China's decision makers have stressed the importance of centralized planning and foreign technology purchases, since early 1978, in an effort to accommodate the interests of influential provincial leaders, provinces and localities have been granted increasing authority in the decision-making process. [13] In particular, factories and local corporations are participating in the survey of the international market and are studying foreign technology in preparation for the purchase of equipment, its application to the production line, and the licensing and hiring of foreign consultants.

Despite the "innovations," however, and some measure of decentralization that is currently being allowed, Chinese customers or end users are still in a "powerless and passive position." [14] According to one Chinese observer, "everything in foreign trade from negotiations to concluding a transaction, exporting and taking payment is handled by the foreign trade department and the enterprise cannot have direct contact abroad." [15] In short, the death of centralism may be highly exaggerated. [16] This is primarily because some kind of control must be maintained over lower-level bodies for the system to function.

Moreover, despite all of these "innovations," imports of major consequence will continue to be determined centrally, if only because the Chinese need to conserve scarce foreign exchange. Perhaps an equally important rationale for centralization is that only the center can accomplish the necessary "comparison shopping to avoid losses" or send personnel abroad "to inspect, to negotiate and to make preparations for construction without wasteful duplication of effort and cost." [17]

The U.S. businessman approaching the China market clearly faces a bureaucratic labyrinth. The basic reason is that the who and how of deciding to purchase major technologies are obscured by multiple and overlapping responsibilities. In particular there is no single or simple pattern of decision making concerning the importation of foreign technology. As Figure 2.3 shows, the decision making is complex. The difficulties of reaching these end users, as is pointed out in Chapters 3 and 5, is considerable and constitutes one of the most burdensome obstacles to U.S.-Chinese trade negotiations.

The decision-making procedure, according to Figure 2.3, begins with a request for foreign products or services from a provincial government, individual plant, or industrial ministry. It also is quite likely that some industrial corporations may be able to request these products or services as end users. [18] Two Chinese officials from the Fourth Ministry of Machine Building (see Figure 2.1) elaborated on this procedure in a December 1979 meeting in Minneapolis with Control Data Corporation (CDC). [19]

In the negotiation for computer technology, the Fourth Ministry, which is the customer or end user, has the responsibility for negotiating

FIGURE 2.3

China: Technology Import Decision-Making Procedure

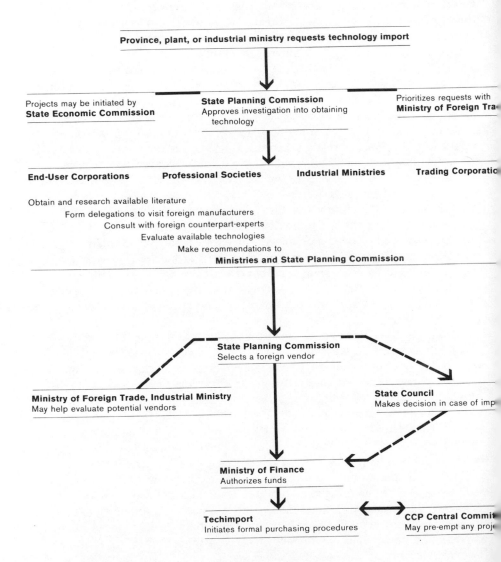

Province, plant, or industrial ministry requests technology import

Projects may be initiated by
State Economic Commission

State Planning Commission
Approves investigation into obtaining
technology

Prioritizes requests with
Ministry of Foreign Tra

End-User Corporations   **Professional Societies**   **Industrial Ministries**   **Trading Corporatic**

Obtain and research available literature
Form delegations to visit foreign manufacturers
Consult with foreign counterpart-experts
Evaluate available technologies
Make recommendations to
Ministries and State Planning Commission

State Planning Commission
Selects a foreign vendor

Ministry of Foreign Trade, Industrial Ministry
May help evaluate potential vendors

State Council
Makes decision in case of imp

Ministry of Finance
Authorizes funds

Techimport
Initiates formal purchasing procedures

CCP Central Commit
May pre-empt any proje

Source: U.S., Central Intelligence Agency, China: Post-Mao
Search for Civilian Industrial Technology (Washington, D.C.: National Foreign Assessment Center, February 1979), p. 8.

the technical aspects of the license, while the Chinese Technology Import Corporation has responsibility for negotiating commercial aspects of the license. These officials also outlined to CDC the Ministry of Foreign Trade's procedure used to procure technology, as follows:

Step	Activity
1	Technical seminar is held.
2	Technical study group is formed and foreign engineers are invited to make presentations to Chinese engineers. At this time a proposal should be announced.
3	The Chinese technical study group completes their study. Internal agreement concerning the study recommendations is then obtained. At this time the Ministry of Foreign Trade asks for commercial prices/terms.
4	Foreign company submits a proposal that includes specifications, training definition, list of equipment, and price list.
5	Foreign company and Chinese customer (Fourth Ministry) negotiate technical aspects of license. At this step a preliminary draft of the contract is created.
6	Foreign company and Chinese Technology Import Corporation negotiate commercial terms, including prices and overall implementation schedule.

It should be stressed that the above procedure may not be universally applied by each end user in exactly this step-by-step way. Nevertheless, as the outline of the procedure followed by the Fourth Ministry shows, the Chinese are very meticulous, even methodical, in their approach to buying U.S. computer technology or any product.

When authorization for undertaking an investigation for obtaining technology has been approved by the appropriate bureaucratic element (see Figure 2.3), other institutions become involved in deciding which product or service to buy. This procedure can be very time consuming, and consequently, frustrating to the U.S. company seeking knowledge of possibilities for sale of its product to the Chinese. Once the Chinese agencies have completed their search for the appropriate product and company (or companies), the proposed purchase is factored into the national economic plans and a vendor is selected (see Figure 2.3). The final phase in the acquisition process is the initiation of formal purchasing procedures by elements of the Ministry of Foreign Trade.

Although there have been innovations in allowing end users to enter into direct negotiations with foreign sellers, this is not a general practice.* Direction from the center is still paramount and controlling. Everything in foreign trade, from the conduct of negotiations to the conclusion of a transaction and taking payment, is handled by the Ministry of Foreign Trade and its subunits.[20] This extreme centralization is not without disadvantages. A Chinese observer writing in 1979 suggested that "for a variety of reasons, for over 20 years there were basically no reforms in the foreign trade system. As the situation developed, a centrally controlled foreign trade system increasingly revealed its drawbacks."[21]

These "drawbacks," according to the Chinese observer, fall into at least three categories. Perhaps foremost is that the centrally controlled system is not able to "bring local initiative into full play." The writer cites as an example Guandong Province, adjacent to Hong Kong and Macao. It has all the resources for development of light industry, yet its "superior conditions" have not been fully developed, although the volume of import-export trade is one-seventh of Hong Kong's trade. Another Chinese writer echoes this theme of ignoring local initiative:

> While operation is controlled by the Peking head office, administration is controlled by the local provincial or municipal bureau of foreign trade. Since the head office is far away in Peking, how can it completely understand the situation in other places in the country? Consequently, what should have been interfered with has been left alone and what should have been left alone has been interfered with. The fact is that the head office is incapable of supervising the branch office. In the circumstances, how can the initiative of the local offices be brought into full play?[22]

Like the Soviet foreign trade system, the Chinese system functions as an integral part of the national economic planning mechanism. Specifically, the Ministry of Foreign Trade receives control figures from both the State Planning Commission and the State Economic Commission for annual and long-range imports and exports. Such figures are based on the overall national economic goals. General import and export plans are then drawn up in accordance with China's political

---

*The first such contract between a U.S. firm and an "end user" was signed between Atlantic Richfield and the China Petroleum Corporation on March 17, 1979, and covered seismic survey work in offshore waters.

relations with each individual trading nation, its existing contractual commitments to foreign partners, the nature of import and export commodities involved, world market conditions, sources of foreign supply and demand, domestic demand and export capability, and the amount of foreign currencies and external financing available. [23]

Once formulated, the general plans are transmitted to the foreign trade corporations (see Figure 2.2) for the making of specific import and export plans. After appropriate review these specific plans become part of the Ministry of Foreign Trade's general plans, which in turn become part of the national economic plan. Once the national plan is approved by the State Council, the Ministry of Foreign Trade has the primary responsibility for oversight of the specific plans.

It is perhaps these laborious and cumbersome planning procedures that prompted one Chinese writer to observe in December 1979 that "all matters, regardless of how trivial, have to be submitted for approval. As official documents are handed down from level to level, actions begin to get slower and slower."[24] Moreover, since international markets tend to change very swiftly, many "golden opportunities" may have been lost by the time final approval from the center has been granted. Zhang Chongwen cites one example of a lost opportunity:

> This year [1979] we arranged outside our country for the import of luan wood and to export to Japan shui-qu willow produced in the northeast. At that time, the price of shui-qu willow was two or three times higher than that of luan wood. But because the local authorities did not have the power to make a decision and had to ask the central authorities for instructions, the matter was delayed for several months as a result of official documents having to travel to and fro. Consequently, the price of shui-qu willow dropped while that of luan wood increased by 50 percent. Despite the fact that deals were made, losses were incurred because we missed the opportunity. [25]

He concludes that enterprises engaged in foreign trade should be given a freer hand in making day-to-day decisions, and the power to act on their own under the guidance of the state's unified planning apparatus. Such a change in procedure would bring local initiative into full play and thereby would enable exports to increase.

Overly concentrated authority, with requirements for approval at several levels, and procedures that are complex, time-consuming, and inefficient, frequently allow good opportunities to slip by, especially in a fast-changing international market. Also in this category

of adjustment to change is the fact that production and marketing techniques, such as packaging and direct appeal advertising, are not
utilized in such a way as to make Chinese products competitive in the
international market.

The Chinese centralized foreign trade system can be criticized
in that it operates in accordance with "objective economic laws" only
with difficulty. Specifically cited is "the method of dividing export
commodities by ports and stipulating that these ports engage only in
trade in selected commodities, . . . [a method which] does not appear to help the port expand exports in accord with local conditions."[26]
Such a procedure obviously does not help develop local initiative to
break into the international market.

Alone, the above criticisms might be read as another attack on
China's bureaucracy in keeping with past tradition, including the tradition of the Cultural Revolution.[27] In the context of the current leadership's drive for modernization, however, such criticism could also
suggest increased attempts at efficiency of organization.

It should be noted that Chinese foreign trade planning apparently
is undergoing a period of change. The traditional foreign trade planning system has usually been described as one of planning with material balances—that is, preliminary export and import targets were de-
rived from the set of aggregate material balances prepared by the
state planning agency (COSPLAN) during the annual planning cycle:
if the material balance showed a deficit, imports were planned; if a
surplus, then exports. The traditional system of planning may have
been adapted to meet the relatively limited demands placed upon it;
with the expansion of foreign economic relations during the late 1970s,
there was a need to introduce new approaches to foreign trade planning.

Such a need may have been manifested in the creation of China's
State Economic Commission (SEC) in 1978, following the first session
of the Fifth National People's Congress. Clearly the Chinese have
been seeking a balance between central control and flexibility in the
operation of foreign trade planning.[28] They also have been separating
the minutiae of long-range planning, which is a State Planning Commission function, from the responsibilities of executing the annual
plans of the nonagricultural sectors (an SEC function).[29] According
to Vice-Minister Yuan Baohua, the process of executing the annual
plan for the industrial and transport sectors is done by the SEC peri-
odically as a "comprehensive, composite organization overseeing the
work of several ministries." Although the SEC does not supervise
foreign trade organizations directly, it has close relations with them.
Moreover, according to Yuan Baohua, "Every time we have a conference, representatives . . . are present to fight for their share of
products for either domestic consumption in retail outlets or in the
foreign trade corporations' export markets . . . we are responsible

for revising the import and export targets. "[30] Nevertheless, despite some harbingers of change toward greater autonomy, the center is still reluctant to cede significant authority in matters of import, particularly instances affecting scarce foreign exchange.*

THE MINISTRY OF FOREIGN TRADE

When the structure of the central government was established in the fall of 1949 by the Chinese Communist regime, foreign trade was not given ministerial stature. Instead, the Foreign Trade Office was created as one of the subordinate units under the Ministry of Trade. In August 1952 the Ministry of Foreign Trade, then called the Bureau of Foreign Trade, was expanded to a full ministry. According to the 1950 Provisional Regulations for the Control of Foreign Trade, the Ministry of Foreign Trade exercises three principal functions: approval and registration of importers and exporters,† approval and licensing of import and export transactions, and fixing prices of import and export commodities. [31]

Since August 1952 the Ministry of Foreign Trade has operated as an independent ministry, subject to the same vicissitudes of centralization and decentralization as the other parts of the Chinese bureaucracy. Before 1966, for example, its work was closely coordinated with the Chinese Communist party Central Committee's Department of Finance and Trade and the State Council's Office of Finance and Trade. Currently it appears that the ministry has relatively more autonomy. Such autonomy, however, does not relieve it of the burden of submitting an annual import and export plan to the State Council, China's leading "executive" body, and upon approval, of supervising its implementation.

The 1975 constitution kept the Ministry of Foreign Trade subordinate to the State Council, but with direct supervision over all the foreign trade corporations (FTCs)[32] as well as the General Customs Administration and the Peking Institute of Foreign Trade. The ministry also works closely with other government agencies involved with foreign trade, such as the China Council for the Promotion of Inter-

---

*Currently, Chinese foreign trade corporations have authority to negotiate only contracts with dollar values of $10 million or less. This is not a very significant amount if one is negotiating for transfers of new technology or building of new plants or factories.

†At the time these provisions were announced, this was an important function for the ministry because of the existence of private enterprises and their participation in import and export activities.

national Trade, the Ministry of Finance, the People's Bank of China, the Bank of China, various insurance companies, the State Planning Commission, the Ministry of Communications, and the Ministry of Foreign Affairs. Figure 2.4 shows the organization of the Chinese Ministry of Foreign Trade.

Externally, the Ministry of Foreign Trade has authority to supervise and coordinate China's trade relations with foreign countries. The ministry can, and does, enter into trade agreements with foreign governments on behalf of the People's Republic of China, and does send trade missions overseas. With regard to trade missions, the Chinese, unlike the Soviets, do not have a law defining the exact legal status of their trade missions abroad. The Soviet Union by statute has defined Soviet trade missions as agencies of the Soviet government. Thus, a contract made with a Soviet trade mission has binding force upon the Soviet state. Although the Chinese have generally followed this principle, the legal status of such contracts is still ambiguous.[33]

Beyond this quasi-diplomatic function the principal responsibilities of the Ministry of Foreign Trade include arranging the exchange of trade delegations with foreign countries, assigning commercial counselors to Chinese embassies around the world (including its Liaison Office in Washington, D.C.), monitoring trade developments and prices worldwide, and training foreign trade cadres.[34]

Located in Peking, the Ministry of Foreign Trade has divided China's trading partners into four groups, or bureaus, on the basis of geography and politics, each in charge of trade with countries within its group.[35] These bureaus are shown in Figure 2.4. The First Bureau is in charge of trade with socialist countries; the Second Bureau supervises trade with Africa; the Third Bureau is in charge of trade with non-Communist Europe, the Americas, and Oceania; and the Fourth Bureau supervises trade with Asia.

Also in the Ministry of Foreign Trade's organizational scheme, shown in Figure 2.4, are a market-research institute known as the International Trade Institute (the Research Institute on International Economic and Market Conditions) and the Peking Institute of Foreign Trade, which is in effect a foreign trade college. As Figure 2.4 shows, functional bureaus exist for planning, accounting, and personnel.[36] The Office of International Conferences is also in the organizational structure.

Assuming an approximation of operational or day-to-day functions between the Soviet and Chinese models, the Chinese Ministry of Foreign Trade operates in the following manner.[37] Besides the minister there is a collegium within the ministry that serves as a top-echelon consultative body for the discussion of major policy questions. The collegium is composed of the minister, deputy ministers, and other "leading personnel" of the ministry. Currently, despite statutory

FIGURE 2.4

Organizational Structure of the Ministry of Foreign Trade

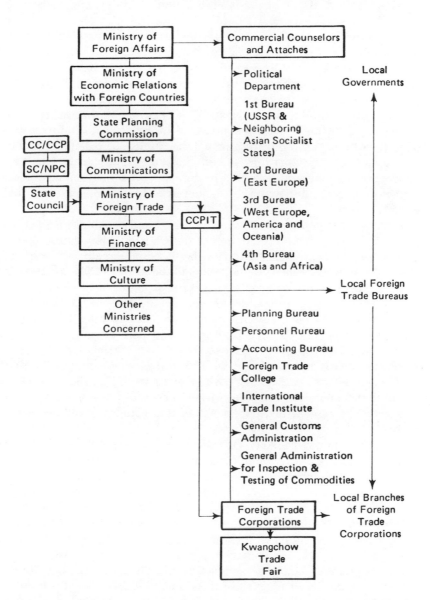

Source: Gene T. Hsaio, The Foreign Trade of China: Policy, Law and Practice (Berkeley: University of California Press, 1977), p. 95.

authority granting it a measure of independence from the minister, the collegium is subordinate to the minister in terms of power. For example, in theory, if the collegium or any individual member disagrees with a decision of the minister, that decision may be appealed upward to the State Council, but in practice few disagreements are reported to the State Council or upper-echelon governmental bodies. The minister occupies a strong position with regard to the collegium, if only by virtue of his long tenure in the position. Also, although the State Council confirms deputy ministers and other collegium members, candidates are recommended by the minister.

Again assuming some parallel, it is probable that in its day-to-day work the Ministry of Foreign Trade is expected to follow a set of well-defined administrative principles: unity of political and economic management, prudent selection of staff, democratic centralism, conduct of all activity according to the plan, one-man management, economic accountability in the conduct of economic operations, and socialist legality.

The first principle—unity of political and economic management —stems directly from the section of the Chinese constitution that states that the Communist party is the "leading core of all organizations of the working people, both social and state." The general party line on foreign trade is proclaimed through major party policy statements at party congresses and at plenary sessions of the party's Central Committee. Such statements are designed to inform ministry personnel of party objectives and to exhort them to improve their performance. For the U.S. business person negotiating with the Chinese, it seems readily apparent that the Chinese government will continue to do business on "a mutually advantageous basis" in those commodity areas that further the Chinese national economic development, economic independence, and the growth of that country's science and technology.

The Communist party also plays an important role in the prudent selection of staff, the second precept of administration. In particular the party obviously can influence a specific appointment or promotion, especially of a party member. More than this, however, the Chinese foreign trade system, and not just the Ministry of Foreign Trade, is in effect an extension of the political system. It is the Communist party that informs "system" personnel of current political and economic objectives and ensures that they are carried out.

The fourth principle—conduct of all activity according to the plan—is certainly a hallmark of the Chinese foreign trade system in general and of the Ministry of Foreign Trade in particular. With this in mind, a brief discussion of Chinese import planning is presented below.

CHINESE IMPORT PLANNING
WITHIN THE FOREIGN TRADE SYSTEM

Chinese planning and its bureaucratic consequences frequently make negotiations protracted and Chinese negotiators inflexible.[38] For example, American business persons may deal with FTCs without ever knowing the identity and special problems of the ultimate end user of their product. Moreover, they may find that the resulting poor communication has given rise to claims that could have been prevented. (More is said about this below in the section on the Chinese foreign trade bureaucracy.) Of importance here is that the Chinese foreign trade system is by and large in lockstep with the plan. The importation of any article into China is based on an import plan as well as on a plan for its internal distribution. Like Soviet foreign trade planning, China's import programs consist of annual, quarterly, and long-term plans, each of which is worked out in the latter half of the preceding year. These programs are produced through the following procedures:[39]

The Ministry of Foreign Trade, in conjunction with related divisions, sets a target figure for each exporting country and each group of goods, in accordance with China's foreign exchange reserves and the possible supply of the respective goods from overseas countries. This target figure also serves as a temporary index of the annual volume of goods to be imported.

The target figure(s) is presented by the Ministry of Foreign Trade to national FTCs, which in turn work out the details. The FTCs, in accordance with the particulars provided by the Ministry of Foreign Trade, process orders for the import of goods from requesting organizations. Meanwhile, those placing orders fill out application forms stating the import demand volume for commodities, keeping within the framework of the target figure set for each government ministry.

The Ministry of Foreign Trade adjusts the target figure(s) on the basis of import demand volume for commodities verified by the government, and then readjusts the annual import programs on a country-by-country, item-by-item basis.

The quarterly programs are based chiefly on the annual import programs, the contracts concluded with each foreign country, and actual changes that might occur during the course of contract execution. They also perform a vital role in materializing and completing annual import programs prior to their expiration date.

Long-term import programs are worked out by the Ministry of Foreign Trade after consultation with each subordinate ministry, and are drafted on the basis of the long-term national economic program (five-year plan), taking into consideration the long-term supply capacity of each exporting country and China's foreign exchange reserves. These plans are executed with the approval of the State Planning Commission, which is responsible for the drafting and execution of long-term economic programs, and the SEC, which is responsible for the drafting and execution of short-term economic programs.

The most important procedures during the course of executing import programs are the formulation and study of application forms that indicate the demand volume of goods to be imported. Since these applications are closely related to the country's economic policy and the production programs of the requesting ministries, a clear-cut system of sharing responsibilities is employed among the national organizations, with responsibilities being borne by concerned production organizations according to the type of goods ordered. Other related organizations participate in reviewing applications, but the final responsibility for overall evaluation and equalization rests with the economic planning bureau in charge.

The Ministry of Foreign Trade is also given the responsibility of formulating a list of applications denoting the import demand volume of commodities. At present these applications are categorized as follows:

Estimated commodity list (estimated cargoes): catalogs for commodities listing only the most important commodities and the amounts that must be purchased during a particular year;

Overall commodity catalog: produced on the basis of an overall listing of goods validated by the government that lists reference numbers, nomenclature of goods, quantity, and value;

Import commodity demand volume cards: containing the basic data concerning specific commodities to be imported, and are produced for use in conducting trade talks and concluding delivery contracts. A list of prices to be used as references is attached to the card when an order is placed with nonsocialist countries.

The requesting organization that is responsible for placing an order fills in an import commodity demand volume card in accordance with its demands for commodities to be imported. This is presented to the ministry in charge of production of the commodities concerned.

If, after an appropriate study, the ministry that receives the card finds that the domestic industry can fully meet the demand, it concludes a delivery contract with the requesting organization for the delivery of domestically produced products. When local production cannot meet the demand and imports are required, the requested volume is placed in a comprehensive annual catalog of commodities to be imported, for presentation to the planned economy organization, the State Planning Commission. The commission, taking into account the economic outlook and supply and demand relations, presents its decision to the Ministry of Foreign Trade while coordinating supply and demand in the light of data provided by that ministry.

The Ministry of Foreign Trade requires that the FTCs under its jurisdiction make a detailed study of the technical data entered on the demand volume cards, including nomenclature, specifications, quantity, use, delivery periods, consignee, and the country with which the order is to be placed or a country-by-country order allocation. Besides the demand volume cards verified by the government ministry, this study is conducted on the basis of the target figures for allocation of foreign exchange provided by the Ministry of Foreign Trade, the data on the domestic demand volume, and the capability of overseas countries to supply the goods.

The FTCs then make a further detailed study of allocations for each exporting country and their technical data and send the results of the study to the Ministry of Foreign Trade, where they are incorporated into a comprehensive catalog of commodities for approval by the national organization. Figure 2.5 summarizes current decision-making functions by the Ministry of Foreign Trade, as based on information from government and business sources.

The discussion of import planning within the Chinese foreign trade system and of the organization of the Chinese foreign trade system emphasized the subordinate relationship of the Chinese FTCs. The ten national FTCs, with headquarters in Peking, are of primary importance to a U.S. firm seeking a commercial contract. Emphasis in the discussion below is on the FTCs as a part of the Chinese foreign trade system and not on the detailed workings of these entities. [40]

In 1978 the 11 national FTCs, averaging about $2 billion turnover each, accounted for virtually all of China's trade. A listing of them is shown in Table 2.1. Other, smaller FTCs concerned with cultural commodities and "domestic" corporations are not shown. The FTCs that are shown are, in effect, "national" FTCs—that is, they have headquarters in Peking, engage in regular merchandise trade, earn "profits," and are legally empowered to sign contracts with foreign companies. [41]

In recent years "domestic" corporations (as opposed to "national" corporations) have been established to deal with specialized commodity transactions and to serve as "consultants" to particular ministries and national FTCs about imports of specialized technology.

The FTCs shown in Table 2.1 earn profits, report on world market conditions and foreign exchange rates, and are legally empowered to sign contracts with foreign companies. In general, they fall into four categories: commodity, technical, cultural, and service.

FIGURE 2.5

Decision–Making Functions by Selected PRC Organizations

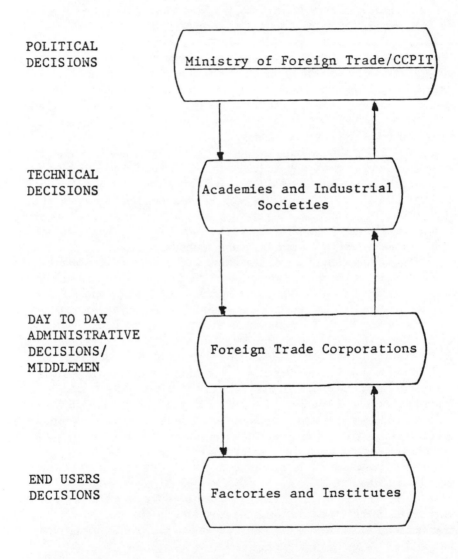

POLITICAL
DECISIONS — Ministry of Foreign Trade/CCPIT

TECHNICAL
DECISIONS — Academies and Industrial Societies

DAY TO DAY
ADMINISTRATIVE
DECISIONS/
MIDDLEMEN — Foreign Trade Corporations

END USERS
DECISIONS — Factories and Institutes

Source: COMTEC DATA, A Directory of Computer Organizations and Corporations: People's Republic of China (Minneapolis:
COMTEC, March 1980), p. F-1.

TABLE 2.1

China's Leading Foreign Trade Corporations

China National Arts and Crafts Import and Export Corporation
(ARTCHINA)

China National Cereals, Oils and Foodstuffs Import and Export Corporation (CEROILFOOD)

China National Chemicals Import and Export Corporation
(SINOCHEM)

China National Export Commodities Packaging Corporation
(CHINAPACK)

China National Light Industrial Products Import and Export Corporation (INDUSTRY)

China National Machinery Import and Export Corporation
(MACHIMPEX)

China National Machinery and Equipment Export Corporation
(EQUIPEX)

China National Metals and Minerals Import and Export Corporation
(MINMETALS)

China National Native Produce and Animal By-Products Import and Export Corporation (CHINATUHSU)

China National Technical Import Corporation (TECHIMPORT)

China National Textiles Import and Export Corporation (CHINATEX)

Source: Jeffrey Schultz, China's Foreign Trade Corporations
. . . Organizations and Personnel (Washington, D.C.: National
Council for U.S.-China Trade, April 1979), p. 34.

Government-owned and -operated Chinese FTCs were not a new concept originating with the establishment of the Chinese Communist regime in 1949. In the 1930s four government corporations that included the China Silk Corporation and the China Vegetable Oil Corporation competed with Western firms in China.[42] Moreover, China's FTCs have been an integral part of the foreign trade system since the very beginnings of the Chinese Communist regime. In fact, China began its state trading operations with six corporations under the Ministry of Trade in 1950.[43] Over the next 30 years, after a long process of expansion, merger, and reorganization, the number of FTCs has increased by only five.

Like their Soviet counterparts, the foreign trade organizations, China's FTCs operate under the supervision and control of the Ministry of Foreign Trade and are wholly state-owned monopolies. In addition to their commercial activities of buying and selling in the international marketplace, they have functions shared with other foreign trade system organizations, including marketing, planning, legal, liaison, and advisory tasks.[44] With regard to commercial activities, China's FTCs purchase foreign goods and sell Chinese products abroad on behalf of their domestic customers and usually have the exclusive trading rights for particular product categories. They handle contacts with foreign firms, conduct negotiations, and conclude contracts—all within the framework of the Chinese foreign trade system. The FTCs generally operate on normal commercial principles, taking into account price, quality, delivery date, and payment terms.

Figure 2.6 shows a hypothetical organizational structure for a Chinese FTC based on the Soviet model. That this Soviet-type organization might apply to its Chinese counterpart is supported by a study that briefly describes the organization.

> The main FTC offices house the general management of the corporations: a general manager (or "managing director"), anywhere from four to twelve deputy general managers ("deputy managing directors"), several product divisions and several functional departments. Product divisions are sometimes numbered and generally deal exclusively in either imports or exports.
>
> A full complement of functional departments usually includes those for general business, planning, accounting, finance, personnel, market research, technical exchange, traffic, packaging, transport, liaison, and advertising, as well as regional bureaus divided along Ministry of Foreign Trade lines.[45]

Many of the FTCs' general administrative duties are carried out by a general coordinating department or a "business office." For the U.S. businessman concerned with doing business with China, these departments and possibly the liaison and technical departments are extremely important in establishing contact. (As will be pointed out in Chapter 3, the establishment of such contact is extremely difficult and time consuming.)

Superficially, at least, the Chinese FTC is similar in many respects to a privately owned corporation in a market economy. A Russian translation of a Chinese handbook on foreign trade in fact refers to these FTCs as "specialized state foreign trade companies."[46] According to the handbook, these companies are "independent, economically self-supporting enterprises concerned with export-import operations," and can sign commercial contracts with foreign companies They are also independent juridical entities, with the right to decide

FIGURE 2.6

Hypothetical Organizational Structure of a Chinese FTC, 1974

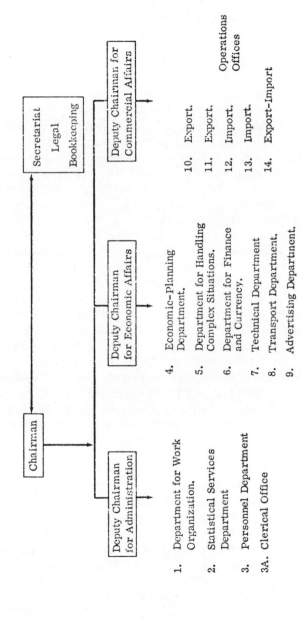

Source: L. A. Feonova et al., Organizatsiia i tekhnika vneshney torgovli SSSR [Organization and technique of Soviet foreign trade] (Moscow: I.M.O., 1974), p. 24.

legal questions having to do with their activities, and to bring suit or enter into arbitration. [47] Moreover, in the absence of a formal agreement with a foreign government, the corporation may enter into a contract, directly or through its agents, with a foreign partner. Also, like its Soviet foreign trade organization "counterpart," the Chinese FTC is legally responsible for its own business losses and profits.

Despite the superficial appearance of independence, an examination of the administrative-legal position of the FTC gives a different impression. Although its civil-legal status perhaps makes it appear independent of the Chinese government and the foreign trade system, in actuality, by the nature of its operation the FTC is merely a middleman in a planned economy. The State Council, for example, allocates working capital to the FTC that is remitted through the Ministry of Finance. [48] Again referring to the Soviet model as an analogy, the FTC administrative superiors doubtless can create or abolish an FTC, appoint its chief executives, and plan and supervise all its commercial operations. It is the State Council, at the apex of the Chinese foreign trade system, that creates, merges, divides, and liquidates FTCs on recommendation from the foreign trade minister. Moreover, the minister of foreign trade has the authority to appoint and remove the chairman and deputy chairman of an FTC, thus giving added emphasis to the assertion that the FTC is very much within the administrative hierarchy of the Chinese foreign trade system.

Another organizational element that is important to the workings of the Chinese foreign trade system, and of the FTC in particular, is the branch corporation. These corporations exist at the municipal, provincial, and regional levels, and serve as the basic statistical and accounting units for the national FTCs. Since 1975 there has been a rapid proliferation of these branches, with a general management structure duplicating that of FTC headquarters in Peking. Apparently most major decisions concerning contract negotiations are left to the branch corporation, provided they are consistent with general guidelines, particularly financial guidelines, of the upper echelons of the foreign trade system, such as the state planning organization, the Ministry of Foreign Trade, or the Bank of China. In effect, little is left to the branch corporations.

To summarize, the link between the FTCs and the center in Peking is that the former are subject on most matters of major import to the discipline and authority of the state bureaucracy controlling foreign trade. The FTCs perform their activities on the basis of planned assignments set by the center. The planning principle in the activities of the FTC is the basic guide promoting the efforts of the FTCs to justify their performance, particularly in their contractual relations with U.S. firms. Thus, to a U.S. firm negotiating with the PRC, it is quite apparent that the FTCs are strictly controlled by the state, which sets the policy, dispenses the financial resources, and plans for the specific types of commodities to be imported.

CHINA'S FINANCIAL AND FISCAL SYSTEM

A number of agencies outside the Foreign Trade Ministry exercise important powers in the conduct of foreign trade, thereby compounding the difficulties of commercial negotiation for the U.S. firm. Organizations concerned with planning and banking are obvious examples of other agencies playing a major role in China's foreign trade system. Since planning bodies have already been alluded to, the discussion below will focus briefly on China's fiscal and banking system,[49] as part of the foreign trade labyrinth.

Banking in China has always reflected traditional Chinese ambivalence toward the proper function of money and its handlers. In Confucian times a virtuous citizen did not seek to accumulate more wealth than was needed to live. Later, as China sought to respond effectively to the Western challenge, this belief tended to undercut official policies aimed at capital development necessary for modernization. During the days of the Canton system, when the West and its traders were kept at arm's length, it was generally the coastal Chinese who were skilled in handling—and profiting from—the flow of money from outside. The Mandarins in the capital accepted the benefits of controlling such money trading through licenses, but regarded those who traded as little more than unworthy mechanics.

A key desire of the PRC, when it was firmly established, was the assertion of complete control over Chinese fiscal and monetary policies. Almost immediately, however, the new government of China encountered the conflict between economic autonomy and the need for development capital. For many years this problem was resolved by dependence on the Soviet Union and its satellites for such credits as China obtained and by various schemes for self-generated capital. After the break with the Soviets, China needed a stronger economy to resist the implied threat from the north and to demonstrate a successful Chinese way of achieving economic and political development. Such is the situation today with China's renewed emphasis on modernization.

The PRC's fiscal and banking system has developed since 1950, and changes still occur. From a somewhat provincial, inward-turned set of institutions, Chinese banks are now becoming significant tools in capital accumulation and transfer.[50] Since political decisions are central to Chinese behavior, it is useful to know something of the structure whereby this is accomplished.

As Figure 2.1 shows, several organizations are significant in China's economic planning and execution. At the top is the Political

Bureau of the National People's Congress, especially its Finance and Trade Department. Titularly equal is the State Council, which sets forth financial policies to implement current plans for development. Those policies are executed by the Ministry of Finance, which is directly responsible for the People's Bank of China and the Bank of China. Together with the Chinese People's Insurance Company, these last three constitute the main instruments for capital development in China.[51]

There are five relatively new organizations that reflect Chinese efforts to upgrade management of foreign trade and investment.

The Financial and Economic Commission, established on July 1, 1979, consists of China's leading economic and financial people. Apparently this is to plan high policy.

The Import-Export Control Commission, established July 30, 1979, under the same chairman as the Foreign Investment Control Commission, has as its apparent purpose to oversee the flow of goods in and out of China, considering the barterlike character of much of Chinese trade.

The China International Trust and Investment Corporation (CITIC), already the best-known of the new set of economic organizations, will probably have a good deal to say about joint ventures. It was approved July 8, 1979, by the State Council.

The General Administration of Industry and Commerce will be the site of registration for authorized joint ventures and will issue a certificate of incorporation.

The State General Administration of Exchange Control is responsible for the unification of China's foreign exchange control and for the supervision of the foreign exchange balance of payments.

How these new bodies will function remains to be seen. At present CITIC has emerged as the most familiar because it handles joint ventures.

In line with the PRC's principle of "self-reliance," China for many years officially avoided direct loans from foreign banks. In those circumstances the role of the Bank of China was limited. China paid for its imports mostly in hard currency through sight letters of credit issued in favor of the exporter. Foreign purchasers of Chinese exports paid cash for Chinese goods through a foreign bank's sight letter of credit presented to the Bank of China's Peking office, or the appropriate mainland branch if goods originated outside Peking.

To import complete plants and heavy equipment during the early and mid-1970s, China engaged in ostensibly cash contracts based on a progress payment scheme.[52] Such contracts normally stipulated a 20 percent to 30 percent payment prior to the first shipment. A per-

centage of the invoice value was paid on each shipment thereafter.
The last two payments usually were 5 percent each and were paid on
acceptance of the plant or equipment and upon expiration of the guarantee period, respectively. Because such payments did not parallel
the exporter's manufacturing costs as they were incurred, the exporter
in effect provided financing until shipment. China was using progress
payments as a means of indirect financing. [53]

China also used a variety of other indirect foreign credits.
These fell into either short-; medium-, or long-term categories of
repayment. Short-term deferred payments ran no longer than 18
months. Many of these were for wheat from Canada and Australia, or
for heavy machinery and equipment.

In the early 1970s, as trade with the West expanded, China ran
a deficit. Much of this was in longer-term credits, up to five years,
from foreign suppliers under deferred payment plans. As a result of
this practice, the PRC's foreign debt by the end of 1978 was probably
close to $3 billion. Most of these credits were extended through sup-
pliers in China's major trading partners in Europe and Japan, at interest rates subsidized by government-supported programs to stimulate
exports. [54]

Where China undertook more extended terms, it was to support
ambitious industrial progress through purchase of turnkey plants,
heavy industrial equipment, and high-priced advanced technology.
Such medium- and long-term contracts usually provided for 10 percent
down payment, 10 percent on shipment of the equipment, and the remainder payable at a nominal 6 percent to 7 percent over five years,
with payment to begin on completion of the plant. Contracts for import of whole plants were usually guaranteed, and thus discounted by
suppliers, again through local export incentive programs, for 80 percent to 85 percent of the total cost. [55]

China was in fact paying interest costs that had been written into
the purchase price by the exporter. This method was expedient when
China preferred not to admit any foreign borrowings. But Chinese officials realized that they had no control of actual costs as long as interest charges were buried in the total contract price. Peking thus
became concerned about the cost of such supplier credits.

Another means whereby China obtained credit was through reciprocal bank deposits. The Bank of China placed nonconvertible
Chinese currency with a foreign correspondent bank, and that bank,
in turn, placed hard currency with the Bank of China for a specific
term. Since the renminbi (RMB) is soft, the hard-currency deposit
was in effect a fixed loan bearing no interest. China has used such
deposits primarily with Japanese, and to a limited extent with European, banks. [56]

During this period direct borrowings were limited to the Bank
of China's London branch, which participated in the London interbank

market to cover short-term deficiencies in hard currency. The Bank for International Settlements estimates that interbank borrowing exceeded $500 million in 1977. But the Chinese recognized that interbank credits, which matured in several months, were a risky way to obtain long-term capital. The other traditional financing mechanisms also proved to be inadequate to meet large capital requirements of the current modernization program.

New Methods of Financing

Constant spending of China's foreign-currency reserves have made it increasingly difficult to offer direct or even progress payments for the technology necessary to its modernization. In order for China to maintain its reserve of hard currency while continuing to acquire foreign technology, it has had to adopt more flexible financing policies and procedures. To bolster foreign-currency reserves, China's economic and financial planners in the late 1970s sought to expand exports, particularly textiles and light industrial products. In addition, the PRC began to expand its tourism industry, to encourage direct investment and remittances by overseas Chinese, and to accelerate the exploitation of its oil and mineral resources. Recognizing the time required to build a solid base of foreign exchange earnings, China offered a surprising solution to its payment problems—it would abandon its strict policy of direct payment or supplier credit in favor of alternative methods of acquiring technology and equipment from Japan, Western Europe, Canada, and the United States. [57]

Profitable trading with the PRC under the system of letters of credit (L/Cs) requires that foreign businessmen have a grasp of the deceptively simple workings of the Bank of China's L/C practices, as well as PRC trading transactions conducted under L/Cs. (Occasionally, small sales or purchases may be transacted against documentary drafts.) Besides being cumbersome, the Chinese L/C system contains pitfalls for the novice China trader who unknowingly may assume certain risks in a trade transaction. The main obstacle, however, is still that China is not a member of the International Chamber of Commerce and does not adhere to its guidelines, the Code for Uniform Customs and Practices for Documentary Credits. [58] Therefore China's L/Cs do not always conform to normally acceptable practice worldwide. The unique characteristics of export and import L/C practices are outlined separately below. [59]

For the most part both import and export transactions require standard documents: an exporter's draft, clean bills of lading, invoices, packing lists, certificates of origin, and inspection certificates. In making and receiving payments China generally deals in sight L/Cs. Usance credits are not used by the Bank of China any more than by any other bank for short-term trade credits. Typically, China's FTCs negotiate purchases on a basis of free on board (f.o.b.) or free alongside (f.a.s.), and sales on cost, insurance, and freight (c.i.f.) or cost and freight (c.&f.).

Exports

The standard payment clause in Chinese export contracts requires the foreign importer to open a confirmed, irrevocable, transferable, and divisible L/C in favor of the importing organization. The L/C must be opened by a designated correspondent of the Bank of China and be payable through sight drafts drawn on the correspondent bank. It must allow for partial shipments and transshipments.

The seller usually requests that an L/C be opened 15 to 30 days before the date of shipment, and that it remain valid for at least 15 days after expiration of the shipping period, as specified in the terms of the purchase contract. The opening date can often extend several months before the date of shipment. Since most contracts for exports do not specify exact dates for shipping, buyers are often without recourse to recoup losses owing to late shipment. Amendments extending the L/C are usually for the account of the buyer.

Chinese exporting organizations require the importer's L/C to be confirmed, thus assuring the Chinese that a foreign bank guarantees payment as long as accompanying documents fulfill the terms of the L/C. Payment cannot be withheld because of defects in the goods received. Documents are usually negotiated (presented and approved) by the Bank of China upon presentation of the exporting organization, and the confirming correspondent's account is charged to pay the Chinese exporter.

Imports

As with Chinese exports, the PRC's importing organizations prefer the L/C as a means of payment. Importers are paid by means of a sight L/C issued by the Bank of China's Peking office or one of the branches. Upon notice that a shipment is ready, the bank will open an irrevocable, transferable, and divisible L/C for sight drafts drawn directly on the Bank of China. The bank also issues revolving letters for long-term routine trading arrangements. Opening and expiration dates are often not as precisely set forth as in Chinese export contracts.

No foreign bank can confirm an L/C on the Bank of China. The bank does not permit foreign banks to act on its behalf, as is usual among other correspondent banks in such transactions. The bank permits its L/Cs to be advised to a foreign exporter through a local correspondent. Moreover, the L/C stipulates that drafts drawn under the credit must be drawn only on the Bank of China, which restricts negotiation of documents to that bank.

From an exporter's viewpoint, such restrictions limit the usefulness of a Chinese L/C. It presents three pitfalls. First, the exporter must send documents to China for negotiation. Briefly, at least, the exporting firm has neither goods nor title documents, nor has it received payment; thus it has no control over the transaction. Second, with confirmation by a local bank, the exporter must deal directly with the Bank of China should discrepancies occur. In the absence of a local bank to act as an intermediary, the exporter must deal with the Bank of China, thousands of miles away. Third, payment of a draft drawn on the Bank of China may take up to three weeks from the date the goods are shipped. The advising bank is not authorized to honor a draft before it is negotiated at the Bank of China. The exporter thereby extends to the Chinese purchaser 20 days or so of interest-free credit.

Until the Bank of China broadens its policy on L/Cs to permit them to be paid through local correspondents, an exporting firm has only one alternative. It may request the advising bank to issue a "silent confirmation." In this way the banks assume responsibility for negotiating documents in the usual manner and then discounting the drafts without recourse to the exporter, providing the documents conform to all terms in the L/C. The advising bank then applies to the Bank of China for reimbursement.

Two fairly typical conditions in Chinese L/Cs may deter banks from issuing silent confirmations. Some L/Cs provide for final examination of goods upon arrival at a Chinese port by the Chinese Commodities Inspection Bureau before full payment is made. To date China has not accepted foreign inspection certificates. Such provisions cancel the irrevocability and make an L/C conditional. Also, some L/Cs require shipping documents to conform to a sales contract. Beyond the scope of banks to determine, such conditions further reduce the usual benefits of documentary credits for export. To avoid these complications, the foreign exporting firm may request that the Bank of China accept its certification that all documents are in order.

Chinese Customs Administration

Besides the banking system, the Chinese regulation of trade is important for the U.S. businessman. As has been indicated, foreign access to the Chinese market is controlled directly by the Chinese foreign trade bureaucracy. The government exercises its tariff control through the General Customs Administration, which is supervised by the Ministry of Foreign Trade. [60]

China currently has a double-column tariff that provides for higher tariffs on imports from countries that do not extend most-favored-nation (MFN) treatment, and lower tariffs on imports from all other countries. Minimum-rate tariffs of between 5 percent and 150 percent apply to the countries extending MFN treatment, with "normal rate of between 7.5 percent to 400 percent applying to the other countries." As a general rule, lower tariffs are applied to construction materials, semifabricates, and machinery, while higher rates are levied on consumer goods such as watches and cigarettes.

THE CHINESE FOREIGN TRADE BUREAUCRACY

The discussion to this point has outlined in some detail those organizations within the Chinese foreign trade system with which a U.S. firm may expect to negotiate or that may have a role, directly or indirectly, in a commercial transaction. Yet in negotiating with the Chinese, the U.S. businessman must be interested in more than an organization chart or a listing of functions. There must also be interest in how the organization goes about its work and its approach to commercial negotiations. No discussion, therefore, would be complete without a brief treatment of the Chinese bureaucracy.

The Chinese foreign trade bureaucracy has its roots in a complex system referred to simply as the "tribute system," which required all foreign states desiring relations with China to undertake elaborate rituals in order to define their status in a hierarchy. Economically, the "tribute system" stimulated an exchange of goods and services between China and other countries and was the only legal means of access to the Chinese market.

The "tribute system" is relevant to understanding Chinese commercial practice today, not only because of parallels in the establishment of an elaborate and complex foreign trade bureaucracy but also because, similarly, there was no body of commercial law that gave the foreign trader clues to workings of the system—only rituals. (More will be said about these "rituals," or interpersonal relations, as an obstacle to commercial negotiations, in Chapter 3.)

Basic to a discussion of Chinese bureaucracy is that Chinese international commercial practice is not presently based on any body of law, but centers on standard contracts that become the "law" for the parties. [61] (Unlike the Soviet Union, where codification was completed in the early 1920s, by Western standards China remains in a formative stage of legal development.) [62] Moreover, as a general rule Chinese standard contracts between FTCs and foreign businessmen are basically the same today as when trade resumed in 1972.[63] (More will be said about commercial contracts in Chapters 3 and 5, but it is noteworthy that in the absence of firm legal rules, such contracts and the negotiation of these instruments assume great importance.)

In noting this lack of concern of the Chinese with formal law, Stanley Lubman, a prominent U.S. lawyer, stated that "it is difficult to convey to Westerners, especially Americans accustomed to the importance of legal rules and lawyers in the United States, the limited application and great ambiguities of the Chinese domestic law."[64] Another lawyer, Gabriele Reghizzi, makes a similar point: "Although a study of Chinese civil law is necessary in order to know the rights and the obligations of the Western trade representatives, . . . bargaining with the Chinese and assisting them in setting up their new plants, factual situations do not always correspond to legal norms."[65] Law, then, usually has been regarded by the Chinese as an instrument of secondary importance but useful in expressing flexible and changeable policies.

Moreover, the Chinese—in Confucian and Communist days alike—have always been suspicious of law as a tool for regulating commercial activity.[66] Worthy individuals know instinctively what is proper behavior, and therefore do not need external rules to guide them. Conversely, unworthy persons, not knowing what is proper, will find a way to twist or evade any set of rules. In 1979 there was some evidence that the Chinese may be discovering that law perhaps has some utility, especially in the commercial area. For example, the promulgation of a new law on July 1, 1979, governing joint ventures, provided a measure of clarity hitherto unavailable and was widely considered to be the first practical step taken by the Chinese government to attract foreign participation in its modernization program. China's vice-premier, Deng Xiaoping, in an interview in July 1979, noted that "In terms of the number of laws, the U.S. ranks first . . . on our part, we have too few laws, and it is imperative that we adopt some."[67]

The diminished importance of China's legal system, especially as it relates to commercial practices, heightens the importance of China's trade bureaucracy. Particularly formidable, as will be noted in Chapter 3, is the difficulty for the U.S. businessman in making the first contacts with this trade bureaucracy. For example, time and again the U.S. businessman has been told to write to the head office, which will route the letter to the relevant department. Under this system information sent to China usually manages to find its way down to the appropriate department. But, as will also be pointed out in Chapter 3, in a trade bureaucracy as large and complex as China's, this "filtering down" of information can take much time. Although there is some indication that now it is sometimes possible for business-men to write to individuals who handle a specific product for import or export, or at least indicate that the attention of a specific department is desired, making the first contact is still difficult and time consuming.

Indeed, the Chinese trade bureaucracy has certain characteristics of government bureaucracies all over the world. For example, the requirement for very strict compliance with contract specifications is not unique to China, for its trade officials, like officials the world over, wish to avoid blame for purchasing or accepting defective foreign goods. Moreover, the notable uncommunicativeness of Chinese bureaucrats with foreigners can be explained, according to Michael Oksenberg, in terms of the traditional desire of the Chinese bureaucracy to maintain secrecy within its own hierarchy.[68]

Even Chinese trade officials have difficulties with their bureaucracy. An official of China National Light Industrial Products noted that "it takes us months—sometimes years—to do what other countries can accomplish quickly, because we common people have little power against bureaucratic regulations."[69] Yet, despite efforts to remove all status symbols, one U.S. observer has noted that "the grade of the Mao suit improves as you go up the ladder."[70] Thus, still another indication that bureaucracies are somewhat the same the world over.

Illustrative of the workings of the Chinese foreign trade bureaucracy is a series of 1976 translations from Foreign Trade Practice, a book that reportedly remains one of the principal texts at Peking's Institute of Foreign Trade.[71] From these translations one can appreciate the methodical and time-consuming approach taken by elements of the foreign trade bureaucracy to accomplish its responsibilities. Prior to trade, for example, there are at least six steps for an FTC to undertake: carry out business arrangements according to a plan, divide the commodities in the plan, examine commodity specifications, consider substitutes, solicit end users' opinions to modify the plan or supplement its content, and efficiently record organizational purchase orders.[72] In this preparatory work it is pointed out that "in the process of carrying out the plan and maintaining contact with business entities both at home and abroad, a great amount of time passes from the moment of initial inquiry, involving complicated conditions and details as well as frequent revisions."[73] Such time-consuming activities in this preparatory work might affect the U.S. firm seeking to make contact with the appropriate Chinese FTC or end user. Other delays are caused by the Chinese need to ensure that plan specifications are "comprehensive" and fit the uses indicated.

To overcome this potential problem, Chinese end users are advised to initiate purchase studies on the basis of new products that are advertised in magazines and to write down the name of the magazine or attach the ad as reference. Similarly, time is consumed while a decision to purchase is made through end users' "mis-estimating the true cost" of a requested item. The FTC would then suggest that substitutes be used. But to do this a form must be used. In short, more time is consumed, and consequently, there is a delay in making the purchase.

The above illustrates the bureaucratic aspects of preparatory work mandated prior to trade. Subsequently, the appropriate foreign supplier must be chosen. Again the 1976 translations of pertinent sections of <u>Foreign Trade Practice</u> illustrate the time-consuming bureaucratic procedures that are used, and consequently, the obstacles that a U.S. exporter may face in selling to China. It is noteworthy that "old trading 'friends'" may receive slightly different treatment. For example, they may receive a form letter inquiry rather than a formal letter of inquiry, which is used for "new friends."

With regard to quotations, the Chinese textbook suggests the following four quotation methods: quotations by telegram, quotation lists, formal letter quotations, and voluntary quotations. In examining the contents of quotations, the first consideration is "whether or not the specifications of the goods that have been quoted are compatible with the nation's requirements." No definition is provided of "nation's requirements," but presumably interpolation from the plan is required. The textbook also counsels caution in assessing foreign price quotations, and stipulates a few of the "ploys" used by foreign firms to win a contract. Specifically singled out are firms that "feel their products are so much better than those of the competition that they can compete without regard to the market price. According to the textbook these firms will intentionally raise their prices. Another ploy is that of firms working with other firms and raising "a fence on the ocean floor." All of these ploys must be recognized and investigated, which of course takes time and delays negotiations.

NOTES

1. Jeffrey Schultz, <u>China's Foreign Trade Corporations . . . Organizations and Personnel</u> (Washington, D.C.: National Council for U.S.-China Trade, April 1979), p. 1. In support of this the author was told in July 1980, by a visitor to China, that no organizational charts were freely available. In asking about this, the visitor, a U.S. businessman, found that even Chinese governmental telephone directories were considered to be classified information and were not available to foreigners. In asking why, the visitor was told that it revealed too much about the Chinese governmental structure.

2. U.S., Joint Publications Research, "On Reform of the Foreign Trade Management System," by Zhou Renhuan and Li Younglin, China Report—Economic Affairs, no. 38 (Washington, D.C.: Foreign Broadcast Information Service, January 21, 1980), p. 83.

3. U.S., Joint Publications Research, "The System of Foreign Trade Must Be Reformed," by Zhang Chongwen, China Report—Economic Affairs, no. 49 (Washington, D.C.: Foreign Broadcast Information Service, March 21, 1980), p. 60.

4. "Soviets Seek to Improve Ties to China," Washington Post, April 8, 1980, p. A-7. Although this is a "journalistic headline" of extremely complex and difficult Sino-Soviet relations, the Chinese are not without social, economic, and political ties with the Soviets. See note 5 and the reference to the recent article by Xiong Fu.

5. U.S., Congress, Office of Technology Assessment, Technology and East-West Trade (Washington, D.C.: Government Printing Office, 1979), p. 259. See also "China in the 1980s," Economist, December 29, 1979, p. 23.

The following observations on problems associated with reforming the economic management system is perhaps illustrative of the current economic dialogues occurring in China.

> For a long time we indiscriminately copied the model of the Soviet economic system of Stalin's time and set up a highly centralized and insular type of economic management which became a system of its own: Capital construction is invested in from above, production plans are arranged from above, materials are allocated from above, products are transferred and marketed from above, profits are handed over above, losses are subsidized from above and wages are paid according to instructions from above. This kind of system artificially severed the natural contacts between the enterprises and caused them to be completely isolated from the market and the customers. . . . In this way, how can economic development avoid becoming ossified? Therefore, to stimulate the economy, a fundamental problem is to emancipate the minds, completely disregard the fetters of old theory and develop socialist commodity economy in a conscious, comprehensive and planned manner. The "greater decision-making power" trail points in Sichuan are making efforts in this direction.

See Xiong Fu, "A Talk Based on Giving Greater Decision-Making Power to Enterprises in Sichuan—A Tentative Discussion of Problems in Reforming the Economic Management System," Hongqi (Beijing), no. 16 (August 16, 1980), p. 21. Translated in PRC Daily Report, September 11, 1980, p. L49.

6. U.S., Joint Publications Research, "On Reform," p. 83.

7. Gabriele Reghizzi, "Legal Aspects of Trade with China: The Italian Experience," Harvard International Law Journal 9 (Winter 1968): 85; and Gene T. Hsiao, The Foreign Trade of China: Policy, Law, and Practice (Berkeley: University of California Press, 1977), pp. 71-73. See also Victor Li, Law and Politics in China's Foreign Trade (Seattle: University of Washington Press, 1977), pp. 339-40.

8. Reghizzi, "Legal Aspects," p. 86.

9. Donald W. Klein, "The Foreign Trade Apparatus," in Law and Politics in China's Foreign Trade, ed. Victor H. Li (Seattle: University of Washington Press, 1977), p. 309.

10. Z. V. Dashkevich and A. A. Zhemchug, Osnovnyye vedenia o vneshne torgovle Kitaya (Moscow: Mysl', 1965), p. 66.

11. See, for example, V. S. Pozdniakov, Sovetskoye gosudarstvo i vneshniaia torgovliya—pravovye voprosy [The Soviet state and foreign trade—legal questions] (Moscow: Mezhdunarodnye Otnosheniia, 1976); and Alexander Eckstein, ed., China Trade Prospects and U.S. Policy (New York: Praeger, 1971), pp. 674-75.

12. Eckstein, China Trade Prospects, p. 675.

13. U.S., Central Intelligence Agency, China: Post-Mao Search for Civilian Industrial Technology (Washington, D.C.: National Foreign Assessment Center, February 1979), p. 9. China has always had strong decentralizing tendencies primarily owing to provincial diversities.

14. U.S., Joint Publications Research, "On Reform," p. 86.

15. Ibid.

16. National Council for U.S.-China Trade, Selling Technology to China: A Workbook . . . (Washington, D.C.: National Council for U.S.-China Trade, December 1979), p. 219.

17. U.S., Joint Publications Research, "How to Improve the Economic Effectiveness of Imported Technology and Equipment," by Wang Furang, China Report—Economic Affairs, no. 7 (Washington, D.C.: Foreign Broadcast Information Service, August 14, 1979), p. 33.

18. U.S., Congress, Office of Technology Assessment, Technology and East-West Trade, p. 265; and U.S., Central Intelligence Agency, The Computer Industry in the People's Republic of China (Washington, D.C.: National Foreign Assessment Center, 1973), p. 7

19. Control Data Corporation, "Interoffice Memorandum—Results of Fourth Ministry Visit," December 28, 1979, p. 1.

20. U.S., Joint Publications Research, "On Reform," p. 86.

21. Ibid., p. 84.

22. Ibid., pp. 85-86.

23. For a more complete description of the planning process, see National Council for U.S.-China Trade, Selling Technology to

China: Proceedings of the Conference on Selling Technology to China (Washington, D. C.: National Council for U.S.-China Trade, December 1979), pp. 22-37.

24. U.S., Joint Publications Research, "The System," p. 61.

25. Ibid.

26. Ibid.

27. "China in the 1980's," Economist, December 29, 1979.

28. U.S., Congress, Office of Technology Assessment, Technology and East-West Trade, p. 269.

29. "Remarks by Yuan Baohua, vice-minister, SEC, in June 1979 to National Council for U.S.-China Trade's Board of Directors' Delegation to China, China Business Review, July-August 1979, pp. 16-17.

30. Ibid., p. 17.

31. Gene Hsiao, "Communist China's Foreign Trade Organizations," Vanderbilt Law Review 20 (March 1967): 305-6.

32. Hsiao, The Foreign Trade of China, p. 73.

33. Hsiao, "Communist China's Foreign Trade Organizations," p. 306.

34. Schultz, China's Foreign Trade Corporations, p. 77.

35. Ibid., p. 78.

36. Ibid., p. 7.

37. John De Pauw, Soviet-American Trade Negotiations (New York: Praeger, 1979), pp. 14-16.

38. Stanley Lubman, "What to Expect at the Canton Fair," Wall Street Journal, April 28, 1972, p. 1.

39. Japan External Trade Organization, How to Approach the China Market (Tokyo: Press International, 1972), pp. 9-10. This book is an English version of the Japan-China Trade Handbook.

40. This discussion of FTCs is based primarily on Schultz, China's Foreign Trade Corporations.

41. In recent years "domestic" corporations (as opposed to "national" corporations) have been established to handle specialized commodity transactions and to serve as "consultants" to particular ministries and national FTCs on imports of specialized technology. For additional information, see ibid., pp. 12-13.

42. Audrey G. Donnithorne, China's Economic System (London: George Allen and Unwin, 1967), p. 486.

43. Hsiao, The Foreign Trade of China, p. 84.

44. Schultz, China's Foreign Trade Corporations, p. 3.

45. Ibid., p. 13. According to the author, "The number of functional departments appears to be fluid, individual FTCs (like their Soviet counterparts) maintaining them as they are needed."

46. Dashkevich and Zhemchug, Osnovnyye, p. 34.

47. Ibid. There is some indication that there is administrative and legal overlap in authority to carry out conciliation and arbitration decisions. See also Schultz, China's Foreign Trade Corporations, p. 4. Of interest is Hsiao's observation that the Chinese system of "economic accountability" actually "originates from the Soviet Union." Hsiao, "Communist China's Foreign Trade Organizations," p. 310. By extension it seems reasonable to assume that components of the two economic systems may be similar in composition and operation.

48. Schultz, China's Foreign Trade Corporations, p. 4.

49. This section is based largely on an unpublished paper by the author and Jon Holstine.

50. Dick Wilson, "The Bank of China's Expanding Role in International Finance," U.S.-China Business Review, November-December 1974, pp. 21-22.

51. The precise relationship among these agencies is still evolving. Responsibilities that fall to one organization or authority may easily be assigned, or appearances may deceive the outside observer. For a range of good discussions see Bohdan O. Szuprowicz and Maria R. Szuprowicz, Doing Business with the People's Republic of China, Industries and Markets (New York: John Wiley & Sons, 1979), pp. 73-74; Mary Goldring, "Tea at the Bank of China," Euromoney, March 1979, pp. 65, 67; and Terry Atlas, "Capitalistic Look at Chinese Bank," Chicago Tribune, April 15, 1979, sec. 5, p. 1. A more recent analysis is Dick Wilson, "How Banks Work in China," Banker 130 (January 1980): 19, 21-25, 27.

52. David L. Denny, "Recent Developments in the International Financial Policies of the People's Republic of China," Stanford Journal of International Studies 10 (Spring 1975): 177-78.

53. Ibid.

54. Alistair Wrightman, "How Japan Finances Trade with China," U.S.-China Business Review, March-April 1975, pp. 30-34.

55. Alistair Wrightman, "Financing China's Steel Imports from Japan," U.S.-China Business Review, September-October 1975, pp. 28-29.

56. Denny, "Recent Developments," pp. 173-74.

57. "The Uncontrollable Stateless Money," Far Eastern Economic Review, September 21, 1979, pp. 44-45; and Melinda Liu, "Rock-Bottom Terms Are a Must for Foreigners," Far Eastern Economic Review, September 21, 1979, pp. 61-63.

58. U.S., Congress, Joint Economic Committee, China: A Reassessment of the Economy, 94th Cong., 1st sess., July 10, 1975, p. 661.

59. For a thorough description, to which this section is indebted, see Katherine Schwering, "Financing Imports from China," U.S.-China Business Review, September-October, 1974, pp. 36-40. An-

other useful discussion is Liu Chao-chin, China's Foreign Trade and Its Management (Hong Kong: Economic Information Agency of the PRC, 1978), pp. 97-105.

60. Schultz, China's Foreign Trade Corporations, p. 78.

61. Stanley B. Lubman, "Trade between the United States and the People's Republic of China: Practice, Policy and Law," Law and Policy in International Business 8 (1976): 4.

62. Hsiao, "Communist China's Foreign Trade Organizations," p. 319.

63. U.S., Congress, Joint Economic Committee, Chinese Economy Post-Mao, vol. 1, Policy and Performance (Washington, D.C.: U.S. Government Printing Office, November 9, 1978), p. 758.

64. Lubman, "Trade," p. 3.

65. Reghizzi, "Legal Aspects," p. 86.

66. William P. Alford, "Law and Chinese Foreign Trade," Problems of Communism 28 (September-December 1979): 81. See also Preston Torbert, "The American Lawyer's Role in Trade with China," American Bar Association Journal 63 (August 1977): 1117.

67. "Walter Surrey's Remarks to Deng Xiaoping," China Business Review, July-August 1979, p. 15.

68. Michael Oksenberg, "Communications within the Chinese Bureaucracy," China in the Seventies 87 (1973): 6-7.

69. Louis Kraar, "China: Trying the Market Way," Fortune, December 31, 1979, p. 51.

70. "China Partly Opens the Door to U.S. Business," Fortune 80 (August 1972): 220.

71. "How China Views Importing: Preparatory Work Prior to Trade," U.S.-China Business Review, January-February 1976, pp. 17-18; "How China Prepares to Buy from Abroad," U.S.-China Business Review, vol. 3 (July-August 1976); and "How China Prepares to Import," U.S.-China Business Review, January-February 1977.

72. Ministry of Foreign Trade, Foreign Trade Practice, rev. ed. (Shanghai: Institute of Foreign Trade, 1972), as translated in U.S.-China Business Review, January-February 1976, pp. 17-18.

73. Ibid.

3

THE DIFFICULTIES ENCOUNTERED IN U.S.–CHINESE COMMERCIAL NEGOTIATIONS

This chapter discusses the procedural aspects of commercial negotiations with Chinese traders, the process of negotiating a business contract with the Chinese government, the probable pattern of the negotiation itself, and the strategy and tactics necessary to pursue successful negotiations with the Chinese foreign trade organizations.

Some of the hindrances and impediments to U.S.-Chinese commercial negotiations discussed in this chapter are the character of the negotiations themselves, the time factor, the difficulty of establishing interpersonal relations, demands for concessions, and the results of the negotiations on contractual provisions that cover price, guarantees, delivery terms and date, and payment.

The process of commercial negotiation, for purposes of this study, is not meant to convey a precise "sequence of demands and offers and their interrelationships,"[1] simply because little information is available about the specifics of the sequence of the demands and offers made during the many U.S.-Chinese commercial transactions conducted each year.

Nor does the process of U.S.-Chinese commercial negotiations mean the mere drafting of the contract. As the discussion in this chapter and the succeeding ones will show, tentative agreement between the parties is a multistage process involving such preliminary stages as "technical negotiations," "arriving at the general terms of the sale," the "license of technology," and "the transfer of services." In addition, as noted in Chapter 4, the securing of a U.S. export license can be vitally important in the completion of a successful U.S.-Chinese commercial transaction. Thus, for purposes of this study, "process" is the sum total of negotiating a U.S.-Chinese commercial transaction, including the establishment of contacts, the arriving at the general terms of the sale, the drafting of the contract, securing the U.S. export license, and the actual delivery of the goods and/or services to the People's Republic of China (PRC).

THE CHARACTER OF NEGOTIATIONS

According to one general view of negotiations, bargaining is a game of chance and skill, something like chess or poker.[2] This view suggests that a skillful negotiator is someone who makes good moves in the same way that a chess master makes good moves. In fact, in discussions of U.S.-Chinese relations the analogy to a chess match is sometimes mentioned. Veronica Yhap, a long-time U.S.-China trader, for example, says that negotiating with PRC officials is "like playing a game of chess. They are superb negotiators and skillful psychologists."[3] Still another observer notes that in Chinese chess, the object is not to capture an opponent's pieces directly, but gradually to surround and isolate them.[4]

Avoiding a costly frontal assault and subtly undermining the enemy is also a basic precept of traditional Chinese statecraft. Granted the U.S. business exeuctive is not an enemy, nor are commercial negotiations exercises in statecraft. Still, in some respects the comparison of chess with commercial negotiations seems apropos, especially if one looks at the game of chess as having three parts: a beginning game, a middle game, and an end game. Successful play of the game depends on successful play of all three parts in toto. With this analogy in mind—the beginning game is analogous to making meaningful contact with the Chinese; the middle game, to the process of negotiations; and the end game, to the signing and fulfillment of the contract—let us examine the character of negotiations with the Chinese foreign trade organizations (FTOs).

In the discussion emphasis is placed on these negotiations as an obstacle to the signing of a contract, whether the U.S. executive/negotiator is a potential buyer or seller. The discussion is not intended to be a "how to do it" guide to negotiations, but merely to present data on the character or process of commercial negotiations with the Chinese.

Julian Sobin emphasized that "If I had a final statement on negotiating with China—it is 'do it your own way.' People will tell you that there are certain rules and regulations and precedents that have been established in trading with China but at our company we don't buy this."[5] Thus, this advice implies that the Chinese, like all traders, will seek certain terms with which they are familiar, but in the final analysis will negotiate an agreement based on common sense and compromise. The only difficulty with this advice is that the company of the negotiator just quoted was selling technology that the Chinese sorely wanted and needed—oil drilling equipment. For companies with products and services that the Chinese may want but do not need as much as drilling equipment, it might be wise to understand the game of Chinese chess as translated into the commercial genre and the process of negotiations.

The author's questionnaire data revealed the following information about the character of U.S.-Chinese commercial negotiations:

Format: Most (73 percent) of the negotiations were held in Peking. Discussions concerning product specifications generally varied from one week to two months in length.

The PRC negotiators: The U.S. firms surveyed reported no set number of Chinese negotiators. In fact, most firms reported a number varying from 1 to 40. Moreover, the majority of firms (80 percent) reported not all of the Chinese negotiators were present throughout all of the sessions. Such a circumstance would, of course, make it difficult to establish a working personal relationship with the Chinese negotiators.

These data are consonant with data reported in a survey of U.S. firms in which 47.1 percent of the companies reported that the size of the Chinese negotiation team ranged from two to four members and another 20.3 percent reported the Chinese team to range from five to seven members.[6] The author's data indicated that the majority of U.S. companies (54 percent) could readily identify a chief negotiator, and that the negotiators had the authority to make on-the-spot decisions with respect to price, quantity, and terms. One U.S. company official stated that "they always say: 'We have to contact end users,' but we know they decide right then and there and to hell with the end users." Yet another U.S. executive, whose company reached several multimillion-dollar agreements with the PRC, observed that the Chinese "Foreign Trade Corporation chief appeared sensitive to the FTC end user relationship [and moreover] the end user chief was very decisive."

Negotiation style: The majority of companies contacted by a 1979 survey (76.8 percent) perceived major differences in negotiation styles, characterized as follows:

Chinese take longer time to make decisions (60.1 percent)
Chinese are more concerned with long-term associations
  (43.5 percent)
Americans are more flexible (42.0 percent)
Chinese are indirect and like to ramble (34.1 percent)[7]

Tactics: From the responses to the author's questionnaire as well as follow-up interviews with company executives, it appears that tactics employed by the Chinese negotiators varied considerably. With regard to the question of whether the PRC negotiators played "a waiting game," for example, the majority of U.S. companies (58.3 percent) reported that the Chinese did not play a "waiting game." This finding correlates with the impression reported by a slight majority of respondents (53 percent) that the Chinese did not use time as an instrument to gain an advantage in their commercial negotiations with U.S. firms. (More will be said about the use of time below.) Of those U.S. companies reporting that the Chinese did play a waiting game, most indicated a waiting time lasting, for the most part, not longer than a few days to a few weeks, although one extreme instance was five months.

With regard to other tactics, an overwhelming majority of U.S. companies (92.3 percent) reported that while PRC negotiators did not alternate between "hard" and "soft" lines by changing team chiefs without notice, they did, in a majority of instances (64.2 percent), mention other Western competitors during negotiating sessions. Chinese negotiators did not, in a majority of instances (76.9 percent), "solicit help" in resolving a bureaucratic snafu.

First Contacts

The beginning of serious negotiations with the Chinese for the most part starts with obtaining an invitation to China. In fact, Erik Kihl, a U.S. Department of Commerce official recommends that U.S. companies not go to China without one. [8] Based on responses to the author's questionnaire, there is no single direct avenue that a foreign seller may use to get an invitation. As might be expected, once an end user shows a real interest in a firm and its commodities, communications become easier and business is expedited. Such "real interest" apparently is not readily and speedily communicated to U.S. firms, however. In fact, according to a 1975 survey, about three-quarters of the U.S. firms reported that the Chinese take a longer time to reply to foreign-trade proposals than do Europeans. [9] In support of this, research indicates that the lack of formal contacts in the PRC, invitation requirements, and lack of response to proposals are major obstacles preventing expansion of U.S. trade with China. * The

---

*Although the study was conducted in 1975, Chase Pacific Trade Advisors indicated to the author in November 1979 that as far as their clients were concerned, the ranking of these obstacles had not changed significantly. Moreover, although the principal obstacle is listed as the lack of market information, for purposes of this study it is assumed

TABLE 3.1

Major Obstacles Preventing Expansion of PRC Trade Activities
(N = 2,574)

Obstacle	Percent
Lack of market information	15.23
Lack of formal contacts in PRC	14.15
PRC invitation requirements	10.22
Lack of response from PRC	9.83
Remoteness of PRC markets	8.59
Inadequate market research	7.77
Western export controls	5.94
Limited currency availability	5.01
Inability to service sales	4.97
Language and cultural barriers	3.61
Unprofitability of sales	3.42
Western competition	3.38
Lack of internal manpower	3.34
Lack of internally budgeted funds	2.29
Lack of patent protection	2.25
Total	100.00

Notes: An average of 3.7 obstacles was indicated by each respondent. The results indicate primarily the frequency of response to individual obstacles. The first six obstacles also show the number of responses ranking those obstacles as most important. Chase indicated to the author in November 1979 that as far as their clients were concerned, the ranking of these obstacles had not changed significantly.

Source: Chase Pacific Trade Advisors, "Results of Survey on Trade and Marketing in the People's Republic of China," October 8, 1975, p. 4.

results of this research are shown in Table 3.1. The table shows that such obstacles ranked above Western export controls and limited currency availability in preventing trade expansion with China.

In short, trading with China offers U.S. executives many unusual challenges, not the least of which is getting a foot inside the trade door. The way in which a firm goes about this can be crucial, as the author's research has shown.

---

that the U.S. company has done its homework and knows what it wants to sell.

One China trader suggests at least five gambits that should be pursued by U.S. firms:

Letters with appropriate enclosures of technical literature directed to the relevant trade corporations and to the China Council for the Promotion of Foreign Trade in Peking;

Direct approaches to members of the commercial section of the PRC's Embassy in Washington;

Attendance at the Canton Fair;

Representation on scientific or industrial delegations to China; and

Engaging an experienced adviser or agent to assist, support, and co-ordinate the seller's approaches to China. [10]

Still another approach used with increasing frequency is the technical seminar. [11] Such a technique involves lectures and some-times demonstrations of equipment by technical specialists sent to Peking and occasionally to other Chinese cities by their companies. These sessions offer an opportunity for sellers' representatives to talk to end-user counterparts. Such direct communication usually is not possible at the Canton Fair. [12] During 1978 more than 80 U.S. firms and several U.S. delegations held such seminars. [13]

First commercial contacts with Chinese can be difficult, as Boeing's early experience shows. Patience and tenacity, however, are requisite for the U.S. businessman. For example, Boeing first detected Chinese interest in jet transports early in 1971 through in-formation gained via European embassies. [14] But efforts to reach the Chinese through third parties and trading firms in Hong Kong brought no response. After President Richard Nixon's visit to China in Feb-ruary 1972, the company renewed its efforts to contact the Chinese through diplomatic channels, but without success. [15] Boeing then tried the simple ploy of writing a letter to Peking's flag carrier, the Civil Aviation Administration of China, on March 7, 1972. About three weeks later Boeing received a cable from the China National Machinery Import and Export Corporation inviting the company to send representatives to visit China and to see the Canton Trade Fair. [16]

The Boeing experience illustrates that there is no tried-and-true gambit for making a first contact with the Chinese. According to Paul Van Slambrouck, a U.S. Department of Commerce official, "sometimes an American businessman will write to one of the Chinese trade corporations and get no response. A few years later the Chinese will answer him and ask him to come to Peking tomorrow." [17] In fact, a U.S. executive who had corresponded for years with a Chinese official who signed himself as M903 was sitting in the dentist's chair in Hong Kong when he learned that M903 wanted to meet him immediately. [18] Years of patience apparently had paid off.

Sobin Chemicals also started business with the Chinese with a letter in 1971. According to Julian Sobin, chairman of Sobin Chemicals, he first wrote to the Chinese when former Secretary of State Henry Kissinger visited China in 1971.[19] In the letter Sobin specified the kinds of trade agreements he could establish with the Chinese. The Chinese did not respond, so the next year Sobin wrote another letter. This time he took a more personalized tack and included a photograph and a resume. He suggested to the Chinese that since he alone made decisions at his $40 million-a-year chemical firm, it would be far easier for the Chinese to deal directly with him; moreover, in dealing with other companies the Chinese would find only the typical bureaucratic maze endemic to large companies.[20]

According to Sobin, this approach was borne out when a member of the Chinese delegation approached him after Sobin's first visit and asked him to see the president of DuPont to assure him that there was no slight intended by the Chinese inviting Sobin and not DuPont. It was simply that there would not have been enough room to put up all the DuPont executives who would have had to make the trip.[21]

In order to negotiate with the Chinese it generally is almost axiomatic that a U.S. company first be invited to Canton or Peking. However, there are exceptions. International Harvester, for example, in 1973 received an unsolicited request from the Chinese to provide a price quotation on tractors. According to a company executive, the contract was negotiated entirely by telex. The result was a $300,000 contract that paved the way for a subsequent $2.5 billion one for other equipment.[22]

First contacts are not all one-sided, with the U.S. business executive resolutely pursuing the Chinese. Sometimes, but probably rarely, contacts can be quite fortuitous. One U.S. company, in the period shortly after the signing of the Shanghai Communiqué in February 1972, adopted the traditional route of making contact by sending information, brochures, and letters through agencies in Hong Kong and the Canadian Embassy in Ottawa.[23] The company, however, received no real sign of interest from the Chinese until about a year later—when, almost miraculously, company executives encountered a Chinese delegation that was visiting one of its licensee's plants in Europe. Subsequently, over a cup of coffee with the U.S. company executives, a Chinese official casually remarked, as if the U.S. firm had never tried to make contact, "We have been trying to figure out how to get in touch with you."[24] As a result of that casual meeting, the U.S. company was invited to Peking to plan two weeks of technical seminars and lectures. In short, there is no tried-and-true method for making a first contact with the Chinese.

The Canton Fair

Although first contacts and negotiations are increasingly being conducted outside of the twice-yearly Canton (Guangzhou) Export Commodities Fair, the fair generally is still an excellent place to initiate business. It should be remembered, however, that the fair is heavily export-oriented and only Chinese commodities are displayed.[25] Foreign trade corporations (FTCs), however, do purchase foreign products during this event held in the spring (April 15-May 15) and the fall (October 15-November 15).[26]

Attendance at the fair is "by invitation only" from a Chinese trading corporation.[27] Quite naturally, owing to the great increase in the number of requests for invitations in recent years, they are issued to firms with which the trading corporations have working relationships or consider the development of relationships to be desirable.[28]

In all probability no contracts will be signed on the first visit. One American, who has represented a number of U.S. corporations, has advised his clients to think in terms of at least three meetings with the Chinese when at the Canton Fair: an introductory session to present the basic proposal; a follow-up discussion with technically qualified trading corporation officials; and a meeting with what the Chinese call "the most responsible person" or the ranking member of a trade group.[29]

There is some indication that the autumn 1979 Canton Fair might be the last.[30] What is contemplated instead is year-round business conducted in a Canton foreign-trade center located at or adjacent to the current fairgrounds. If this occurs, it will mean easier access for business people.

At recent fairs as many as 5,000 negotiators from China's ten product-related trade corporations have conducted business negotiations.[31] By and large these representatives are not consumers, end users, manufacturers, or suppliers. Usually the U.S. business executive will be facing a team of four or five Chinese negotiators, each with different duties. As the discussions proceed, the Chinese team members are likely to "change hats." For example, the role of interpreter is passed around; and once the job changes, the previous interpreter will not understand if spoken to.[32] Moreover, the composition of the team may change without explanation. If it gets really interested, it will bring in a product expert. According to executives who have conducted negotiations at the fair, it is not unusual to find competitors sitting at adjacent tables during trade discussions.[33] Also, some of the Chinese negotiators at a session may abruptly get up and leave, while others may randomly wander in, perhaps even interrupting the flow of conversation.[34]

Once first contacts have been made, the U.S. company enters a new phase, perhaps analogous in parlance to the middle game play.

Technical Negotiations

Like commercial negotiations with the Russians, negotiation of contracts with the Chinese is normally a two-stage procedure, with technical clarification as the first. The negotiating logic for the Chinese is very simple: Why discuss price and other contract terms with the U.S. company before they know exactly what the seller proposes to sell? Thus, commercial negotiations to establish the terms and conditions of the transaction usually take place only after the Chinese have absorbed every possible technical detail, sometimes including design and research matters that a company may regard as proprietary. [35]

Perhaps the reason for absorbing every possible detail is explained, in the words of one Chinese writer:

> The equipment and technology that we import must be of a truly advanced kind, and for this reason we must organize well our overseas inspection and technical intelligence work, understand the various performance characteristics of equipment from different countries, and know about differences in quality of equipment and prices. [36]

There is some evidence that since 1979 the Chinese have begun to put greater stress on the "most suitable" rather than the "most advanced" technology, indicating a recognition that certain technologies, such as labor-saving farm machinery, may not be appropriate for China's needs. [37] If this is true, then the Chinese will be all the more interested in what kind of technology is under consideration before they begin to consider price and other commercial terms.

In evaluating which technology to buy from whom, the Chinese take into consideration four fundamental criteria: novelty, reliability, competitiveness, and suitability for China. In many instances China has demonstrated a preference for technology with an established reputation for performance. [38] Thus "novelty" and "competitiveness" may be downplayed somewhat for "reliability" and "suitability." (Certainly this was the case in China's decision to buy equipment from the Control Data Corporation, which is detailed in Chapter 5.)

Intensive negotiations between Techimport and the High Voltage Engineering Corporation (HVEC) of Burlington, Massachusetts, during August 1978 for the $5.2 million purchase of a tandem accelerator illustrate how the Chinese aim to extract the maximum technical information.[39] The purpose of this exercise, of course, is to wear down the U.S. negotiators with highly technical questions in order to enable the Chinese (Techimport in this case) to get the best possible contract terms.

Although the Chinese initiated correspondence with HVEC as early as 1975, nothing came of the initial contacts, possibly because of the political confusion in China occasioned by the succession struggle involving the Gang of Four. It was not until early 1978 that HVEC was invited to Peking for preliminary talks.[40] After these talks the Chinese sent their own ten-man delegation to the United States to visit HVEC and to talk to one of the firm's major competitors as well. The company was then invited to Peking in August to discuss the possible purchase of the HI-13 tandem accelerator.

HVEC sent its best people, including both engineers and management decision makers. The projected two-week visit lasted 32 days, with the company team meeting 35 times with its Chinese counterparts. During the technical negotiation phase the scientist members of the Chinese negotiating team steadily questioned HVEC about an improved version of the HI-13. According to HVEC negotiators the Chinese intended to extract the maximum technical information and wear down the U.S. team with highly technical questions in order to enable Techimport to get the best possible contract terms.[41]

The HVEC negotiators countered with a threat to break off negotiations and leave without concluding the contract. After the second U.S. threat to leave without signing a contract, the Chinese quickly moved to an agreement. Thus, HVEC's patience and endurance yielded dividends. Not only was it able to obtain a favorable contract but it also was given the opportunity to meet with end users of its equipment to talk about possible follow-on business.

In any event, technical negotiations are integral to large and complex transactions, particularly where the Chinese may be acquiring plants, processes, or complicated equipment or systems. Such negotiations, which can include a wide variety of subjects—such as plans, specifications, drawings, warranties, involved delivery and payment terms, training arrangements, spare parts, schedules, inspection procedures, and technology transfer—have enlarged agreements into weighty volumes. For example, Boeing's first contract for the sale of ten Boeing 707 aircraft to China ran well over 100 pages.

In technical negotiations one basic issue in discussions can be quantification of the parts and spare parts lists. For example, with Caterpillar the biggest issue was the Chinese refusal to accept Caterpillar's recommended spare parts list.[42] The Chinese composed a list apparently based on the experiences they had had with parts prototypes from other countries. Moreover, the Chinese list showed that they were preparing for technical problems that U.S. engineers had already solved. Thus, according to the company, "many talks ensued," leading to a modification of the list "toward some of Caterpillar's original suggestions."

Also, in technical negotiations U.S. companies have found that often it is difficult to get any information about the Chinese factories and industrial processes, even where this knowledge would be helpful in determining how the foreign technology could be put to its best possible use.[43] One U.S. business executive was successful in persuading the Chinese to answer some questions about their factories. After about 15 minutes the Chinese, obviously uncomfortable, ended the session with "That's enough. Now let's get back to the technical exchange."[44]

In reality it is sometimes difficult to separate technical and commercial negotiations. The two stages may go on concurrently. The sale of ten Boeing 707 passenger airplanes to the China National Machinery Import and Export Corporation (Machimpex) is a case in point. The actual negotiations, which took almost six months to complete, can be divided into four phases, according to company officials.[45] The first phase, begun in April 1972, was basically a "getting to know you" introductory period. Boeing's delegation consisted of four people from sales and engineering who presented Machimpex officials with general information on the company and its products. This effort took about two and one-half weeks. At the end of that time company officials had no idea whether the Chinese were interested in making any purchases.

The second phase, which began on May 18, 1972, and lasted through the end of the month, was concerned primarily with technical questions and specifications. It was during this period that the Chinese told Boeing that they were seriously considering the purchase of 707s. Boeing then enlarged its team to nine, to include additional contract and spare parts specialists. According to the chief Boeing negotiator, "We could see from the outset that we were very far apart on our basic approaches to contractual matters."[46]

The third phase, which took place between the middle of June and the middle of July, was in effect the commercial phase in which "contractual principles," such as payment, delivery, excusable delay, guarantees, and inspections, were discussed. During this part eight of the team returned to Seattle to obtain additional data and to arrange for a Department of Commerce export license.

The fourth, or "wrap-up," phase was concerned with the finalization of the contract. After the 125-page contract was reviewed and signed on September 9, 1972, the $125 million contract price was more than 20 times the sum involved in the largest Chinese-American transaction to that time.

In the words of one of the Boeing participants, "The Chinese had been gracious hosts but, when it came to the essentials of working out final contract terms, they went over every technical and financial detail with the meticulousness of the highest-paid corporation lawyer."[47] Moreover, this Boeing executive described the chief Chinese negotiator as one of the best lawyers he had ever seen, and as speaking English better than the young woman who was his interpreter.

It follows from this discussion that the U.S. company must include its best technicians in any substantive trade negotiations. The president of one Midwest machinery firm was startled when Chinese engineers wanted to know the chemical composition of a lubricant used in its machinery. The man explained that he did not know the composition, and hurriedly wired home for the answer.[48] By not including technical personnel on the negotiating team, this company may well have lost a sale.

It also is apparent that the Chinese make every effort to extract the maximum amount of information from the negotiations. They increasingly tend to use contractual arrangements that will yield as much information and experience to the Chinese as possible. One company summed up its experience with Chinese technological negotiations by noting that they want all of the information necessary to guarantee the successful transfer of the technology for which they are paying.[49] After the Chinese were completely satisfied that they could make full use of the company's technical process, commercial negotiations were initiated.

THE TIME FACTOR IN THE NEGOTIATING PROCESS

The previous section provided a brief overview of the character of negotiations with the Chinese and what the U.S. business executive might expect in negotiations with the Chinese. Implicit in this discussion was the importance of the time factor in the negotiating process. This section discusses that important element. Almost all questionnaire respondents stressed the need for patience in dealing with the Chinese. On the same subject one executive observed in an interview that "the Chinese have got all the time in the world."[50] China's being the longest continuous civilization in history reinforces this observation. Contrast this with the fact that U.S. civilization is one of the youngest and still in the process of change. Time appears more important to Americans.

According to an unpublished paper on Chinese manners, one should never present a clock to a Chinese person as a gift.[51] The Chinese consider a clock a bad omen, since the word for clock and the word for end or death have the same sound.

To sum up, one U.S. executive has suggested that "unless you have a ten-year view, there's no point in being here [China]."[52] Reinforcing this point, a former Chinese minister to the United States suggests that "an American is apt to be in too much of a hurry. He should make up his mind that if he has an article the Chinese want, they will buy it eventually."[53] This observation was written in 1919, and seems to be applicable today.

Negotiations move slowly for several reasons. As mentioned above, Chinese buyers will try to learn as much as possible about the technology related to a seller's product before the decision is made to purchase it. Second, the Chinese often request extremely detailed price breakdowns so that weak points in the seller's offer can be found, or substitutions of foreign or domestically made components can be proposed to the seller. Third, the Chinese negotiators may not have the authority to make quick decisions on important price aspects of negotiations.[54] In such cases they may request adjournment of the negotiations and the U.S. firm may have to wait days before the Chinese are prepared to resume negotiations.

An official U.S. Department of Commerce publication suggests that "it takes time and patience to enter the China market successfully, whether exports or imports are involved and whether a large or small firm is participating in the transaction."[55] One large U.S. company, Pullman Kellogg, has built a profitable relationship with the Chinese "by being just as clever and patient as they are," according to one of its managers.[56] The company's senior liaison man in Peking put it in even stronger terms: "We weren't going to lose our shirts. You cannot sit there like a weenie or give in because you're tired."[57] Pullman Kellogg's problem was to persuade Chinese officials to release the last installment on five plants that had been completed. Their liaison man spent 11 weeks patiently explaining how Pullman Kellogg had met its contract on one of the plants—until Chinese officials agreed. Summing up, the company negotiator said, "It's long hard work, but the Chinese are fair."

An executive of a large retail chain that imports large quantities of Chinese merchandise put it another way when he said that in addition to being hard bargainers who take a lot of time to negotiate business, Chinese trade officials "seem to know everything about markets and prices."[58] As was seen earlier, this observation may not be entirely accurate, since the Chinese themselves believe that they have a lot more to learn. But even if their negotiators were only slightly conversant with world markets and prices instead of being paragons of such knowledge, their U.S. negotiating counterparts would still have to be patient and flexible.

The experience of RCA in China is instructive because it provides a capsule view of the patience necessary to conduct business

with China. In 1973 RCA was asked to prepare a proposal for building a color television picture tube plant. According to an RCA vice-
president, RCA was picked because many of the technicians in China
had been educated at the RCA Institute and knew of RCA's leadership
in electronic developments.[59] RCA "at tremendous expense" prepared the proposal, only to see it lost in the Chinese bureaucratic
hierarchy as a result of the internal upheavals associated with the
Cultural Revolution. According to RCA, a few years later the Chinese
came back and asked RCA to update its proposal and include plans for
an integrated circuit factory. The company then felt it was in a bind
because it knew of the U.S. export controls on such technology, so it
did not reply immediately to the Chinese offer. Only after some prod-
ding by the Chinese did RCA send a negotiating team to China. RCA's
experience is perhaps an example of a U.S. company using time to its
own advantage.

Even with these experiences in mind, there is no easy answer
to the question of how long it takes to conclude a commercial transaction with the Chinese. It can take years, as in the case of RCA, or
65 days, as in the case of Clark Equipment Company of Buchanan,
Michigan. Following major airplane purchases from Boeing and
British Aircraft, the Chinese FTC, Machimpex cabled Clark on February 19, 1973, asking for information relating to c.i.f. or c.&f. delivery for a single unit of Clark's model CT50E towing tractor.[60]
The company responded immediately with a price. Machimpex then
requested a discounted price for 20 tractors. On March 30, Clark
cabled an answer and asked for a letter confirming the sale. On
April 2, Machimpex cabled confirmation and sent a confirmation letter 11 days later, thus ordering $150,000 worth of equipment without
ever having met representatives of the seller face to face. In short,
where there is a need by the Chinese for a product and no apparent
direct competition, it is the U.S. firm that can afford to wait.

More than half of the respondents to the author's questionnaire
(53 percent) did not believe that the Chinese used time as an instrument to gain an advantage in the negotiating process. This would imply that the lengthy periods needed for completion of a commercial
transaction are more the result of the communication requisite within
the foreign-trade bureaucracy regarding the product of the U.S. company and the best contract terms. One of the "dissenting" respondents
reported that it was his impression that "time is used to wear down
Americans who are accustomed to rapid time schedules." An executive in another company, perhaps typical of the 53 percent who said
time was not used as an instrument to gain an advantage, observed
that "since we take a firm stand on our pricing policy, extended negotiation time does not have any effect on us."

The time spent in actual negotiations with the Chinese varied
from two to three days to two years. In other words, there was no

apparent rule of thumb about the time necessary to negotiate a successful contract.

THE DIFFICULTY OF ESTABLISHING
INTERPERSONAL RELATIONS

U.S. business people who have had little previous contact with their Chinese counterparts tend to consider them an enigma.[61] The purpose of this section is to describe briefly some of the basic Chinese character traits and societal influences that may have a bearing on the difficulties of establishing interpersonal relations.

Most Chinese business practices are based on customs and traditions. They present a sharp contrast with the informality and pragmatic nature of U.S. business practice. For example, an individual apparently insensitive to the cultural nuances of Chinese methods of doing business, behaved almost as a kind of caricature of a "big businessman" in China.[62] The result was that in one instance he was asked to leave the meeting in which he was taking part. In short, the U.S. executive who can adapt to the Chinese way without losing his own identity will enjoy a distinct advantage.

The Chinese place a premium on trust in relationships, and it takes a lot to gain their respect. Those who have long-standing relationships with the Chinese are known as "old friends"—people who can be counted on personally and, in turn, can be relied upon to recommend other trustworthy parties. According to William Whitson, a long-term China trader, "earning the term 'foreign friend' is the American trader's goal in the negotiating process. The status is not easily won."[63]

In order to achieve such recognition in the Chinese lexicon of relationships, a U.S. negotiator and his company must have earned the genuine respect of his Chinese counterparts. As one company doing business with China observed, "To the Chinese an indication of anger is a demonstration of a loss of self-confidence."[64] Therefore, the length of time necessary in most instances to establish meaningful contact with the Chinese is a function of the Chinese emphasis on "getting to know each other"—that is, sizing up their U.S. business counterparts and testing their friendliness and sincerity.[65] As if to aid the Chinese in this endeavor, most of the respondents in the author's questionnaire (93 percent) indicated that the establishment of personal relationships helped to complete the negotiations, and most of the respondents (93 percent) also believed that gestures of goodwill helped in their negotiations.

Hierarchy and Kuan-hsi

The Chinese have learned to feel more secure in a hierarchical society.[66] The U.S. concept of social equality is alien, if not incomprehensible, to them. Within a family each member has his or her own place above and below others. Within a clan the separate families are graded according to status. The various clans in a community are similarly positioned. When two strangers meet, the decision on which has superior status is reached quickly. No two nations are seen as equal, and much diplomatic effort is spent on establishing national rank within the world community. Between two friends (or nations) the one in the superior position may permit the other to act as an equal, but neither ever forgets their true position and the privilege may be revoked at any time. If, when two strangers meet, the first immediately treats the second as an equal, the latter is likely to assume that the first is a social-climbing inferior who is attempting to establish an underserved status; the first is almost sure to be snubbed. Unless the status of two strangers is immediately apparent, courtesy requires a polite exchange of largely meaningless pleasantries until gradually the one in the dominant position is revealed.

It is this hierarchical element, albeit simplified here for purposes of this discussion, that helps to explain why the Chinese, in the course of their commercial negotiations—preferably at the beginning—are accustomed to dealing with those individuals who have the authority to make the agreement.[67] A bit of advice from a 1925 issue of the Chinese Economic Monthly highlights this Chinese preference for dealing with corporate decision makers:

> Apart from a clear and definite understanding, another desideratum is to make sure that the person with whom one deals has full authority to make the agreement. Managers of old-style firms usually handle all such matters themselves, and do not delegate their powers to assistants. If a customer approaches an assistant about a transaction, he is generally referred to the manager, because the assistants in these firms have been carefully trained under strict discipline not to go beyond their powers.[68]

It is important to understand that, ideology aside, the Chinese viewpoint and behavior patterns are much affected by unique social theories that can be traced to Confucius. In Western culture we can say that we are taught sets of principles—the Golden Rule, the Ten Commandments, and such—that in effect are lists of "do's and don'ts" intended to guide behavior. A good or respectable man is one who has voluntarily accepted the righteousness of these principles and acts

accordingly. Conversely, among the Chinese less attention is given
to principles; emphasis instead is placed on prescribing behavior patterns. The idea is that what a person thinks or believes is not really
important; if one acts like a good and respectable person, that is what
one will be. Hence, the individual tends to be taught precisely how to
behave in all the relationships and circumstances that a person of his
or her status is likely to encounter.

As mentioned above, the Chinese rarely recognize social equality.
It also has been demonstrated that the Chinese distrust total strangers
and will make efforts to avoid them. Nevertheless, the Chinese do
welcome contact with strangers whom they meet through relatives,
friends, or professional associates. They are much interested in establishing relationships that have a quality called kuan-hsi. (Kuan-hsi
is the Wade-Giles transliteration. The Hanyu-Pinyin rendering of
this term would be guanxi.) The term means "relationship," but it
has a semantic value that suggests mutual benefit. Friendship may
be involved, but it usually is not. Kuan-hsi is in effect a contract between two individuals for providing each access to certain goods and
services that otherwise would have to be provided by strangers.

If an American is introduced to a Chinese businessman and con-
verses with him, his interest is almost sure to concern what the American has that could be of benefit to him. This would seem cynical and
selfish, except that he fully expects the American to learn what he has
that could be useful. Thus the conversation is meant to be a mutual
exchange of biographical data. Family background, education, social
position, economic status (including current income), and other kuan-
hsi connections are revealed by each person. If what each has to offer the other is acceptable, kuan-hsi is established. Inevitably, what
one of the two can offer is more valuable than what the other is able
to contribute. The one with more to offer is in the stronger position,
and therefore has the privilege of defining the terms of the contract.

It is a definite contract that, although very personal, is also
known publicly in every detail. Social pressure to uphold the terms
of agreement is powerful. One who fails to meet accepted obligations
suffers sharp reprisals and may well be ostracized. Certainly that
person's other kuan-hsi will be jeopardized.

The main purpose of the superior-subordinate positions in kuan-
hsi is to facilitate the original agreement to terms. Once the superior
partner has determined the exact nature of the goods and services to
be exchanged, the ranking system assumes a passive function. Each
partner has equal obligation to honor the agreement. Neither party
may make demands not originally specified. The subordinate partner
is entitled to reject unreasonable requests by the superior.

Every person is likely to have kuan-hsi with both superiors and
inferiors. The exchange of goods and services would be economically

pointless if what each party had to offer was the same. Thus, basically kuan-hsi is a means whereby two people supply what neither could obtain without the other. The institution has been described as the "'old-boy net' carried to the ultimate conclusion." It is more than that. The average Chinese depends almost exclusively on the kuan-hsi network for social and economic sustenance. It is most unusual for a Chinese to seek help from someone unknown or to expect reliable information from a person to whom he or she has not been properly introduced. Since little of consequence is likely to be transacted outside the network, an individual must establish kuan-hsi in anticipation of all foreseeable needs. Considering the variety of constraints within which the individual Chinese must operate, the importance of kuan-hsi can hardly be exaggerated.

In order to ascertain the U.S. executive's knowledge of kuan-hsi, in the author's questionnaire to U.S. firms the question was asked, "Are you familiar with the term Kuan-hsi?" The response was surprising. Half of the respondents indicated that they were familiar with the term. In fact, one of the respondents familiar with the term suggested that by itself the term usually refers to a "personal relationship." One U.S. company wrote that kuan-hsi was a "very important concept," and the fact "that we had an established relationship with the FTC and the end user was instrumental in the conclusion of our second and most recent deal."

Language

In any negotiating milieu differences in language are barriers to effective communication. "What did he mean?" may be more important than "What did he say?" The Chinese language is no exception. In the "early days" of Chinese-U.S. trade, the number of Chinese who could speak English was small. The U.S. trader who could speak Chinese was a rarity and came to occupy a key position as a facilitator of trade between the two countries. [69]

Reversing this pattern, some U.S. companies of late have benefited substantially by having members of their negotiating team fluent in Chinese. For example, during Boeing's negotiations to sell three aircraft, one of the company's spokesmen answered a Chinese negotiator's question by saying, "You're talking to the wrong employee," realizing that the official translation would be taken as meaning it was an improper or embarrassing question. [70] The Boeing spokesman was a Chinese-American who understood and spoke Chinese fluently. At another point in the negotiations, the Boeing negotiators saw that the Chinese were perplexed as to why aircraft designers built in special accommodations for dogs in jumbo jets. The puzzle was solved when the Chinese learned through the same spokesman that in the aircraft business "doghouses" refer to the compartments used to store food trays on 747s. Later the Chinese decided to buy three 747s, complete with doghouses, for about $160 million. [71] Knowledge of the Chinese language in this particular negotiation helped to provide some important clarification.

Another author writing about U.S.-Chinese business negotiations confirms the importance of using the Chinese language during negotiations. He states unequivocally that he could not have negotiated 25 agreements in the short time that he was in Canton, Peking, and Shanghai if he did not speak Chinese fluently. [72]

Nevertheless, there have been U.S. negotiators who have stated flatly that all negotiations should be conducted in English. [73] One observer suggests that "there is no necessity to learn Chinese because most traders in the PRC speak excellent English." But it should be noted that the use of English in China is uneven. Whereas some people and some organizations are proficient in English, there are others with lesser abilities. In a discussion of the efficiency of training of Chinese technicians, one author pointed out that the competence of the Chinese interpreters provided has been crucial, and noted:

> China has not been able to train interpreters in the necessary spectrum of technical subjects fast enough to keep up with the number of contracts signed. . . . Interpreters simply have not been familiar with the range of technical terms necessary to explain plant installation and machine assembly and have often been helped out by American technicians who speak Chinese. [74]

In short, it would appear that anyone signing a business contract with a Chinese party would be well advised to take the trouble to understand the Chinese contract—to learn, for example, that legal arguments that begin with "is causing" or similar present tense constructions can be very tenuous in Chinese, a language whose verbs have no tenses. [75]

Use of an Intermediary

An independent consultant who played host in 1978 to a Chinese shopping tour of the U.S. computer industry, suggested that "the expertise of people like myself comes in knowing what the Chinese will respond to." [76] In contrast with this singular viewpoint, many companies report that advisers and consultants are not essential for China trade. [77] Boeing, for example, did not use them in its negotiations

for the sale of 747s. Nor did the Coca-Cola Company, when it negotiated its exclusive cola rights, use an intermediary. One of the basic
reasons cited for this viewpoint is the belief that contracts are awarded
first on the basis of technical competence and thorough preparation.
In any case, although Coca-Cola did not use outside consultants, it
did use its own Chinese-American chemist, Peter Lee, in the negotiations. Specifically Mr. Lee, holder of a Ph.D. in chemistry who
worked in the company's quality-assurance department, acted as
Coca-Cola's "principal liaison" with the Chinese in correspondence,
day-to-day meetings, and the discussions leading to the agreement. [78]

The majority of respondents to the author's questionnaire (85
percent) did not use an intermediary to approach the Chinese. Of interest is that more than half of the companies responding reported
that it was the Chinese who first approached their company about the
proposed deal. In cases where the Chinese approach the U.S. company, an intermediary might be unnecessary.

THE DEMAND FOR CONCESSIONS IN NEGOTIATIONS

An official U.S. Department of Commerce publication advises
U.S. businessmen to consider, among other questions, the following:
"Am I prepared to resist granting concessionary terms to penetrate
this market?"[79] If the answer to this question is in the negative, the
U.S. businessman, according to the U.S. Department of Commerce,
might want to reconsider entering the Chinese market.

David Cookson, an experienced trader with China, notes that
many companies have sacrificed profits in order to establish a foot-
hold in the Chinese market. He states that "unless one has overriding
excess capacity to dispose of," he does not recommend a prolonged
subsidizing of Chinese business.[80] Too often a U.S. company finds
that orders dry up when more realistic prices are introduced.

One good method of extracting concessions is for negotiators to
refer to the competition. Chinese negotiators do this consistently.
In fact, Cookson advises the U.S. business executive to expect to be
confronted with negotiators who have copies of competitors' offers
conspicuously on their laps as they discuss the transaction.[81] Moreover, he suggests that their expressions indicate that the product under consideration is overpriced, overrated, and devoid of merit.
After a few days of sessions like these, together with changes of negotiators who one day speak no English yet the next day are word-per-
fect translators, a company's negotiators can begin to doubt the
strength of their own arguments.

Still another observer notes that a seller may expect that whatever lines of inquiry appear at his sessions will be repeated at meet-

ings with his competitors.[82] As has been noted previously, the buyer of Chinese goods also may expect that during negotiations his competitor may be sitting at an adjacent table. One U.S. buyer wanted to purchase some antique mandarin robes for his department store but was told by the Chinese "that they're too expensive." When the buyer pressed for an explanation, he was told, "The Macy's buyers said so."[83] Thus, the Chinese thrive on the whipsaw technique, where appropriate, to gain concessions. An executive of a U.S. company negotiating to sell mining technology observed, "We would talk, then they would leave, obviously to talk to other people, then come back and talk some more."[84]

The basic reason for such tactics would appear to be to persuade the U.S. negotiator to grant concessions. U.S. executives, the Chinese might reason, are fearful of returning home empty-handed, so unnerving tactics—such as making sure that the negotiator knows that a potential contract might be signed with a competitor—are designed to gain the most desirable contract terms.

A Boeing Company executive, and a member of the sales team that sold ten 707s to the Chinese in 1972, stated that "the Chinese would never make a decision or purchase one product without a look at all other available possibilities."[85] In order to emphasize this, he noted that at the same time the Boeing team was negotiating the contract for the 707s, representatives of Lockheed Aircraft Corporation were discussing additional aircraft sales with the Chinese in Peking. This practice is specifically alluded to in an article in a Chinese economic journal:

> We must adopt international practice of having firms in
> each country quote prices and tender bids so the best may
> be selected for importation. We must do comparison
> shopping if we are to avoid losses.[86]

One company, Control Data Corporation (CDC) of Minneapolis, Minnesota, had an experience different from those of the previously mentioned companies. The Chinese "wanted their [computer] system quite badly,"[87] for they had accumulated a great deal of seismic data pertaining to oil exploration and needed the processing capability that the company's Cyber 172 computers could provide.

According to a CDC executive who was conversant with the negotiations, "the contractual negotiations were somewhat easier than otherwise might have been the case."[88] As in the case of International Harvester, the Clark Equipment Company, and now CDC, the U.S. company had products the Chinese needed and were willing to pay to obtain. Quite obviously they made no effort to extract concessions above those normally required in transactions of this type.

The majority of responses to the author's questionnaire (76.9 percent) indicated that U.S. companies believed that they did not negotiate concessionary terms to establish a position in the Chinese market. Paradoxically, half of the respondents indicated that they had made concessions on price. An overwhelming number (84.6 percent), however, indicated that they did not make concessions concerning terms of financing. Other concessions granted by U.S. companies, as reported by the respondents, included free service and spare parts, free training, lower-than-normal delivery costs, and free packing.

THE RESULTS OF NEGOTIATIONS

Previously it was mentioned that negotiation of a contract with the Chinese FTOs is a two-stage procedure, involving first technical clarification and then commercial negotiations. The second stage could take place after technical negotiations or in conjunction with them. In any case the process of commercial negotiations with the Chinese FTOs, especially the middle and end phases, revolves around the drafting of a contract by the U.S. company. The result of negotiations, then, is a signed commercial contract, often complete with the technical appendixes.

Writing in 1925, one observer noted:

> Chinese businessmen trust verbal agreements as much as written contracts. . . . One thing, however, is very important in verbal or written agreements. The understanding between the two parties must be perfectly clear. [89]

This customary Chinese desire for a clear and definite understanding is reflected in current practice. Gabriele Reghizzi has observed that the Chinese desire to describe all details relevant to the transaction in the contract itself, in order to avoid subsequent misunderstandings. [90] Benjamin P. Fishburne III suggests that "some engineer someday is going to pick up that document [contract] and decide whether to pay you or not to pay you, based on the clause that is written there, and it would be useful if he could understand what it is all about." Thus, it behooves the U.S. firm to be very careful in the drafting of its contracts with the Chinese. [91]

An article published in 1979 about the strict enforcement of contracts between Chinese enterprises and the state planning agencies indicates the current Chinese desire for a clear and definite contractual understanding:

> Once signed, economic contracts must be strictly carried out. This is not just a simple economic question, but a

question of correctly dealing with the relations between the enterprises and the state, and between the parts and the whole. It is a question as to whether or not the four modernizations can be realized at a high speed. Therefore, after the contracts are signed, they must be strictly carried out. Those units that do not carry out their contracts must shoulder not only moral and economic responsibilities, but also administrative and legal responsibilities. For this reason, it is necessary to formulate "Contract Laws," to have all parties strictly abide by contract discipline, and to establish and strengthen relevant supervisory institutions for the carrying out of economic contracts.[92]

If the Chinese government views this contract discipline in the same light when negotiating with foreign buyers and sellers, then it follows that they are not going to negotiate contract terms lightly.

In their commercial relations with the United States, the Chinese have adopted many standard Western contractual terms. Moreover, they have used contract terms to their advantage, gaining the greatest protection possible, whether they are in the role of the buyer or the seller.[93] In fact, one trader has characterized Chinese purchase contracts as "bind[ing] the seller very tightly" and, perhaps with some exaggeration, their contracts of sale as "little more than statements of intent."[94] Supporting this contention, a well-known U.S. lawyer suggests that "not surprisingly the Chinese seek to safeguard their interests to the maximum extent possible."[95] This asymmetrical quality of Chinese contracts perhaps reflects a profound distrust of Western legalism and lawyers, as was noted in Chapter 2.

Preston Torbert, a prominent U.S. lawyer, noted that "the Chinese believe that lawyers are troublemakers, pettifoggers, shysters, and—this is perhaps the most damning of all—that they are utterly superfluous."[96] In fact, traditionally law in China has had a lowly status. In Chinese philosophy law circumvents the cardinal virtue of human-heartedness and is therefore subject to manipulation.[97] A popular Chinese saying suggests matter-of-factly that "it is better to enter the lair of the dragon than a court of law."[98] Considering this background, one can understand the Chinese aversion to law and lawyers.

Erik Kihl responds, however, by suggesting that the Chinese aversion to lawyers is "rapidly changing."[99] This is because the Chinese are almost of necessity, by virtue of increased trade with the West—particularly the United States—having to abide by international law and trade agreements. With respect to contracts it should be noted that in recent years, in an effort to maximize export earnings, the Chinese government has begun to encourage countertrade and a wide variety of contractual arrangements not previously practiced. It is now permissible to do the following:[100]

Accept raw materials into China for processing and reexport;
Accept components into China for assembly, further processing, and reexport;
Enter joint ventures where the Chinese side supplies the factory shell and raw labor and the foreign partner brings in the raw materials, if needed, and the equipment, and supplies the training of labor, technology, and supervision (if required); the foreign partner receives the product at a reduced profit until the costs, including a profit, are paid off; and
Enter into joint-venture arrangements of various types in Hong Kong, and possibly elsewhere outside of China.

According to official Chinese sources, there are currently at least seven types of trade contracts:[101]

1. Straight sale, straight purchase, or the combined form, called "reciprocal trade." Under the straight-sale formula, export is not conditioned by import, nor is import conditioned by export. In either case a contract is concluded when the seller and buyer have reached an agreement on the quality, quantity, specifications, and price of a given commodity, as well as the date of delivery and the terms of payment.

2. Barter. Under this arrangement sale and purchase are carried out at the same time, one kind of commodity is exchanged for another, or a given amount of merchandise is exchanged for another. In any case a relatively even balance of trade is to be maintained.

3. Consignment. Here an export corporation or consignor entrusts a reliable agent or consignee abroad to sell certain types of goods in accordance with the terms agreed upon by both parties, and the consignee may claim a given amount of commissions for the service. In general this formula applies only to the sale of new commodities totally unknown to the external market, or commodities not yet well known to foreign consumers, or objects d'art such as jade or paintings, which normally are purchased only after the customer has actually inspected the object. The price of a consigned commodity is determined either by the consignor or by the consignee, on the basis of actual market conditions or by special agreement between the two. Since consigned commodities are delivered to the consignee before payments are made, the amount involved usually is very limited and specific contractual terms stipulate payment settlement, commissions, and related matters.

4. Agency, sole or general. Under this arrangement an export corporation entrusts a selected firm abroad to sell a given type of commodity or commodities with a specific trademark in a designated area for a given period of time. In the case of sole agency, the export corporation or principal is not allowed to sell to other consumers the type of commodities already entrusted to its agent or to appoint subagents within the designated area during the stipulated period of time unless otherwise provided in the contract.

Generally the commodity prices involved in an agency contract are determined by the principal and the amount of commission is proportional to the amount of sales, on a percentage basis. The average period of agency for a new agent ranges from three months to a year, and it may be extended on the basis of the agent's satisfactory performance.

The principal terms of an agency contract usually specify the foundation and purposes of the contract, commodity descriptions, quality and specifications, the minimum amount of goods to be sold, the area and time period of agency, remunerations for the agent or agents, prices, payment settlement, delivery conditions, and claims and arbitration.

5. Conditional agency. A conditional agency contract provides the agent a certain amount of commission or profits for the sale of certain commodities for an export corporation. The only difference is that under a conditional agency contract, the agent must make a deposit as security money. It is refundable upon satisfactory execution of the contractual terms.

6. Distributorship. Under this formula a single firm or group of firms abroad undertakes to buy from an export corporation a certain type or types of commodities for resale within a designated area during a given period of time. The buyer is responsible for his own gains or losses, and the seller undertakes not to sell the same type of commodities to a third party within that area during the stipulated period of time. The terms of payment are negotiable. If the buyer fails to fulfill the contract due to objective circumstances, that is, circumstances beyond the control of the buyer, a settlement may be made in accordance with the principle of "mutual benefit." Otherwise, the buyer is obligated to compensate the seller for any losses.

7. Fixed distributorship. An arrangement based on relatively long-term large transactions, a distributorship contract assures the buyer of the sources of supply of certain types of commodities within a stipulated period of time. The prices for these commodities are generally lower than those of commodities sold to other buyers without a distributorship contract. Resale of these commodities by the buyer is not restricted by area of time. At the same time the seller is free to market the same types of commodities in any area at any

time. Under the contract the buyer is responsible for his own gains
or losses.

New and versatile arrangements are being worked out, particularly in the area of joint ventures. One commercial "memorandum
of understanding," for example, calls for a 15-year arrangement in
which China will build engines for export using technology developed
in the United States during the past 20 years. [102] Such a transaction
for a long period of time suggests that China attaches considerable
importance to the arrangement, possibly because it could become a
major earner of foreign exchange for the country.

According to legislation approved July 1, 1979, all joint-venture
proposals have to be submitted to the Foreign Investment Control
Commission for authorization. (This bureaucratic element has been
referred to in Chapter 2.) Of importance for contract negotiation is
that the new law, while specifying that a foreign partner will generally
contribute at least 25 percent of the investment, has not specified an
upper limit. Generally the Chinese have said that they intend to maintain a substantial interest in all joint ventures, thus precluding virtually total ownership by foreign corporations. [103] Also, even though
a foreign partner may contribute more than 50 percent of a joint venture's investment, it does not necessarily follow that the foreign concern will have a final say in decision making. [104] This reality puts a
premium on spelling out detailed arrangements before the final contract is signed.

In short, Chinese contractual practices—new and old, distrust
of legalism and lawyers—are all the more reason for the U.S. business executive, not his lawyer, to be thoroughly familiar with Chinese contracts in order to negotiate successfully. Of particular importance are those contractual aspects that serve as hindrances to
negotiation. No attempt will be made here to be exhaustive in the
treatment of the drafting of such arrangements, since several authors
have already written extensively on the subject. [105] Instead, the following highlights the difficulties of the final contract phase of the negotiation process. The basic features and peculiarities of Chinese
commercial contracts are discussed below under the general rubrics
of sales contracts, purchase contracts, and payment. Again the focus
is on these contractual elements as part of the hindrances to be overcome in the process of negotiation.

Sales Contracts

When negotiations with a U.S. firm reach the stage of strictly
commercial concerns, and the transaction is not a sizable or com-

plicated one, the Chinese FTC normally offers one of its own form contracts and urges its adoption. [106] Most business with the Chinese is in fact done on preprinted, standardized forms, with the FTC and its foreign trading partner filling in the blanks. U.S. firms in "virtually every instance" buy on the basis of standard contract forms. [107] Usually these contracts are placed before them on a take-it-or-leave-it basis. It should be noted, however, that the Chinese apparently have begun to realize that if they are to increase their exports (and sorely needed foreign exchange earnings), they have to do a better job of meeting their buyers' needs. For example, Chinese negotiators have shown a willingness to copy samples brought to them by importers, and they have begun to offer exclusive U.S. distributorships for some textile and light industrial products. [108]

The Chinese state trading corporations use two standard types of contract forms for sales of their goods, although the particular forms within each class vary slightly; these "contracts" are the one-page "sales confirmation" and the "sales contract." (Copies of these types of contracts are reproduced in Appendixes D and E.) It is important to note that these form contracts represent the commercial terms of the transaction only. Any technical aspects of the negotiations usually are covered in appendixes to the contract and, depending on the size of complexity of the transaction, can run many pages. The "sales confirmation" is a simple standard form, usually printed in both Chinese and English, on one sheet of paper. There are blank spaces for the bare essentials of the transaction, such as the buyer, the description of the goods, quantity, and price. [109] Also included are certain conditions relating to documentation instructions, and letter-of-credit procedures. Some "sales confirmations" may include a standard clause providing for the finality of Chinese inspections of quantity, weight, and quality of goods. The second common form, the "sales contract," is very similar to the "sales confirmation" but includes clauses dealing with force majeure and arbitration.

Chinese negotiators generally are very reluctant to delete or modify terms that appear on the printed contracts. Negotiations concerning the addition of unique terms or conditions are particularly difficult. [110] Notwithstanding this, one U.S. commercial negotiator recommends that buyers press for inclusion of terms they believe genuinely essential. [111] According to this negotiator, they should not be satisfied with oral assurances that despite the contractual provisions, the buyer's apprehensions are unfounded. To the Chinese "honor the contract" generally means the written contract.

Purchase Contracts

Although there is no standard contract for Chinese purchases from the United States, certain common features apparently do prevail.[112] For standard products the contracts are most often simple, one-page documents, usually in English, although sometimes in Chinese as well. In contracts that involve substantial sums of money, both languages may be used, with an accompanying statement that both versions are equally authentic. Generally these more complex Chinese purchase contracts are about four pages in length.[113] (An example of such a contract is reproduced in Appendix F.) As mentioned, these purchase contracts differ basically from the sales contracts in that they tend to bind the foreign supplier much more tightly than the sales contracts bind the Chinese FTC.

Thus, it is small wonder that when Chinese corporations purchase abroad, they prefer to use their standard form contracts.[114] However, variations are possible, particularly in transactions with "old friends"—U.S. companies long active in the trade.[115] In these transactions special clauses often are used to codify practices that have arisen in relationships with particular foreign companies.

Standard-form preprinted contracts cannot, of course, encompass the totality of large and complex transactions, particularly where the Chinese may be purchasing a plant, industrial processes, or complicated equipment or systems. Large and complex transactions, such as Boeing's sale of aircraft or Control Data's sale of computers, result in very lengthy contracts. Control Data's contract for complete equipment for a large seismic data processing center, signed in Peking on December 22, 1978, had 16 chapters and 8 annexes, and ran to 123 pages.[116] (In order to provide an overview of the size and complexity of this contract, the contract summary, the annexes, and significant portions of the contract are reproduced in Appendixes A, B, and C.) More will be said about CDC's negotiations of this contract in Chapter 5. Suffice it to say here that the negotiations were arduous and lengthy.

Payment

Chinese sales contracts negotiated before the spring 1975 Canton Fair normally specified payment in Chinese currency, the renminbi (RMB or yuan). This meant that the buyer—or, more precisely, the buyer's bank—had to purchase the currency from the Bank of China in order to pay the Chinese seller.[117] In 1975 several Chinese FTCs began to sign contracts in which payment was designated in U.S. dollars, thus shifting the foreign exchange risk from U.S. buyers.

The standard payment clause for Chinese goods calls for confirmed, irrevocable, transferable, and divisible letters of credit that are payable on sight. Normally letters of credit are the mode of financing China trade. Previously letters of credit included a margin above the original price to cover excess delivery or extra insurance requirements.[118] The following two clauses taken from contracts with the Chinese illustrate this:

> The usual allowance of trade margin of 5 percent more or less to the quantity stipulated overleaf should be added to the necessary letter of credit. . . .
> If additional risks are required to be covered or the insurance is to be made for the percentage of the invoice value over what has been mentioned in this contract, the buyers should put forward their requests for the sellers' further approval. . . . The additional premium incurred therefrom shall be borne by the buyers who shall agree to have it to be drawn through negotiation of the relative L/C, or to be refunded to the sellers immediately after receipt of the sellers' debit note.[119]

Recent sales contracts apparently do not stipulate these additional premiums:

> The buyers, upon receipt from the sellers of the delivery advice specified in clause 12(1)(a) hereof, shall 15-20 days prior to the date of delivery, open an irrevocable letter of credit with the Bank of China, Peking, in favor of the sellers, for an amount equivalent to the total value of the shipment.[120]

The payment clause in a Chinese seller's contract specifically requires that the letter of credit allow transshipments and partial shipments; that the letter reach the seller at a specified date—often 30 or more days before the date of shipment (usually expressed simply in terms of a two-month period); and that it remain valid 15 days after expiration of the shipment period.[121]

In any case, pricing and payment considerations must be paramount in negotiating with the Chinese. A U.S. Department of Commerce official advised one firm "that one of the best things they could do if they were a little tight would be to add 10 percent for bargaining purposes."[122] The president of the firm chose to ignore this advice, and did not include the 10 percent in the contract price. In the last meeting the Chinese negotiator said that the team liked the company's price but that they would have to take 10 percent off before the Chinese FTC would sign. The president of the firm was in a bind; 10 percent was his profit margin, so all he could say was "no."[123] The chief Chinese negotiator responded by saying, "I don't understand, please explain." Negotiations continued in this manner for two more days until the president of the U.S. firm came down to about 6 percent. This example shows that U.S. companies must plan their price strategy in advance of the negotiations and adhere to it.

Until very recently, when the Chinese purchased goods or services, they preferred to pay cash.[124] In fact, one well-known China trader observed in February 1978 that in financial dealings the Chinese are very conservative. "They're like my parents, who thought a checkbook was one of Satan's works. They are cash-on-the-barrelhead customers, and proud of it."[125] Perhaps one reason for the Chinese unwillingness to accept deficit financing is that they are aware that for many years before 1949, Western banks and trading companies had strong influence in China and that debt service of foreign loans required a level of taxation that was extraordinarily onerous.[126]

In the past, payment, under large contracts with U.S. firms—for Boeing aircraft, M. W. Kellogg ammonia plants, Bucyrus Erie blast-hole drills and shovels—was on a strictly cash basis.[127] Recently there have been indications that the Bank of China has sought funds in the Eurodollar market, perhaps foreshadowing major borrowing abroad.

THE FINAL SIGNED CONTRACT

Chinese trade contracts, depending on amounts and complexity, are mostly written in both Chinese and English with equal force.[128] The principal terms of the final signed contracts may vary, depending on such diverse factors as the relationship of the U.S. firm to the Chinese party, the time of the contract signing, the nature of the products or services, and the correlation of both parties' bargaining strength. In general, contract terms include payment, shipping, insurance, commodity inspection, quality guarantee, penalty for late delivery, force majeure, and arbitration.

The majority of firms responding to the basic questionnaire (78.6 percent) that had completed a signed contract with the Chinese indicated that their final contract contained the maximum specificity possible. They were satisfied that they had obtained the best possible deal. The majority of these firms did not believe that a better contract might have been achieved if there had been more time for advance preparation. Of interest is that one firm used its contract signed six years earlier as a "base line" for its 1978 transaction, in order to "expedite contract conclusion." The decision to take this approach, according to the company, was based in part on "our perception of the volatility of the [Chinese] policy toward large ticket purchases." Another U.S. firm suggested that it might have achieved a better contract if it "had placed more emphasis on the economic value of technical features" of its product.

NOTES

1. See, for example, Otomar J. Bartos, Process and Outcome of Negotiations (New York: Columbia University Press, 1974), p. 16. Also see I. William Zartman, The Negotiation Process, Theories and Application (Beverly Hills, Calif.: Sage, 1978), pp. 13-27.

2. Zartman, The Negotiation Process, pp. 31-32. One observer suggests a dance analogy: "With the Chinese it [negotiation] is a sensuous, formal, highly courteous retreat and advance type of dance." The author explains that this is not only a subtle way of hard bargaining but also a practical necessity because the state trading corporation negotiators must check requirements and capabilities with their own factory managers and farmers. "Forget About the Rabbit Routine," Forbes 109 (January 15, 1972): 41.

3. "In Search of Roots," East-West Markets, July 24, 1978, p. 22. Veronica Yhap is sometimes referred to as "Dragon Lady."

4. "The Taiwan-Peking Game, like Chinese Chess, Is Subtle," New York Times, January 11, 1979, p. A-2.

5. Julian M. Sobin, The China Trader (Washington, D.C.: Mass Communications, Inc., 1978), interview with Robert W. Johnson. Series of tapes.

6. Rosalie Tung, "Summary of Findings of U.S.-China Trade Negotiations Study" (Eugene: Graduate School of Management, University of Oregon, February 1980), p. 3.

7. Ibid.

8. Erik Kihl, "Market Overview of Activities in China," in China: Proceedings of China-Telecom (Brookline, Mass.: Information Gatekeepers, 1979), p. 38.

9. James A. Brunner, "Frequency Distributions: U.S.-People's Republic of China Trade Survey" (Toledo, Ohio: Department of Marketing, University of Toledo, 1975).

10. U.S., Congress, Joint Economic Committee, Chinese Economy Post-Mao, vol. 1, Policy and Performance (Washington, D.C.: Government Printing Office, November 9, 1978).

11. "Entering the China Market," Business America 2 (February 26, 1979): 3-4.

12. Ibid. Recent reports indicate that the Canton Fair is not the all-important avenue for initiating trade with the Chinese that it once was. See in particular "Canton Fair Last of Kind?" Journal of Commerce, May 19, 1980, p. 12.

13. "Entering the China Market," p. 4. Also see "Improving the Chinese Side," China Business Review, January-February, 1978, p. 30. This article indicates some of the problems that U.S. companies have been having with these technical seminars.

14. Aviation Week and Space Technology, March 15, 1971, p. 30. This is considerably before the issuance of the Shanghai Communiqué in February 1972.

15. "China Buy Signals New Markets," Aviation Week and Space Technology, September 18, 1972, p. 21. The Civil Aviation Administration of China would be the end user of the Boeing equipment.

16. Ibid. Also see Aaron L. Coldiron, "The Boeing Experience in China: A Brief Overview," Appendix 8 of Law and Business, Inc., Doing Business with China: Legal, Financial, and Negotiating Aspects (New York: Harcourt Brace Jovanovich, 1979). In the later there is some slight discrepancy regarding FTCs.

17. Paul Van Slambrouck, "Trading with China: As Awkward as Chopsticks," Christian Science Monitor, September 12, 1978, p. 1.

18. "How to Dicker with the Chinese," Time, February 19, 1979.

19. Interview with Julian Sobin, November 1979.

20. Ibid.

21. Ibid. Also see "China's Door Is Open but It Takes Time to Get In," Chemical Week, January 24, 1979, p. 33.

22. Sobin, The China Trader, interview with Robert J. McMenamin.

23. National Council for U.S.-China Trade, Selling Technology to China. Workbook (Washington, D.C.: National Council for U.S.-China Trade, December 1979), p. 121.

24. Ibid.

25. U.S., Department of Commerce, Doing Business with China (Washington, D.C.: Department of Commerce, March 1979).

26. Interview with Julian Sobin, November 1979.

27. U.S., Congress, Joint Economic Committee, China: A Reassessment of the Economy, 94th Cong., 1st sess. (Washington, D.C.: U.S. Government Printing Office, July 10, 1975), p. 518.

28. U.S., Congress, Senate, "The China Trade," by K. H. J. Clarke, Congressional Record, December 20, 1973, p. S23475.

29. "China Partly Opens the Door to U.S. Business," Fortune, August 1972, p. 220.

30. "Canton's Autumn Trade Rite," Business China, October 17, 1979, p. 144. See also "Canton Fair Last of Kind?" p. 12.

31. Van Slambrouck, "Trading with China," p. 1.

32. Interview with Julian Sobin, November 1979.

33. Japan Air Lines, Executive Business Guide to China (Tokyo: Japan Air Lines, 1980), p. 34. Also see Stanley Lubman, "Trade Between the United States and the People's Republic of China: Practice, Policy and Law," Law and Policy in International Business 8 (1976): 19. He notes that "sometimes the raised voice of an exasperated foreign friend may be heard by other 'foreign friends' awaiting their turn outside."

34. Ibid.

35. Louis Kraar, "China's Narrow Door to the West," Fortune, March 26, 1979, p. 64.

36. U.S. Joint Publications Research, "How to Improve the Economic Effectiveness of Imported Technology and Equipment," by Wang Furang, China Report—Economic Affairs no. 7 (Washington, D.C.: Foreign Broadcast Information Service, August 14, 1979), p. 33.

37. Ibid.

38. National Council for U.S. China Trade, Selling Technology to China, p. 104. Also see "Making a Decision on 'Purchase of Foreign Technology,'" China Business Review, May-June 1978, pp. 9-10; "China's New Priorities for Technology Development," China Business Review, May-June 1978, pp. 3-8.

39. For a more detailed account of this transaction, see "FTC Branches and End Users May Now Sign Contracts Directly," China Business Review, November-December 1978, pp. 5-6.

40. Ibid.

41. Ibid.

42. "Export Trade with China," China Business Review, January-February 1979, p. 65.

43. Japan Air Lines, Executive Business Guide, p. 38.

44. Ibid.

45. "Exporting to China: Two Examples of Timing," U.S.-China Business Review, July-August 1974, p. 5.

46. "How Boeing Sold 707's to Peking," New York Times, September 18, 1972, pp. 37, 39.

47. Ibid., p. 37.

48. "Cashing in on the China Trade," Dun's Review, November 1978, p. 107.

49. Basic questionnaire data.

50. Kraar, "China's Narrow Door," p. 68.

51. Control Data Corporation, "Chinese Manners" (Minneapolis, Minn.: CDC, November 1977).

52. Kraar, "China's Narrow Door," p. 68.

53. Guaranty Trust Company of New York, Trading with China: Methods Found Successful in Dealing with the Chinese (New York: Guaranty Trust Co., 1919), p. 24.

54. J. Dingle, "Technical Selling in China," as quoted in Stanley Lubman, "Trade Between United States and the People's Republic of China: Practice, Policy and Law," Law and Policy in International Business 8 (1976): 35.

55. U.S., Department of Commerce, Doing Business with China, p. 6.

56. Kraar, "China's Narrow Door," p. 69.

57. Ibid.

58. "Patience Prescribed in Selling to China," New York Times, May 16, 1979, p. D-4.

59. "How RCA Got Offer to Build a TV Plant in China," Christian Science Monitor, October 25, 1978, p. 1.

60. "Exporting to China: Two Examples of Timing," U.S.-China Business Review, July-August 1974, p. 5.

61. U.S., Department of Health, Education and Welfare, "Introducing Metalinguistic Instructional Material into Language and Area Studies Programs: A Syllabus for American-Chinese Intercultural Training," by William K. Carr (Washington, D.C.: Department of Health, Education and Welfare, April 1974).

62. David C. Buxbaum, "Negotiating with the Chinese," Doing Business with China: Legal, Financial and Negotiating Aspects (New York: Harcourt Brace Jovanovich, 1979), p. 167.

63. William W. Whitson, Doing Business with China: American Trade Opportunities in the 1970's (New York: Praeger, 1974), p. 453.

64. "How to Dicker with the Chinese," p. 58.

65. R. K. Nelson, "China Briefing: Chinese Electronic Society Visit to CDC, October 23 & 24, 1973" (Minneapolis, Minn.: CDC, October 15, 1973), p. 18. Also see "How to Succeed in Business with China? U.S. Firms Find Friendship Is the Key," Asian Wall Street Journal, April 9, 1980, p. 3.

66. This section is based on U.S., Department of Health, Education and Welfare, "Introducing Metalinguistic Instructional Material," pp. 6-13.

67. Sobin, interview with Robert Johnson.

68. "Unwritten Code of Chinese Commercial Law," Chinese Economic Monthly 2 (June 1925): 2.

69. George C. Allen and Audrey G. Donnithorne, Western Enterprise in Far Eastern Economic Development (New York: Macmillan, 1954), p. 45.

70. William Wong, "Chinese-Americans Help U.S. Employers Bridge the Language Gap in China Trade," Wall Street Journal, July 3, 1979, p. 30.

71. Also see "How to Dicker with the Chinese," p. 58.

72. Patrick Boarman, ed., Trade with China (Los Angeles: Center for International Business, 1973), p. 105.

73. Whitson, Doing Business with China, p. 417.

74. "How China Prepares to Import: Foreign Quotations," China Business Review, January-February 1977, p. 32.

75. National Council for U.S.-China Trade, Selling Technology to China, p. 6.

76. Kraar, "China's Narrow Door," p. 68.

77. Wong, "Chinese-Americans," p. 30.

78. Ibid.

79. U.S., Department of Commerce, Doing Business with China, p. 6.

80. David Cookson, "In Negotiating with the Chinese There's No Magic Formula," China Business Review, March-April 1977, p. 53.

81. Ibid.

82. "China Buy Signals New Markets," p. 21.

83. "Trading with China," Christian Science Monitor, November 12, 1978, p. 1.

84. "Cashing in on the China Trade," p. 107.

85. "China Buy Signals New Markets," p. 21.

86. U.S., Joint Publications Research, "How to Improve," p. 33.

87. Hugh Donaghue, "Overview" (Washington, D.C.: Control Data Corporation, 1979), p. 2.

88. Ibid.

89. "Unwritten Code of Chinese Commercial Law," p. 1. This same point was made in C. Y. Chou, "How to Sell to the People's Republic of China," Journal of Commerce, August 31, 1979, p. 2.

90. Gabriele Reghizzi, "Legal Aspects of Trade with China: The Italian Experience," Harvard International Law Journal 9 (Winter 1968): 97-98.

91. Benjamin P. Fishbourne III, "Drafting and Negotiating Contracts in China," paper given at China Telecom Conference, Washington, D.C., June 21, 1979, p. 6. In his paper this author states that "The Chinese, as well as I, hate legalisms, Latin phrases, heretofores, hereinaboves, and all that nonsense."

92. U.S., Joint Publications Research, no. 73845, p. 21.

93. William Boone, "The Foreign Trade of China," China Quarterly, Autumn 1975, pp. 169, 179.

94. Quoted in Marc Palay, "Legal Aspects of China's Foreign Trade Practices and Procedures," Journal of International Law and Economics 12 (1977): 113-14.

95. National Council for U.S.-China Trade, "China's Standard Form Contracts and Related Legal Issues in U.S.-China Trade," by Eugene A. Theroux, in Standard Form Contracts of the People's Republic of China, special report no. 13 (Washington, D.C.: National Council for U.S.-China Trade, June 1975), p. 1.

96. Preston M. Torbert, "The American Lawyer's Role in Trade with China," American Bar Association Journal 63 (August 1977): 1017.

97. National Council for U.S.-China Trade, Selling Technology to China, pp. 61-62.

98. Ibid.

99. Kihl, "Market Overview," p. 38.

100. U.S., Department of Commerce, Doing Business with China, p. 14.

101. Liu Chao-chin, China's Foreign Trade and Its Management (Hong Kong: Economic Information Agency of the PRC, 1978), pp. 32-38.

102. "An Unusual Deal Is Set by China," New York Times, December 8, 1979, p. 29.

103. "China Is Establishing Two Key Commissions for Joint Ventures," Wall Street Journal, August 1, 1979, p. 2.

104. Zhang Jingfu (Minister of Finance), "Presentation at the First National Bank of Chicago," July 16, 1979, pp. 2-3. Also see "Rong Yiren: The Man to See about Joint Ventures," China Business Review, September-October 1979, p. 7.

105. See in particular articles by Gene T. Hsiao and Alan H. Smith cited in bibliography.

106. National Council for U.S.-China Trade, "China's Standard Form Contracts."

107. Ibid.

108. Japan Air Lines, Executive Business Guide, p. 44. For an excellent article on exclusive distributorships, see Sally Winder, "Exclusives from the PRC," China Business Review, November-December 1977, pp. 25-26.

109. National Council for U.S.-China Trade, "China's Standard Form Contracts."

110. Ibid., p. 1.

111. Ibid.

112. James A. Brunner and George Taoka, "Marketing Opportunities and Negotiating in the People's Republic of China," Baylor Business Studies, Fall- Winter 1977, p. 17.

113. National Council for U.S.-China Trade, "China's Standard Form Contracts."

114. U.S., Congress, Joint Economic Committee, China: A Reassessment of the Economy.

115. Interview with Hugh Donaghue, March 1980.

116. Control Data Corporation, "Contract for Complete Equipment for a Large-Size Seismic Data Processing Center," Contract no. 78 ME-45090F (Minneapolis, Minn., December 22, 1978).

117. U.S., Congress, Joint Economic Committee, Chinese Economy Post-Mao, p. 786.

118. Alan H. Smith, "Standard Form Contracts in International Commercial Transactions with the People's Republic of China," International and Comparative Law Quarterly 21 (January 1972): 140.

119. Ibid.

120. U.S., Congress, Joint Economic Committee, Chinese Economy Post-Mao, p. 786.

121. Ibid.

122. Kihl, "Market Overview," p. 41.

123. Ibid.

124. "A China Connection for U.S. Companies," New York Times, February 26, 1978, p. D-1.

125. Ibid.

126. National Council for U.S.-China Trade, "China's Standard Form Contracts."

127. Ibid.

128. Howard M. Holtzman, Legal Aspects of Doing Business with China (New York: Practising Law Institute, 1976), p. 151.

4

HINDRANCES AND IMPEDIMENTS
ON THE U.S. SIDE TO U.S.–CHINESE
COMMERCIAL NEGOTIATIONS

The previous chapters have discussed the Chinese organizations charged with commercial negotiations and the process of negotiating with Chinese Foreign Trade Organizations (FTOs) and end users. This chapter is concerned with obstacles in U.S.-Chinese commercial negotiations originating from the U.S. government's policies and actions.

The focus in this chapter is particularly on restrictions pertaining to the licensing and financing of U.S. exports. The purpose is not to present an exhaustive description of U.S. export licensing procedures and other U.S. governmental restrictions, but to show that a process of dual negotiations must be conducted by any U.S. firm transacting business with the People's Republic of China (PRC). For purposes of this study, dual negotiations are defined as the requisite negotiations conducted either concurrently or sequentially with both the pertinent elements of the Chinese foreign trade system and the appropriate agencies of the U.S. government. Of importance to a U.S. firm are the complexity and time-consuming aspects of many of these negotiations with the U.S. government, especially in cases involving the export of technology to the Chinese government.

RESTRICTIONS ON U.S. EXPORTS

Many of the present U.S. controls affecting exports to Communist countries, including the PRC, were fashioned at the height of the cold war. On February 26, 1949, even before the establishment of the PRC, Congress passed the Export Control Act, authorizing the executive branch to prohibit the exportation from the United States, and the reexportation from other countries, of any articles, materials, or supplies necessary to further U.S. foreign policy or the national security.[1] The Export Control Act declared it to be the policy of the United States to "exercise the necessary vigilance" over exports to ensure this security, and empowered the president to prohibit or curtail the export of "any articles, materials, or supplies, including technical data, except under such rules and regulations as he shall prescribe."[2] Of importance is that the act placed national security considerations over the economic advantages of foreign trade.

In keeping with the act, selective trade controls were imposed by the Department of Commerce to prevent the export of strategic goods to parts of China controlled by the Communists. In October 1949, with the establishment of the PRC, the list of goods requiring a license for export to China included articles of strategic importance, such as aviation fuel and truck tires. By March 1950, U.S. controls on exports to China were equivalent to those on exports to the Soviet Union and Eastern Europe. With the outbreak of the Korean War in June 1950, U.S. controls on exports to the PRC were tightened even more, so that virtually all trade ceased.

In theory the Export Control Act extended equally to all countries, but in actuality licenses for exports to Western countries were usually easy to obtain. By law almost all exports from the United States must be licensed. Most exports are permitted under a blanket authority called a "general license." With a general license each proposed export does not require a specific application. In most cases involving the export of advanced technology to the Communist countries, specific "validated licenses" are required for each proposed export. These exports seem to give U.S. government agencies charged with export control their most vexing problems.[3]

Despite the fact that "most of the time, the licensing system works routinely, effectively, and without conflict," according to the House Subcommittee on International Trade and Commerce, the system is unwieldy and is now one in which any interested agency can, and does, withhold approval of licensing applications.[4] In fact, in 1978, 16 percent of all license requests for export of articles to China required over 90 days for the Department of Commerce to process.[5] Illustrative of the export licensing obstacles that a U.S. firm can face is the experience of the Digital Resources Corporation of Houston in its sale to China of seismic data processing systems valued at $5.5 million. In October 1976 this company filed an application for a validated export license with the Office of Export Administration in the U.S. Department of Commerce for the sale of seismic exploration equipment to China. Almost 30 months later, after the company had redesigned its computer equipment in accordance with strict Department of Commerce export control criteria, the company received approval to export its equipment. Similarly, Control Data Corporation, whose case is presented in more detail in Chapter 5, did not receive an export license for the sale of its computers until more than two years after it signed its sales contract with the Chinese.

Perhaps because of these types of occurrences, there has been much pressure on Congress, particularly in recent years, to alleviate the delay problem. The number of export licenses processed by the Department of Commerce has been increasing at an annual rate of nearly 20 percent—from 54,000 in 1977 to 65,000 in 1978 to an estimated 70,000 to 80,000 for 1979.[6] Yet cases requiring more than 90 days for completion have been increasing even faster: from 1,032 in 1977 to 1,988 in 1978—nearly a 100 percent increase. Typical of legislation to speed sales of technology and to eliminate delay in the processing of licenses is the Export Administration Act of 1979, which was passed by Congress on September 29, 1979. In order to implement this legislation, the Department of Commerce in July 1980 announced proposed rule changes for processing export license applications.

Debates in both the House and the Senate on the Export Administration Act of 1979 highlighted two major themes that since 1969 have surrounded the passage of amendments to legislation affecting U.S. trade relations with the Communist world: the importance to the U.S. national interest of a favorable trade balance and, therefore, of a viable export sector.[7] Major provisions of the 1979 act, a lengthy document of many pages, are summarized as follows:

> The Act finds that the ability of U.S. citizens to engage in international commerce is a fundamental concern; that exports contribute significantly to the national security and well-being of the United States; and that over-restriction or uncertainty in the exercise of export controls can be detrimental to the interests of the United States. On the other hand, export of goods or technology without regard to whether they make a significant contribution to the military potential of recipient countries may adversely affect the national security of the United States.
>
> The Act declares it to be the policy of the United States to minimize uncertainty in export controls and to encourage trade. Export controls are to be utilized only after full consideration of their economic impacts and only to the extent necessary to protect U.S. national security, to further significant foreign policy goals, or to protect the domestic economy in cases of short supply.
>
> A qualified general license, as proposed in the Senate bill, is established and a detailed procedure for processing export-licensing applications, including deadlines, provisions for multiagency consultation, and applicant notifica-

tion and consultation is outlined. Qualified general licenses, in lieu of validated licenses, are to be encouraged to the maximum feasible extent.

U.S. firms or enterprises (excepting educational institutions) entering into commercial agreements with controlled countries must now report these agreements to the Secretary of Commerce if they cite an intergovernmental technical cooperation agreement that will result in the export of unpublished technical data.

In cases where reliable evidence shows diversion of dual-use items to military use, the Secretary of Commerce is authorized to deny all further exports to the end user responsible for the diversion until such time as it ceases.

Validated licenses may not be required in cases where foreign availability has been demonstrated, except in cases where this provision is waived by the President. In these cases, the Secretary of Commerce must publish the details of the basis and estimated economic impact of the decision.

The Commodity Control List (CCL) may be indexed, i.e., annual increases in performance levels of items subject to controls identified and items automatically deleted on the basis of these stipulations.

The President is enjoined to consider alternative actions and the following criteria before curtailing exports for foreign policy purposes:

—the probability that such controls will achieve the intended foreign policy purpose in light of other factors, such as foreign availability;
—the reaction of other countries;
—the likely effect of the controls on the U.S. economy; and
—the ability of the United States to effectively enforce the controls. [8]

In short, the present act, while representing a liberalization of export controls on goods and technologies to the East, particularly China, does express congressional concern that U.S. national security interests be protected. This concern is embodied in that portion of the act that allows the president flexibility in the use of export controls to further foreign policy aims.

Recent events have highlighted Soviet expansionist tendencies in their border areas, and have exacerbated tensions between the United States and the Soviet Union. Concomitantly, economic and political relations between the United States and China have improved dramatically. The Carter administration, in a low-key manner apropos of this improved relationship, in March 1980 decided that sales to China of technology and equipment that could have dual uses, meaning military as well as civilian, would be considered on a case-by-case basis. [9] Specifically included as a category that was previously excluded is "certain aircraft, including helicopters, designed, modified or equipped for cargo or personnel carrying."[10] It should be noted, however, that the Munitions Control Newsletter (just quoted) is for guidance only and that no actual sale can be authorized until a U.S. manufacturer comes forward with a contract and request for an export license.[11]

U.S. EXPORT REGULATIONS

On June 10, 1971, President Richard Nixon announced the lifting of the 21-year embargo on trade with China. At the same time the president's announcement also terminated U.S. export controls on a list of commodities that, though large, was about 70 percent as comprehensive as that allowed for the Soviet Union.[12] It should be noted, however, that despite the removal of some restrictions, in U.S. law freedom to export is considered to be a privilege and not a right. Moreover, in many cases, particularly with regard to items involving sensitive technology, such as computers, explicit permission from the government is required. Over time such governmental permission, or controls, came to extend to three categories of items: exports of commodities and technical data, reexports of U.S.-originated commodities and technical data from one foreign country to another, and U.S.-originated parts and components used in a foreign country to manufacture a foreign end product for export. Although U.S. policies changed radically in the 30-odd years subsequent to passage of the Export Control Act in 1949, the bureaucracy that grew to administer the controls has survived nearly intact.

Pursuant to the Export Administration Act, the licensing system, through which permission to export is granted, is administered by the U.S. Department of Commerce. This agency has jurisdiction over most commodities and unclassified technical data, and, as was mentioned above, issues two types of export licenses—general and validated. In addition to the Department of Commerce's Office of Export Control, the Office of Munitions Control of the U.S. Department of State administers the licensing of arms, ammunition, implements of war, and related technical data. Besides the Commerce and State Departments, other major agencies concerned with export regulation are the Energy Research and Development Administration (formerly the Atomic Energy Commission), the Treasury Department, the Department of Justice, the Department of Agriculture, the Maritime Administration, and the Federal Power Commission.

Although it is not strictly charged with export regulation, the Department of Defense is directly concerned in cases pertaining to the export of advanced technology to the PRC. Section 5 of the Export Administration Act of 1969 directs the Department of Commerce to seek information and advice from other executive departments concerned with aspects of foreign policy and operations bearing on exports, and Section 709 of the Defense Appropriations Act of 1975 requires the Department of Commerce to refer to the Department of Defense all export licenses for goods or technology destined for Communist countries. [13]

In administering the licensing system the most difficult and vexing problems arise for the most part from the exports that require a validated license—about 5 to 10 percent of all commercial transactions. [14] A license application is shown in Figure 4.1 to illustrate the complexity of the application process. Applications requiring a validated license are specified in the Department of Commerce's Commodity Control List. The list contains those products, commodities, or technologies that fall into the following general categories:

—products and technical data that the U.S. government determines capable of contributing significantly to the design, manufacture, and utilization of military hardware, or that fall under the COCOM strategic control system; petroleum and other products or commodities in short supply; and

—some devices related to nuclear weapons and explosive devices; certain nuclear power facilities; and crime control and detection equipment that is controlled for foreign policy reasons. [15]

Currently, the list contains some 200 entries that are grouped in the following categories:

Group	Types of Commodities
0	Metalworking machinery
1	Chemical and petroleum equipment
2	Electrical and power-generating equipment
3	General industrial equipment
4	Transportation equipment
5	Electronics and precision instruments
6	Metals, minerals, and their manufacture
7	Chemicals, metalloids, and petroleum products
8	Rubber and rubber products
9	Miscellaneous

FIGURE 4.1

Export License Application

FORM DIB-622P (REV. 3-75)
(FORMERLY FC-419)
Form Approved: OMB No. 41-R.0735

CONFIDENTIAL — Information furnished herewith is deemed confidential and will not be published or disclosed except in accordance with provision of Section 7 (c) of the Export Administration Act of 1969, as amended.

U.S. DEPARTMENT OF COMMERCE
DOMESTIC AND INTERNATIONAL
BUSINESS ADMINISTRATION
BUREAU OF EAST-WEST TRADE
OFFICE OF EXPORT ADMINISTRATION
WASHINGTON, D.C. 20230

APPLICATION FOR
EXPORT LICENSE

DATE RECEIVED (Leave Blank)

CASE NO. (Leave Blank)

DATE OF APPLICATION

APPLICANT'S TELEPHONE NO.

1. APPLICANT'S NAME

STREET ADDRESS
CITY, STATE, ZIP CODE

2. PURCHASER IN FOREIGN COUNTRY
(If same as ultimate consignee, state "SAME AS ITEM 3"; if same as intermediate consignee, state "SAME AS ITEM 4.")
NAME
STREET ADDRESS
CITY AND COUNTRY

3. ULTIMATE CONSIGNEE IN FOREIGN COUNTRY
NAME
STREET ADDRESS
CITY AND COUNTRY

4. INTERMEDIATE CONSIGNEE IN FOREIGN COUNTRY.
(If none, state "NONE", if unknown, state "UNKNOWN.")
NAME
STREET ADDRESS
CITY AND COUNTRY

5. COUNTRY OF ULTIMATE DESTINATION

6. APPLICANT'S REFERENCE NUMBER

7. (a) QUANTITY TO BE SHIPPED | (b) COMMODITY DESCRIPTION AS GIVEN IN COMMODITY CONTROL LIST (Include characteristics such as basic ingredients, composition, type, size, gauge, grade, horsepower, etc.) | (c) EXPORT CONTROL COMMODITY NUMBER AND PROCESSING NUMBER | (d) TOTAL SELLING PRICE AND POINT OF DELIVERY (Indicate F.O.B., F.A.S., C.I.F., etc.)

UNIT PRICE | TOTAL PRICE

TOTAL

8. FILL IN IF PERSON OTHER THAN APPLICANT IS AUTHORIZED TO RECEIVE LICENSE
NAME
STREET ADDRESS
CITY, STATE, ZIP CODE

9. IF APPLICANT IS NOT THE PRODUCER OF COMMODITY TO BE EXPORTED, GIVE NAME AND ADDRESS OF SUPPLIER.
(If unknown, state "UNKNOWN.")

10. END USE OF COMMODITIES COVERED BY THIS APPLICATION. DESCRIBE FULLY

11. IF APPLICANT IS NOT EXPORTING FOR HIS OWN ACCOUNT. GIVE NAME AND ADDRESS OF FOREIGN PRINCIPAL AND EXPLAIN FULLY

12. ADDITIONAL INFORMATION (Attach separate sheet if more space is needed.)

13. APPLICANT'S CERTIFICATION. — The undersigned applicant hereby makes application for a license to export and certifies as follows: That all statements herein, and in any documents or attachments submitted in support hereof, are true and correct to the best of his knowledge and belief; and that (a) he has read the instructions on the fifth copy of this application and is familiar with the U.S. Department of Commerce Export Administration Regulations; (b) this application conforms to such instructions and regulations; (c) unless Item 14 is completed, he negotiated with and secured the export order directly from the purchaser or ultimate consignee or through his or their agents abroad; (d) all parties to the export transaction, the exact commodities and quantities, or the exact technical data, and all other terms of the order and other facts of the export transaction are fully and accurately reflected herein; (e) documents and records evidencing the order and other facts of the export transaction to which this application relates will be retained by him for 2 years from whichever is later: the time of (i) the export from the United States, or (ii) any known reexport, transshipment, or diversion, or (iii) any other termination of the transaction, whether formally in writing or by any other means, and made available to the Department of Commerce upon demand; (f) any material or substantive changes in the terms of the order or other facts of the export transaction as reflected in this application or any certification made in connection therewith, whether the application is still under consideration or after a license has been granted, will be reported promptly by him to the Department of Commerce; and (g) if the license is granted, he will be strictly accountable for its use in accordance with the Department of Commerce Export Administration Regulations and all terms and conditions specified on the face of the license.

Type or Print _____ (Applicant (Same as Item 1)) | SIGN HERE IN INK _____ (Signature of person authorized to execute this application.) | Type or Print _____ (Name and title of person whose signature appears on the line to the left)

14. ORDER PARTY'S CERTIFICATION. (See § 372.6 (c) of the Export Administration Regulations.) — The undersigned order party certifies to the truth and correctness of Item 13 (d) above, and that he has no information concerning the export transaction that is inconsistent with, or undisclosed by the application and agrees to comply with Items 13 (e) and 13 (f) above.

Type or Print _____ (Order Party) | SIGN HERE IN INK _____ (Signature of person authorized to sign for the Order Party) | Type or Print _____ (Name and title of person whose signature appears on the line to the left)

This license application and any license issued pursuant thereto are expressly subject to all rules and regulations of the Department of Commerce. Making any false statement or concealing any material fact in connection with this application or altering in any way the validated license issued, is punishable by imprisonment or fine, or both, and by denial of export privileges under the Export Administration Act of 1969, as amended, and any other Federal statutes.

FOR OFFICIAL USE ONLY

ACTION TAKEN	VALIDITY PERIOD	AUTHORITY	RATING	DV	TECH. DATA			
☐ APPROVED								
☐ REJECTED	MONTHS		END USE CHECK	RE-EXPORT	SUPPORT DOCUMENT	TYPE OF LICENSE	(Licensing officer) (No.) (Date)	
DOCUMENTATION							(Review officer) (Date)	

NOTE: Submit the first four copies of this application, Form DIB-622P (with top stub attached), to the Office of Export Administration, Room 1617M, Domestic and International Business Administration, U.S. Department of Commerce, Washington, D.C. 20230, retaining the quintuplicate copy of the form for your files. Remove the long carbon sheet from in front of the quintuplicate copy. Do not remove any other carbon sheets. See Special Instructions on back of quintuplicate. Reproduction of this form is permissible, providing that content, format, size, and color of paper and ink are the same.

ORIGINAL
O E A FILE COPY

Source: U.S. Department of Commerce.

93

Each entry on the list contains a general description of the technical commodity, the countries for which validated licenses are required, and, in some instances, limitations on exports that restrict the number or dollar value of items that may be exported. For export-. control purposes all countries are divided into eight separate country groups. China, which now has most-favored-nation status, is treated separately in country group "P."

In describing the export-control system, the chairman of the House Subcommittee on International Economic Policy and Trade suggested:

> Lost in a growing blizzard of paper, the Department and its advisory agencies are unable to devote the amount of time necessary to evaluating the really critical technology transfers. We know we are controlling a lot that need not be controlled. We are not certain we are adequately controlling what really needs to be controlled. This is a dangerous situation that cannot be permitted to continue. We must learn to focus our limited export control resources on critical technologies and products. [16]

Although it is still too soon to evaluate the revised procedures created by the Export Control Act amendments of 1979, the procedural aspects of negotiations with the U.S. government for an export license can still be very lengthy for firms exporting to China. Indicative of this time-consuming process is that the number of export licenses processed by the Department of Commerce has been increasing at an annual rate of nearly 20 percent: from 54,000 in 1977 to an estimated 70,000 to 80,000 for 1979. [17] Moreover, those cases requiring more than 90 days for completion, because of national security questions, have been growing even faster: from 1,032 in 1977 to 1,988 in 1978—nearly a 100 percent increase.

The Export Control Act amendments set a 90-day statutory deadline on all licensing decisions not requiring interagency review. For those cases needing such a review, the time limit is as follows: 30 days to refer the application to other departments and agencies, 60 days by other departments and agencies, and 90 days after receipt of recommendations to issue or deny the license. All told, this new procedure for interagency review could take at least 180 days. [18] Again, regardless of the pros and cons of how stringent U.S. export regulations should be, the central point here is that the procedural aspects of such negotiation with the U.S. government for an export license for high-technology items, even in the best of circumstances, can be time consuming for firms exporting to China.

THE PROCEDURAL ASPECTS OF NEGOTIATIONS
FOR A VALIDATED EXPORT LICENSE WITH THE
DEPARTMENT OF COMMERCE AND OTHERS

As was mentioned above, the procedure for applying for a validated license is not an easy one, especially in cases involving the export of technology to China. The basic point here is that the mere existence of a bureaucratic apparatus—no matter what its predisposition to act—is ipso facto a cause for some delay, because a U. S. company must negotiate with that bureaucratic apparatus in order to secure a result. This is not to suggest that there should or should not be governmental oversight or control of exports, but merely to note that some delay is almost inherent in the export control system. In fact, a 1979 report by the comptroller general stated the following:

> The government's complex system for reviewing and determining commodities that should be controlled is complicated by vague criteria, insufficient funding, and low priorities. As a result, decision-making is sometimes inadequate, occasionally slow, or both. Items may remain on the control list and exporters may needlessly lose sales simply for lack of a decision. [19]

Since this U. S. governmental apparatus is so very important to the U. S. company seeking a validated license to export to China, let us examine it in finer detail.

The U. S. Department of Commerce's Office of Export Administration (OEA) receives all export license applications. The current export licensing structure and the consulting agency system are shown in Figure 4.2. Most of the applications—generally for exports to "free world" destinations—are approved without referral to another agency. [20] The current OEA licensing procedure is shown in Figure 4.3.

Initially export license applications are received in the Operations Division, where they are logged in and entered into a computerized information system. The purpose is to check the application against a list of known or suspected violators of export control laws.

The application itself requires detailed technical information on the product or process to be exported, the quantity to be exported, unit selling price, and total sales receipts. Details concerning the foreign buyer, including intermediate and final consignees, as well as the end use of the product, must also be shown. (A portion of the form is reproduced in Figure 4.1.)

After an initial review the application is routed to one of three licensing divisions—computers, electronics, or capital goods and pro-

FIGURE 4.2

The Current Export Licensing Structure

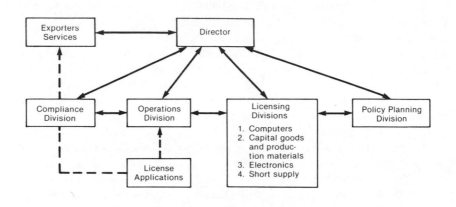

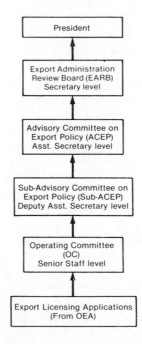

Source: U.S., Comptroller General, Export Controls: Needs to Clarify Policy and Simplify Administration, ID 79-16 (Washington, D.C.: General Accounting Office, March 1, 1979), p. 35.

duction materials. Here the technical staff, in reviewing the application, concentrates on the following criteria:

The function and uses of the equipment
Its level of sophistication
Its normal pattern of military/civilian uses in the United States and
  in the country of destination
The unrestricted availability of comparable equipment elsewhere
The suitability of the equipment for the proposed end use
The likelihood of diversion from the stated end use to less acceptable
uses
The economic/commercial implications of the transaction for the
  United States.[21]

If the staff is not familiar with the end user, it may consult informally with the Export Information Service of the Department of Commerce, as well as with technical people in other agencies. However, it is important to note that at this level only a limited number of cases are decided.[22]

Once information has been gathered and analyzed, the application is forwarded to the Policy Planning Division for review. At this stage the division determines whether it has sufficient data to make a decision or whether other federal agencies must be consulted. Applications referred to the formal interagency review process almost always concern products or processes with dual civilian-military use capabilities. The items most frequently involved include numerically controlled machine tools, semiconductor processing equipment, high-strength materials, high-temperature polymers, nuclear-related materials, computers, electronic testing and measuring equipment, magnetic recorders, and integrated circuits. Since all interagency decisions must be unanimous, delay of export applications for those types of products and processes is virtually ensured.

It is possible for a U.S. company to obtain an advisory opinion from the OEA on the likely disposition of the export application. However, in some instances, as will be shown in the Control Data export license case, this process can be as time-consuming as the formal application. Moreover, the OEA's advisory opinion is delivered orally and is not binding.

An illustration of the frustrating delay that can result from a U.S. firm's applying for an export license can be seen in the following licensing history, described in an October 1978 report of the comptroller general.[23]

In August 1977, according to the report, an applicant sought a license to export semiconductor manufacturing equipment to an Asian country. Its letter of credit was due to expire in mid-October, and

FIGURE 4.3

Office of Export Administration Licensing Procedure

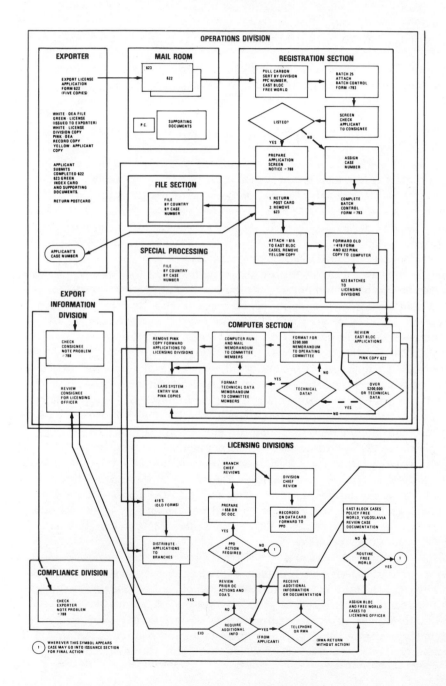

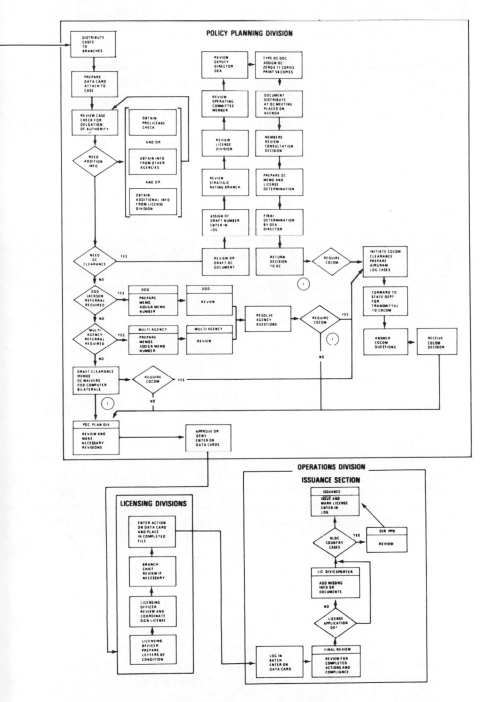

Source: U.S., Congress, House, Committee on International Relations, Subcommittee on International Trade and Commerce, Export Licensing of Advanced Technology: A Review, 94th Cong., 2d sess., 1976.

the equipment was scheduled to be shipped by mid-September. Specifically, in August 1977 the application was received by the OEA. The value of the equipment was roughly $8,100. The Licensing Division reviewed the application for about 12 days, then referred it to the Policy Planning Division. The Policy Planning Division referred the application to the Department of Energy after five days—one day after the scheduled shipping date.

The application still had not been approved by the scheduled expiration date of the letter of credit. Therefore, the applicant's letter of credit had to be extended, and a new shipping date for mid-December was arranged after consulting with the consignee. The applicant called an OEA licensing officer twice in the last two weeks of October to determine the status of the case, and each time the licensing officer replied that he had no information. At the end of October, after 42 days of review, the Department of Energy recommended approval.

In early November, four days after the Department of Energy recommended approval, the applicant again called the licensing officer, who said he still had no information on the status of the application. The applicant asked an official in a Department of Commerce regional office to inquire about the application; he did, but also to no avail. The applicant during this period mistakenly believed that the Defense Department was holding up the application, although the application had not been referred to Defense. In mid-November, the OEA sent the application to the Subgroup on Nuclear Export Coordination, which recommended approval without controversy. Six days later the OEA's Policy Planning Division recommended approval, and the application was approved eight days later, at the end of November. On the day after the Policy Planning Division recommended approval, the applicant cabled the consignee asking him to send more information about the intended use of the equipment, stating that this information might help the government make a favorable decision.

On December 1 the applicant again asked the licensing officer for information about the application, but the officer again said he had nothing to report. Five days later the applicant received the license.

One of the comptroller general's conclusions was that "applicants will continue to face a potentially costly and frustrating discovery game as long as export license applications are separately managed by several semiautonomous bureaucracies during the decision making process."[24] Although the Export Administration Act amendments of 1979 did establish a system of "suspense points" in the licensing process at which an application either would have to be decided or escalated to higher levels for further consideration, the semiautonomous bureaucracies were not eliminated.

Another potential obstacle inherent in the U.S. export licensing procedure that can result in delay to the U.S. firm is that cases involving transactions with the Chinese must be submitted to the North Atlantic Treaty Organization's (NATO) Coordinating Committee on Export Controls (COCOM), a multilateral organization formed in November 1949. COCOM includes all the NATO countries except Iceland, plus Japan. Only with the unamimous consent of the 15 participating governments can an item on the COCOM restricted list be exported to a Communist country.

During the Korean War a special China Committee (ChinCom) was established as a part of COCOM to administer restrictions on trade with China and North Korea. For a while these restrictions were more severe than those applied to the Soviet Union and its allies, but this "China differential" was eliminated in 1957 and ChinCom ceased to operate as a special body.[25] Now the same COCOM controls apply to both the Soviet Union and China.

In actuality there are three COCOM lists, organized according to the technical specifications and applications of the items contained in them:

1. A munitions list that includes all military items;
2. An atomic energy list that includes sources of fissionable materials, nuclear reactors, and their components; and
3. An industrial/commercial list.

Since by their very nature munitions have distinct military purposes and strategic importance, much of COCOM's activity and debate center on the industrial list and on requests by the members for "exceptions."

The new COCOM list has 149 items; and to get the unanimous consent of the 15 COCOM countries for "exceptions" to them is a difficult task at best, owing both to the procedural unwieldiness and to the fact that each participating government applies the COCOM controls in its own way.[26] In recent years there have been many complaints from the U.S. business community that the COCOM countries not only interpret the controls differently but also enforce them with varying degrees of rigor and have different provisions for controlling the reexports of their exports to unauthorized destinations. In referring to the COCOM system, the chairman of the House Subcommittee on International Economic Policy and Trade stated in March 1979 the following:

COCOM is a completely secret and completely informal understanding, and U.S. firms are convinced that many of our COCOM partners, through interpretation or evasion manage to export products and technology to the East for which our government does not grant licenses. This does nothing for our national security; it merely loses business for our country.[27]

Regardless of whether this is entirely accurate, the fact that the COCOM bureaucratic apparatus exists cannot help but complicate the process of the U.S. firm's dual negotiations and subsequent completion of its commercial transaction with China. Moreover, since the bureaucracy that handles U.S. participation in COCOM is headed by the Department of State and is largely separate from the licensing bureaucracy of the Department of Commerce, a U.S. firm might in fact be involved not just in dual negotiations but in triple ones. In any event, the March 1979 report by the comptroller general is not optimistic: "Present agency actions and proposed changes indicate that U.S. performance in COCOM may worsen, since the U.S. licensing system is becoming more, not less, complex."[28]

DUAL NEGOTIATIONS—A CASE STUDY

From the above, it would appear that even if there were no basic doubt that a U.S. business person could ultimately obtain an export license, validated or general, the time-consuming administrative procedures mentioned above accentuate the impact that U.S. restrictions have on trade with China in general, and the consummation of any commercial transaction with it in particular. No matter how successful negotiations with the Chinese foreign trade corporation (FTC) may be, the process of securing an export license can make or break the commercial transaction.

The dual negotiations conducted simultaneously by Control Data Corporation (CDC) of Minneapolis, Minnesota, with the Chinese and U.S. governments are a case in point. The contract involved the sale of two medium-scale computers to China for oil exploration. The negotiations, lasting for more than two years, concerned not only CDC and the Chinese FTC Techimport but also the U.S. government, France, and even the Soviet Union. The brief case study developed below is based on interviews with CEC officials as well as information in company documents, and treats only CDC negotiations with the U.S. government. (Other aspects of the negotiations are presented in Chapter 5.)

In December 1973, CDC's foreign subsidiary, Control Data France (CDF), and its French partner, Compagnie Générale de Géophysique (CGG), entered into formal negotiations with Techimport for the sale of two computer systems valued at $7 million. A contract was signed on August 14, 1974. An export license was granted on October 20, 1976, more than two years later; the systems were installed in September 1977 and were accepted by the Chinese in mid-November 1977. All told, the total elapsed time for this transaction was one month short of four years.

After the signing of the contract, an export license application was submitted to the French government. The application was quickly approved and submitted to COCOM at the same time that CDC applied for U.S. approval for a reexport license for France. The United States put in for an exception to the COCOM process in the spring of 1975, thus delaying approval of the case until full consideration could be given to it by the various U.S. agencies involved.

While this transaction was being debated among the agencies concerned, another complication arose. The USSR signed a contract with CDC for a similar system for oil exploration, to be delivered in approximately the same time period. Application for license approval was submitted to the U.S. government.

The CDC export license application detailed the technical specifics of the transaction. The 83-page application spent five pages describing the end user and end use. In a section of the end use statement, it was stated:

> China National Technical Import Corporation has stated in writing that the end user is China National Oil and Gas Exploration and Development Corporation. . . .
> All equipment systems will be operated in the same building. The design of the equipment configuration has been defined so the systems can process 250,000 seismic records per month, within which one-fourth of the throughput of the second Cyber 172-4 will be used for other processing (well logging gravity, magnetism and reservoir engineering) and one-fourth of the throughput is for the research on a new seismic processing method. [29]

Upon receiving CDC's request for an export license, the Department of Commerce's Office of Export Controls set up an operating committee that included computer specialists, to determine whether adequate safeguards could be provided for the two CDC Cyber 172s. Besides the technical experts mentioned above, the committee consisted of officials from the Department of Commerce, Department of State, and Department of Defense. [30] One major problem confronting the committee was the fact that CDC's Cyber 172 had the capability of being utilized to track ballistic missiles. This, however, was not the first U.S. sale of computers to the Chinese. In October 1973, Geospace of Houston, Texas, contracted to sell $5.5 million of seismic surveying computer equipment, including a Raytheon model 704 computer. In November 1975 another U.S. company concluded a $23 million contract with the Chinese for oil exploration equipment with computer components and intermediate software by Interdata Corporation of New Jersey.

Countering the government suggestion that CDC Cyber 172 computers had dual use possibilities, CDC argued that the Chinese already had computer technology equivalent to that of the United States. In order to prove its point, CDC exhibited an East German 1040 Ryad computer that was being used in China and that appeared to rival the Cyber 172 in every major respect. [31]

After almost a year of deliberation on both the PRC and the USSR transactions, CDC received conditional approval of these cases on March 9, 1976. The conditions were that the Chinese accept certain safeguards to ensure proper end use. However, CDC was very surprised at the level of safeguards being imposed for these systems. In addition to having free access to the site and submitting periodic reports to the U.S. government, the conditions called for CDC to have a man on-site for three years. These conditions posed a serious dilemma for CDC—and, as it turned out, for the U.S. government. Previous experience with the USSR convinced the Americans that they would in all likelihood accept them verbatim. They had done so in the past in order to purchase other systems, though larger in size. On the other hand, CDC was convinced that the Chinese, as a matter of principle, would reject any conditions. This problem was raised with a number of U.S. government officials by CDC, but to no avail.

CDC finally agreed to attempt to negotiate with the Chinese on a best-effort basis and to try to gain acceptance of some, if not all, of the conditions in order to satisfy U.S. government concerns. CDC officials arrived in Peking about one week after the Tien An Men Square riots and the expulsion of Deng Xiaoping. Along with the expulsion of Deng there was a very rapid ideological reversal of his philosophy of reliance on Western products and experts.

Shortly after CDC officials arrived, it became apparent that the Chinese were going to reject any condition, even the most innocuous. They maintained that this issue of safeguards was an internal problem between CDC and its government, and it should not involve either Control Data France or the PRC. The Chinese further stated that although the loss of this computer purchase would be very costly for them, they would not accept any conditions imposed by the United States.

The company then changed its strategy. CDC proposed an amendment to the contract that called for a technical assistance agreement whereby it would provide a Western expert on-site for a period of three years. CDC was able to justify this approach on the ground that the training of the Chinese technical personnel had already been completed in France, and that since delivery of the system was at least a year away, they would need additional assistance after the installation and acceptance of the equipment. The company had never raised the U.S.-proposed condition that a man must be on-site for three years. The Chinese initial response to this proposal was a tentative rejection based on the then-prevalent philosophy of self-reliance.

CDC, however, was able to finally convince them that such an amendment to the contract was in their best interests, and they finally negotiated an agreement for two people to be on-site for one year and one person for an additional year. Even though the Chinese agreed to this contract amendment, they refused to sign it, on the ground that such an agreement would be meaningless if the export license was not issued, but they also indicated their willingness to sign once an export license was granted. In early May, CDC's Washington-based negotiator returned to the United States and presented this technical assistance agreement to the U.S. government. At the same time, CDC learned that the USSR had agreed to all of the conditions proposed by the United States.

During the following months the U.S. government wrestled with the dilemma that it had created for itself. It was dissatisfied with what was considered to be a minimum set of conditions, although the most critical one was contained in the contract amendment with the PRC. On the other hand, the Soviet government had accepted the safeguards in toto, and was now expecting quick approval of its computer system. There was the further political problem of having to demonstrate equal treatment to both countries in the area of trade. Therefore, to approve the Russian license and not the Chinese would appear, in the eyes of the general public, to be tilting toward the Soviet Union. Another problem was that COCOM had approved the Chinese case and still had to consider the Russian case.

During August the USSR exerted a great deal of pressure to obtain its system, and the U.S. government finally forwarded the case to COCOM, where it was promptly held up by the French government. The latter was not about to release this U.S. case of trade with the Soviet Union until a decision had been made on what France considered to be "its" sale to the Chinese. CDC then had to convince the French that it was not in their best interest or CDC's to delay approval of the system for the Soviet Union, and in early September COCOM approved that transaction.

CDC scheduled further negotiations with the Chinese concerning this matter in mid-September, only to have them postponed again because of the death of Chairman Mao. Meanwhile, Secretary of State Kissinger became involved in the case, and he urged its approval by the U.S. government. CDC finally returned to the PRC in the second week of October, and upon arrival was advised by the U.S. government that notification of official approval would be waiting at the Liaison Office in Peking. However, approval was not received until October

20—seven days later. During this time the U.S. government kept asking whether CDC had obtained a signed amendment, while the Chinese kept asking whether the U.S. government had approved the export license.

NOTES

1. U.S., Code, 63 Statute 7 (1949), as amended 50, app. secs. 2021-32 (1964).

2. U.S., Congress, Office of Technology Assessment, Technology and East-West Trade (Washington, D.C.: U.S. Government Printing Office, 1979), p. 112.

3. U.S., Congress, House, Committee on Commerce and International Relations, Subcommittee on International Trade and Commerce, Export Licensing of Advanced Technology: A Review, 94th Cong., 2d sess., 1976, p. v.

4. "Faster Process Ahead for China Sales?" China Business Review, July-August, 1977, p. 55.

5. Ibid.

6. "China Recognizes Form 629: Permits Monitoring of Sensitive Equipment," China Business Review, July-August 1979, p. 55.

7. U.S., Department of Commerce, "Processing Export License Applications: Procedures and Time Limits," Federal Register, vol. 45, no. 132, p. 45891. For background on the debates in both the House and Senate on the Export Administration Act of 1979, see U.S., Congress, Office of Technology Assessment, Technology and East-West Trade, p. 125.

8. U.S., Congress, House, "Export Administration Act of 1979," Congressional Record, Public Law 96-72, September 29, 1979.

9. U.S., Department of State, Munitions Control Newsletter (Washington, D.C.: Department of State, March 1980).

10. Ibid. See also "U.S. Willing to Sell China Copters, Transport Planes," Washington Post, March 19, 1980, p. 2.

11. China has shown a strong interest in the model 212 Bell helicopter for seismographic surveying, oil exploration, and forestry management. "Bell Helicopter Lifts Off," U.S.-China Business Review, November-December 1979.

12. Luke T. Lee and John B. McCobb, Jr., "United States Trade Embargo on China, 1949-1970: Legal Status and Future Prospects," New York University Journal of International Law and Politics, Spring 1971, p. 8.

13. U.S., Congress, House, Committee on Commerce and International Relations, Subcommittee on International Trade and Commerce, Export Licensing of Advanced Technology, p. 71.

14. U.S., Congress, Office of Technology Assessment, Technology and East-West Trade, p. 127.

15. U.S., Congress, House, Committee on Science and Technology, Subcommittee on Domestic and International Scientific Planning, Analysis, and Cooperation, testimony of Rauer Meyer, director of the Office of Export Administration, U.S. Department of Commerce (Washington, D.C.: Government Printing Office, October 4, 1978).

16. U.S., Congress, House, "Export Administration Act Amendments of 1979," Congressional Record, March 1, 1979, p. H1046.

17. "China Recognizes Form 629," p. 22.

18. U.S., Congress, House, "Export Administration Act of 1979," sec. 10.

19. U.S., Comptroller General, Export Controls: Need to Clarify Policy and Simplify Administration, ID 79-16 (Washington, D.C.: General Accounting Office, March 1, 1979), p. 18.

20. Ibid.

21. U.S., Congress, House Committee on International Relations, Subcommittee on International Trade and Commerce, Export Licensing of Advanced Technology, p. 71; and U.S., Congress, Office of Technology Assessment, Technology and East-West Trade, p. 132.

22. U.S., Congress, House, Committee on International Relations, Subcommittee on International Trade and Commerce, Export Licensing of Advanced Technology, p. 71.

23. U.S., Comptroller General, Administration of U.S. Export Licensing Should Be Consolidated to Be More Responsive to Industry, ID 78-60 (Washington, D.C.: General Accounting Office, October 1978), pp. 10-11.

24. Ibid, p. 12.

25. U.S., Congress, Office of Technology Assessment, Technology and East-West Trade, p. 154.

26. U.S., Comptroller General, Export Controls, p. 11.

27. U.S., Congress, House, "Export Administration Act Amendments of 1979," p. H1046.

28. U.S., Comptroller General, Export Controls, p. 16.

29. Control Data Corporation, "Control Data Export License Application for Dual CDC Cyber 172's Seismic Data Processing Center" (Minneapolis, May 29, 1975), p. 30.

30. "CDC Gets the Green Light: Export Controls," U.S.-China Business Review, November-December 1976, p. 51.

31. Ibid.

5

OVERCOMING HINDRANCES AND
IMPEDIMENTS IN U.S.–CHINESE
COMMERCIAL NEGOTIATIONS

Previous chapters have stressed the importance of understanding the specific hindrances and impediments that complicate negotiations for both the Chinese and the Americans. It was implied that overcoming these hindrances and impediments is what successful negotiation is all about. Also implied was that the finding a commonality of interest in a given commercial negotiation assuredly helps in overcoming impediments to negotiation and, thus, in achieving a successful commercial transaction.

In this chapter, using primarily the experience of one U.S. company—Control Data Corporation (CDC) of Minneapolis, Minnesota —those aspects of commercial negotiations reflecting commonality of interest and other key elements of U.S.-Chinese commercial negotiations are highlighted and discussed. Specifically discussed are the CDC commercial negotiations for the sale of equipment for seismic data processing centers to China conducted between 1973 and 1978. Some of those key elements discussed in Chapter 3 and referred to in the CDC negotiations are the difficulty in establishing contacts with the Chinese and the results of negotiation. The CDC contractual negotiations are important because they represent the sale of significant high-technology items to China and also because by themselves they represent, in dollar terms, a significant share of the total trade turnover for the years in which the transactions occurred. Also of importance, especially in the case of the first transaction, which took more than two years to complete and involved the sale of two medium-scale computers to the People's Republic of China (PRC) for oil exploration, is that these negotiations illustrate the frustration, "political maneuvering and sometimes sheer lunacy" that may characterize commercial negotiations[1] with any country.

For purposes of this study, commonality of interest is the maximization of any and all opportunities for compromise during the commercial negotiations. Such compromise can result in the elimination of specific hindrances and impediments that could have delayed or thwarted commercial negotiations. Thus, commonality of interest, or its absence, can affect U.S.-Chinese commercial negotiations and, therefore, like the bureaucratic context that also influences these negotiations, can ultimately contribute to their success or failure.

In a larger context, commonality of interest can also imply a basic, almost urgent, need by the Chinese for the U.S. firm's product so strong that it is almost mandatory that they secure the product from the U.S. firm, assuming successful negotiations. Such instances are rare but have occurred, as in the case of the sale by International Harvester Corporation of its airplane tow trucks (see Chapter 3). Unfortunately, products made by CDC, while unique and needed by the Chinese, are not without competition.

Price and cost, for example, are conflicting interests that must be resolved in any negotiation. One way to resolve price issues, aside from haggling in negotiating sessions, is by approaching decision makers on an "old-friend basis" (see Chapter 3). Thus, reaching commonality of interest is in effect negotiating from the bureaucratic top down. CDC, for example, in its efforts to establish contact with the Chinese used a consultant who was an acquaintance of Premier Chou En-lai.

The majority of respondents in this study (84.6 percent) indicated that price and cost were not the only considerations in their negotiations with the Chinese. Other considerations mentioned were the technical specifications and quality of service. In fact, one company singled out the "reliability of the Western supplier" as being very important.[2] Thus, from the standpoint of commonality of interest, considerations other than price can be very important to a U.S. firm in executing a successful commercial transaction with the Chinese foreign trade monopoly. However, as was indicated in Chapter 3, and as will be shown in the case of CDC, price considerations also are extremely important, and it takes a great deal of ingenuity on the part of the U.S. firms to negotiate with the Chinese foreign trade corporations (FTCs) on this issue.

Interestingly, unlike the Soviet experience, most of the companies responding (86 percent) indicated that their negotiations were enhanced by having apparent access to Chinese political decision makers, as well as to FTC officials. Such access was viewed as an important asset in promoting a commonality of interest between the parties. Going beyond commonality of interest, a majority of responding companies felt that the uniqueness of their product also contributed to the success of their negotiations.

CONTROL DATA CORPORATION—A CASE STUDY OF
U.S.-CHINESE COMMERCIAL NEGOTIATIONS

As will be shown below, the CDC computer systems are relatively singular, and therefore are products necessary to the fulfillment of the Chinese plan—and, perhaps even more important, necessary in earning the foreign exchange necessary to finance imports.
Of late China has emphasized the three "balances" that must be maintained for successful commercial relations and trade.[3] First of all,
it is important to strike a balance between imported projects and domestic capacity for economic development.[4] Just as important is the
balance between imported technology and the national capacity to as-
similate it. Finally, and perhaps most important, the Chinese believe it is important to maintain the "import-export balance." Thus,
any U.S. company doing business with the Chinese is confronted at
the outset by a very real policy that militates against frivolous utilization of scarce foreign exchange.
    Since 1971 CDC has been actively interested in marketing com-
puters to China to complement its sales of computers in other parts
of the world. In 1978 CDC had world mainframe computer sales that
constituted about 6 percent of the total world mainframe computer
market. The company reported consolidated net earnings of $124.2
million in 1979, with earnings from the computer part of the business
amounting to $70.8 million, 57 percent of the total. Total assets em-
ployed by CDC in 1979 were over $6 billion.[5]
    CDC has become the world's largest computer services firm
through the combination of its Cybernet services network and the acquisition of the Service Bureau Company (SBC—formerly owned by
IBM) and, more recently, other international computer services enterprises. SBC's strength lies in commercial rather than scientific
computing, providing a complement to the primary emphasis of Cybernet.

THE CHINESE NEED FOR COMPUTERS

    One of the "clinchers" in the CDC sale of computers to China
is that the latter wanted the CDC system "quite badly."[6] In fact,
since 1964, China has relied heavily on imports of computers, as
Table 5.1 shows. According to the table, during the period 1964 to
1975 about 16 different computers were sold to China. Ten of these
were primarily parts of seismic or geophysical exploration systems
of the type marketed by CDC.
    With regard to imports, a 1973 CIA report noted that China ap-
parently employed Japanese and West European computers "for its

TABLE 5.1

Typical Sales of Computers to China, 1964-77

Year	Type of Computer	Supplier, Country, and Order Value
1964	Unidentified	SERCEL, France; seismic exploration system
1965	ARCH 1000	Marconi-Elliott, U.K.; process-control system
	NADAC 100 (five units)	SEA, France; plant automation systems
1966	ELLIOT 803	Elliot Computers, U.K.; medical research use
1967	ICL 1903 ICL 1905 }	ICL, U.K.; unknown destination
1973	UNIVAC	SERCEL, France; seismic research system
	RAYTHEON 704	Geospace, U.S.; seismic control, $5.5 million
1974	IRIS 60 MITRA 15 (two) }	SERCEL, France; oil-exploitation management
	CDC 172 (two) CDC 170 }	CGG, France; oil-exploration ship, equipment $5 million
1975	INTERDATA	U.S.; oil-exploration system, $23.0 million
1976	MITRA 30	CII, France
	BURROUGHS B7700	Burroughs, U.S.; license denied
	RIAD EC-1040	East Germany; reported one installation in China
	HITAC M 160-2 HITAC M 170 }	Hitachi, Japan; Central Meteorological Office
	Unidentified	Hungary; petroleum-control system
	MITRA 125 (two)	SFIM-CII, France; civil aviation use in China
	PDP 11/45 (two)	Digital Resources, U.S.; seismic exploration
1977	UNIDATA 7738	Seimens, West Germany; power-station use
	IBM 3032	U.S.; for Bank of China in Hong Kong, $20 million
	IBM 360	U.S.; process-control application

Source: Compiled by 21st Century Research.

few major data management tasks."[7] The report also notes that "these tasks will grow in importance with the increasing complexity of China's economy and ultimately affect domestic computer design and production." Although precise figures for computer imports are not available, it is unlikely that imports will exceed much more than $100 million in any given year.[8]

The basic reason for this appears to be that the Chinese leadership is intent on building its own viable computer industry and has confined its purchases of computers to "prototype purchasing."[9] Table 5.1 shows that no two systems were alike and were purchased from companies in France, the United Kingdom, United States, and Japan. Nevertheless, despite such "prototype purchasing," Chinese contracts for computers have been increasing. During 1973 and 1974 such contracts amounted to an estimated $6 million to $7 million per year and rose to about $25 million for each of the years thereafter to 1978. In the latter year, primarily as a result of the $69 million CDC contract for the sale of a seismic exploration computer system, imports of computers reached at least $100 million.

Even without imports China has come a long way in the development of its own computer/electronics industry since 1958. In that year it produced its first computer, the AUGUST 1st, from designs provided by the Soviet Union.* In 1965, only three years after the introduction of such computers in the USSR, China produced a second-generation computer based on transistors. Third-generation computers, based on integrated circuits, were produced "within about two years of such Soviet models."[10] Figure 5.1 shows the use of computers in the Chinese economy.

Although not indicated in Figure 5.1, in recent years a shift in the primary use of computers by China appears to have taken place. Most noticeable, and of particular importance from CDC's point of view, is China's demand for computers with specific applications, particularly in petroleum exploration. As shown in Figure 5.1, a significant percentage of computers imported by the Chinese have been for process control at imported turnkey plants or for end uses for which domestic computers are not available, such as analyses of weather data, management of banking operations, and air traffic control.

In its "China Briefing" (October 1973) CDC highlighted the observations of a group of six U.S. computer scientists who had written a report on the state of the Chinese computer industry. These observations are relevant today. According to their report:

---

*This first Chinese computer was based on design specifications for the Soviet URAL-2, and appeared only six years after the Soviet Union built its first BESM-1 machine.

FIGURE 5.1

PRC Use of Computers

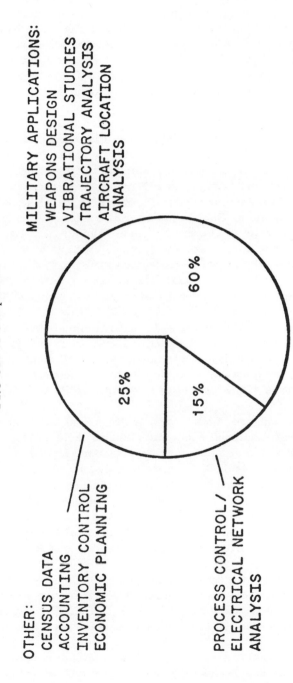

MILITARY APPLICATIONS:
WEAPONS DESIGN
VIBRATIONAL STUDIES
TRAJECTORY ANALYSIS
AIRCRAFT LOCATION
ANALYSIS

OTHER:
CENSUS DATA
ACCOUNTING
INVENTORY CONTROL
ECONOMIC PLANNING

PROCESS CONTROL/
ELECTRICAL NETWORK
ANALYSIS

60%

25%

15%

Note: Bohdan Szuprowicz, "CDC's China Sale Soon Focusing Western Attention," Computerworld, November 1976, p. 34, suggests that "at least 50 percent of all computers made in China are used for military applications such as nuclear and missile programs and in weapons systems design and shipbuilding."

Source: Control Data Corporation.

There is very little meaningful crystal ball gazing we
can do about the future of Chinese computing, yet a few
remarks in this vein seem in place. First, the Chinese
we talked to indicated a strong interest in what they called
the "super computer"—i.e., very big and very fast machines such as the CDC STAR computer and the Burroughs
B6700. One guesses they will continue the trend toward
bigger and faster computers, perhaps next attempting a
very large step. [11]

As will be mentioned below, there is little doubt that the Chinese
need for the large CDC mainframe computers and CDC's corporate
staff perception of this need were key elements in spurring CDC's
huge marketing efforts beginning in 1971.

An article in a Chinese economic journal in March 1979 also is
significant in highlighting China's need for computers. The author
suggests that "the level of electronics [in a country] is an important
indicator of modernization," and cites as one example of the current
state of the level of the Chinese electronics industry the fact that "The
Ministry of Foreign Trade can complete within one minute monetary
transaction tasks with the offices it maintains in London and Tokyo and
can query the computer center through the terminals for data." [12]
The author of the article then suggests that it is important for a developing country such as China to secure high-speed, quality data-
handling computers as well as the adjunct peripheral equipment. However, one computer does not make an electronics industry, nor does
it testify to a nation's capabilities in electronics. He notes:

Under the guidance of Marxism-Leninism and Mao Zedong
thought, using national economic plans as the criteria, and
on the foundation of mass bookkeeping, our nation's socialist
accounting work is destined to become advanced. But owing
to the destruction and interference of Lin Biao and the "gang
of four," it still lags rather far behind the advanced levels
of the rest of the world in the use of electronic technology.
Recognition of backwardness leads to the abolition of backwardness and an overtaking of the advanced countries. [13]

China's plan for the development of its computer science in
1978-86 was outlined in a major speech by Fang Yi, vice-premier of
the PRC State Council, on March 18, 1978, at China's National Science
Conference.* Specifically, China should manufacture giant computers,

---

*In addition to this title, Fang Yi is also minister in charge of
the State Scientific and Technology Commission and de facto head of
the Chinese Academy of Sciences.

as well as putting a range of computers into serial production. By 1985, according to Fang Yi, China should "have acquired a group of comparatively advanced specialists in computer science research and . . . to have built a fair-sized modern computer industry."[14] In short, the implication is that China needs computers and computer technology to become a modern, developed state.

Fang Yi also noted:

> In the next three years we should rapidly develop basic research on computer science and related disciplines, lose no time in solving the scientific and technical problems in the industrial production of large-scale integrated circuits, and make a breakthrough in the technology of ultra large-scale integrated circuits.[15]

Parenthetically, the fact that Fang Yi noted that China must "make a breakthrough in the LSI [large-scale integrated circuit] technology" may indicate a backwardness in such advanced technology that would put China a number of years behind the United States. This lag is noted in the report of a visiting U.S. Institute of Electrical and Electronic Engineers delegation in the fall of 1979. According to the head of the delegation, Chinese computer development lags at least ten years behind the West. Moreover the PRC cannot catch up without outside help.[16] Thus, a market of great potential in fourth-generation computers for U.S. firms could exist. In this regard, according to Fang Yi, China would aim "to 'popularize' microcomputers and 'to put into operation' giant ultra-high-speed computers." It is no wonder, then, that CDC, from the very beginning of Chinese resurgence of trade with the United States in the early 1970s, was very interested in establishing a meaningful market relationship in order to sell its computers.

As of January 1980, China is believed to have more than 50 different models of foreign computers installed, with a total inventory of about 1,000 units.[17] Many of these units—perhaps about 20 percent of the total—are relatively small and slow, almost obsolete, machines. By contrast, about 170,000 general-purpose computers, excluding minicomputers, are believed to be in operation in the United States, and about 12,500 in the civilian sector of the Soviet Union.

Currently China's electronics industry is known to have the following five groups: components, instruments, computers, communications, and consumer products. Overall there are at least 200 major plants, 500 smaller plants, and 1,500 "neighborhood" factories. The Fourth Ministry of Machine Building has overall jurisdiction over the planning and production of electronic components and computer systems.

It also can be seen from the brief treatment of China's need for computers that even before entering negotiations, CDC's bargaining position was quite advantageous. This was particularly true because mainframe computers had high priority in Chinese import planning, if only for "prototype purchasing." Consequently, scarce foreign exchange was most likely to be allocated for purchase of these products. Conversely, if CDC's product had not had high priority in Chinese import planning, the company's bargaining position would have been a relatively weak one; and although its products might not have been rejected out of hand, pressures for countertrade at the very least would have been quite strong.

With regard to entering the Chinese market, the basic task for CDC in the early 1970s was to adopt appropriate strategies for entering the market and to make first contact with the interested Chinese users of CDC products and the Chinese authorized to negotiate and sign the final contract.

CDC CORPORATE STRATEGIES

CDC's initial strategy in 1971/72 can be summarized as follows: to assess China as a viable market for the future; to determine the political climate for business; to get China acquainted with CDC.[18] As early as June 1971, a CDC memorandum suggested that "we, just as our competitors must be doing, should develop a plan for eventually marketing selected lines of our computers in China."[19] The memorandum thought it "highly probable" that the U.S. government would allow selected exports of certain mainframe computers. Moreover, it was "more than likely," according to the memorandum, that China would import rather than manufacture its own computers "for the foreseeable future."

Considering this optimistic assessment of the market for computers in China, CDC's corporate staff was faced with the immediate task of how to proceed. The 1971 memorandum referred to above suggested two courses of action that occupied the CDC corporate staff for the next two years. These courses of action for marketing computers in China centered on establishing marketing contacts through Canadian and/or Hong Kong channels. (More will be said below about these first contacts.) The important thing to note is that like any company beginning a new venture, CDC was in many respects "flying blind." A 1974 CDC memorandum highlights this particular aspect:

> I am quite certain an American could not get a visa to visit
> there at the present time, but a Canadian could. We'd
> start by writing a few letters through Hong Kong and state

the purpose of the proposed visit. Who knows, maybe we'll get a hit that could lead to something.[20]

In light of its market assessments and in order to facilitate marketing strategies and to pool information, CDC established a corporate "task force" in September 1973. Its first meeting was held on September 21. In retrospect, of importance is not so much what was discussed, but the tenor of the meeting, which indicated an attempt by a major U.S. corporation to come to grips with the basic problem of how to enter the China market.

Communication among the members of the company's China task force and with the company as a whole was a prime item on the agenda, as was outlining the requisite "position papers" to be prepared on "major corporate product strategies for China."[21] The marketing strategy adopted was to sell the "entire range of total services and to engage in appropriate cooperative activities with the PRC."[22] In December 1973 a CDC memorandum suggested:

> This marketplace for U.S. high technology, and in particular computer and telecommunications technology, is developing in a quantum jump that is much faster than . . . many experienced China-watchers had anticipated seven months ago. The tremendous opportunity this gives Control Data is exciting to witness.[23]

One basic reason for this optimism was the expectation that the Chinese would give high priority to their computer sector. Moreover, according to the CDC memorandum:

> In the increasingly relaxed U.S.-China political climate, China would be looking toward U.S. technology to speed modern industrial development, which, in 1973, has resulted in an absolutely astounding record of 20-25 complete U.S. large plant sales valued at between $1.0-$1.5 billion.[24]

Notice the continuing CDC emphasis on the political situation in China. (More will be noted below about this.) Doubtless the company was also buoyed by a joint U.S.-China communiqué released on December 5, 1973, following Secretary of State Henry Kissinger's sixth visit to Peking. According to the communiqué, "the Chinese and U.S. agreed to take steps to further trade relations."[25]

A 1977 CDC market assessment is instructive for its insight into the strategies that the company debated and subsequently adopted. In assessing the potential market for computers CDC estimated that in 1977, China would need at least 5,000 computers for industrialization "in the near future."[26] According to company marketing experts, it was reasonable to assume that China was capable of producing about 150 computers a year, with a growth rate of about 25 percent per year. Therefore "the potential market for computers is in the order of at least 1,000 machines in the near future." In dollar terms, according to CDC expectations, this might amount to as much as $250 million.[27]

Moreover, CDC believed that the potential market for original equipment manufacturer's (OEM) peripherals also was promising, but did not estimate the dollar value that might be involved. China would be able to pay for this Western equipment "with increasingly larger amounts of oil."[28] It was this optimistic assessment of the market in China that spurred CDC to approach the marketing of its computers with vigor.

On the basis of this assessment, CDC's objectives in the short run were to pursue immediate prospects, particularly with regard to selling OEM disk drives and tape drives, and to pursue contact and possibilities with China's Academy of Sciences. CDC's long-range plans were much more ambitious, including such projects as selling large systems for nuclear research and for use in the petroleum industry, education, and weather forecasting. Also included were the sales of licenses for peripheral equipment.

The major competition, according to CDC corporate strategists, was probably from such Japanese manufacturers as Hitachi, Fujitsu, NEC, Mitsubishi, and Toshiba. However, they saw Japan's computer industry as being "weak in service and support of its customers." China, according to the plan, was an ideal customer because it neither required nor desired the normal computer sales support "beyond the initial training of its technicians."[29]

With regard to U.S. competition, IBM was without peer "because of its monopoly in the EDP field," according to CDC. CDC's marketing plan, however, suggested that although IBM is strong in some areas, and although the Chinese have made extensive studies of IBM equipment, "IBM does not provide as good a price or performance as CDC in scientific or educational environments."

The company's strategy therefore became a twofold one of "pursuing immediate prospects" and of "further improving relationships with Chinese foreign trade corporations." The first move would yield immediate revenue, according to the plan, while the second one would, it was hoped, lead to "future sales, technical sales and joint ventures." Just how successful these CDC corporate strategies proved to be will be discussed below.

As a means of implementing its corporate sales strategies, the company in September 1973 replaced its China "task force" with a corporate China office. The new office was to participate directly in the development and implementation of CDC's corporate strategy for marketing computers to the Chinese. Such participation would include long-range planning and assistance to the International Development Committee, the Management Committee, and other members of top management.[30] According to the company's job description, the person in charge of the office would be an assistant to the executive vice-president and would report to the executive vice-president and chairman of the International Development Committee. Other duties would include the following:

> Developing contacts and liaison at the highest levels of
> PRC government and embassies, China Academy of Science, Ministry of Foreign Trade, and selected Chinese
> Foreign Trade Corporations (FTC).[31]

Also of importance was that the new office would cooperate closely with U.S. officials at the Department of State, Department of Commerce, National Academy of Science, and other agencies. The new office was particularly charged with "keeping abreast of social, political and economic factors as they relate to the evolving corporate strategy for the PRC." It is noteworthy that in establishing a new China office, CDC was clearly making a commitment to the future. In this regard the marketing plan cited above makes the following point: "It is important that we maintain an image which indicates that [we] . . . are interested in building a long term relationship with China, rather than an image of a company which only reacts to their immediate requirements."[32] Again it is important to emphasize that CDC realized from the beginning that commercial negotiation involved much more than sitting down at a table, offering a product, and determining a price. For entry into the China market, it was first necessary to find in the Chinese foreign trade labyrinth the right person or organization to market the product—in other words, to make contact with the end user.

FIRST CONTACTS

Establishing contact with Chinese foreign trade organizations (FTOs) and end users, as was pointed out in Chapter 3, is a major obstacle in undertaking commercial negotiations for most U.S. firms. For CDC establishing first contacts with the Chinese was particularly difficult.

The company first became interested in the PRC as a potential market about the time of U.S. rapprochement with China in 1971/72.[33]

The first CDC contact was a proposal sent July 16, 1971, to the Chinese Ministry of Science and Technology via the Chinese Embassy in Ottawa.[34] In essence the proposal offered to export to a Canadian firm certified CDC peripherals and mainframes that were "refurbished and modified as appropriate."[35] Also of interest to the CDC corporate staff at this time was information relayed by the president of another U.S. firm that China found it "more politically desirable" to deal with Canada than either the United States or Japan. In addition the CDC contact mentioned that "presumably, France would also be relatively high on the Chinese acceptability list."[36] CDC later learned through contacts that the Canadian government believed that a direct approach by CDC would be better.

As can be seen from still another CDC memorandum, the corporate staff leaned also to the direct approach in contacting the Chinese. The staff's perception was as follows:

> One approach is through the foreign trade corporations (FTC's) which are controlled by the Ministry of Foreign Trade since foreign trade is a state monopoly. . . .
> The first step in establishing business contacts with the PRC is to select the appropriate FTC. It is best initially to contact the main office in Peking . . . although responsibility for the import or export of particular commodities is often delegated to various branch offices, and negotiations may ultimately be with them. Just as in East Europe, normally all negotiations are handled by the foreign trade officials—contact with end users is rare. PRC trade missions in foreign countries have been known to take the initiative in contacting Western firms when the Chinese have a strong interest in their products. . . .
> The initial proposal submitted to the appropriate FTC in Peking should be sufficiently detailed and comprehensive to allow the Chinese to evaluate it commercially. Price quotations are not recommended. However, full information about CDC, its activities and its products is essential. It is further recommended that the firm indicate a willingness to provide further details, answer any questions, and arrange personal follow-up meetings.[37]

CDC was convinced that "all indications here pointed to computers being a high priority item on the Chinese shopping list, therefore a reply should be expected to a CDC proposal."

In order to begin the direct approach, CDC entered into an agreement in October 1971 with a Washington-based consulting firm that had good contacts with China Resources Company of Hong Kong as well as with Chinese officials in all parts of the government, for the purpose of "strengthening the company's position in dealing with officials of the PRC."[38] In fact, one of the principals in the firm was a former acquaintance of Premier Chou En-lai, and thus was in a position to be very helpful. According to the contract with CDC, the consultant

> will assist CDC in analyzing the market potential for its products and services in the PRC; will accompany certain of the company's business and technical officials to the PRC to cooperate with and advise CDC in the detailed sales negotiations; will assist in the development of the finance package necessary to assure the success of the transaction; and will assist in obtaining export licenses in Washington, D.C.[39]

The CDC contract with the consultant lasted from October 1971 to June 1973. Although there is no clear evidence that the consultants were actually able to secure a contract for CDC, they were able to "open doors" to China and arrange contacts that might otherwise have eluded CDC.[40] One CDC official, commenting on the arrangement with the consultant, stated that "if this looks like a five-step process to get from CDC to the correct purchasing agency of goods and services in China, it is."[41]

In December 1971 the consultant informed CDC that China was interested in buying computers through a barter arrangement.[42] According to the consultant:

> I think the best Christmas gift for me to give to you is to tell you: it is a deal. The [PRC] are going to buy your computers. The question not decided yet is: how many? This has to be determined by whether we ask for cash or accept their barter. As soon as I receive the catalogs, I will have them sent up north right away. Then I will sit down with them to discuss the nitty-gritty of barter. Perhaps they will buy more than just two 3600 at this time.[43]

During the next six to eight months the CDC consultant had other meetings with China Resources, and in early September 1972 met with the deputy director of the National Machinery Import and Export Corporation. During this meeting they discussed the Chinese plan to acquire several computers and the possible method of payment.

CDC officials, however, were realistic in their assessment of the situation, for in a March 1972 memorandum the question of export licenses was raised—a question that was to come up many times during the lengthy history of the negotiations for CDC's first contractual sale of computers to China.

> The Chinese were not willing to give him a letter of intent unless he would give some assurance that a U.S. Government export license would be forthcoming. This is one of the reasons he returned to the U.S., in order to discuss the export problem with White House officials. As you may be aware, just prior to the President's trip to China he recategorized the People's Republic of China placing them in the same category as the USSR and East Europe. Therefore, [the consultant] . . . was given oral assurance that under the proper conditions we would get export approval for a 3600. He still has some concern as to whether the conditions will be palatable to the PRC.[44]

As mentioned previously, the consultant had strong indirect ties to China Resources, Hong Kong's oldest and best-known agency representing Chinese state trading companies. The organization of China Resources is shown in Figure 5.2. At the time China Resources had 11 Chinese partners, all of whom had addresses in Hong Kong.[45]

In November 1972 the consultant mentioned in a letter to CDC that during his recent month-and-a-half trip to China he was "given to understand that as soon as they have an opportunity to examine all the documents which Control Data submitted, they will notify Control Data for business discussion."[46]

Other CDC contacts with the Chinese were made during 1971/72, all with the basic purpose of getting the Chinese to know about CDC. For example, in April 1972, CDC sent a letter to the China National Machinery Import and Export Corporation telling about CDC and its personnel.[47] The Chinese did not acknowledge the CDC letter until June 15.

In their reply the Chinese indicated that they had received the brochures and other literature that were forwarded to them by China Resources. They also expressed interest in CDC's equipment and asked for a price list on typical configurations.[48] The fact that CDC's letter was answered directly by the Chinese was "a good sign" since apparently only about one out of every 50 or 60 corporate letters is answered directly by Peking.[49] Normally responses are channeled through organizations such as China Resources.

In September 1972, CDC sent a letter to China National Machinery Import and Export Corporation responding directly to the Chinese letter of June 15. In the letter the subject of prices for CDC computers was addressed:

FIGURE 5.2

China Resources Organization

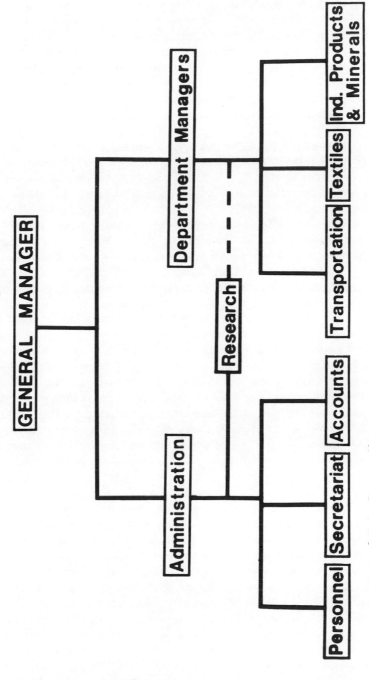

Source: Control Data Corporation.

123

You will note that we have quoted prices for typical configurations of our Cyber 72, 73, and 74 computer systems.
Various combinations can be developed depending upon the
size of the memory, the number of central processing
units, and various configurations of peripheral equipment.
. . . Configurations vary depending on the needs of the
customer and therefore, individual units may be added
or taken away from each of these peripheral sets. In that
case the price of the individual item is either added or sub-
tracted from the total prices.[50]

With the letter CDC enclosed information on the pricing of software and guidance material to allow the Chinese "to configure their
own computer systems."[51] Thus, the CDC letter constituted another
element in that part of the familiar game of doing business—"getting
to know you."

Still other CDC contacts with the Chinese during early 1971/72
included a meeting with Chinese officials in Bucharest, Romania, in
April 1972 and an "exchange of business views with China Resources
officials over dinner in Hong Kong in July.[52] The basic purpose of
these far-flung contacts was to familiarize the appropriate end user
with CDC computers.

As was mentioned in Chapter 3, lack of formal contacts in the
PRC was one of the principal obstacles preventing U.S. firms from
getting to the negotiation stage in a successful U.S.-Chinese commercial transaction. Thus, in the development of computer sales, CDC
was essentially attempting to gain contact with decision makers. The
company's first real contact as a U.S. corporate entity with potential
Chinese "buyers" of computers came in October 1973, with the visit
to the United States of the Chinese Electronic Society. It was this
visit that enabled CDC to gain a "jump on its other U.S. competitors."[53]

The general purpose of the visit was to make a comprehensive
study of U.S. electronic computers. It was a result of Henry Kissinger's visit in February 1972 to Peking, where, among other things, the
exchange of scientific and technical groups between the United States
and China was discussed.[54] The visit of the Chinese group also provided CDC with an opportunity to "convince the Chinese that CDC
technology is and will continue to be state-of-the-art."[55]

The visit proceeded without problems, and in a follow-up letter
in January 1974, CDC expressed its "appreciation" to the society for
its visit. The letter went on to suggest "the establishment of a series
of seminars on computer contacts at a location to be designated at
your convenience."[56] The purpose of these seminars was to provide
CDC and the Chinese with further opportunity to get to know each other.

THE FRENCH CONNECTION

Despite the efforts of CDC to establish contacts with Chinese end users and decision makers, perhaps the most important factor in securing substantive contact, and therefore substantive contractual negotiations, with the Chinese was the CDC decision to take a foreign partner in the sale: Compagnie Générale de Géophysique (CGG) jointly signed the contract with CDC's wholly owned subsidiary, Control Data France (CDF).* CGG was in the very incipient stages of responding to a proposal tendered in a letter by the China National Technical Import Corporation (Techimport). The proposal was for a data processing center to be installed at an unknown location along the Chinese coast intended to process the data of at least 15 land crews exploring for oil in the eastern sedimentary basins of China. Since 15 land crews exploring for oil were estimated to develop about 15,000 records per month, the high-sea exploration boats were developing an estimated 150,000 records per month, and the shallow-water boats 30,000 records, Techimport would need one or two Cyber 70 series central computers to process all of these records. The Chinese estimated that "the design of the equipment configuration will be 250,000 seismic records per month, within which one-fourth of the throughput of Machine II is for the disposition of other processing, one-fourth of the throughput is for the research of the new processing method."[57]

One of the basic assets of CGG was that the company had been selling oil exploration equipment to the Chinese for over ten years and had earned their respect. They were in a sense "old friends." CGG personnel in fact did much of the negotiating, particularly in the final commercial stages. Also, the Chinese insisted that CGG sign the contract along with CDF. Thus, in effect CGG was to be the prime contractor responsible for all of the special-applications software for the computer systems and for much of the software training. CDF was to be responsible for installation and warranty of the computer system.

The Chinese proposal received by CGG in late February 1973 covered all kinds of equipment used for the acquisition and the processing of seismic data for offshore and onshore oil exploration.[58] CGG/CDF did not know at that time whether Techimport's letter was an inquiry or a request for a proposal. Therefore, in late May they couched their reply in such a way that it could be considered as a proposal. A portion of the letter is as follows:

---

*CGG and CDF are combined here to simplify the account of the negotiations.

We offer the world's largest selection of electro-mechani-
cal peripherals for sale to other computer system manufacturers worldwide. With this peripheral equipment,
Control Data offers, on a worldwide basis, a single source
support with all the accompanying operating software and
service beyond that of simply supplying the peripheral
equipment itself. We sell this complete unit of peripheral
equipment and operating software at a lower price to other
computer system manufacturers. For purposes of illustration, this lower price may be one-half the price charged
to the final retail customer. The difference between the
higher price to the final retail customer and the lower
OEM (wholesale) price to the computer manufacturer to
whom we sell peripheral equipment allows him to absorb
the cost of adding his system integration, software development, system marketing, installation, training, support
and other related costs. This permits Control Data's
wholesale customers to sell their total systems at a competitive retail price.[59]

In addition to the emphasis on lower price, also of importance
was the company's statement in the letter that it was important to
"establish contacts . . . on a direct basis [emphasis added] as it is
unnecessary and often less efficient to work through intermediaries
especially when dealing with friends."[60]

CGG/CDF's approach turned out to be the right one, since the
Chinese suggested in mid-July that discussions begin as soon as possible; the first meeting took place on August 4 in Peking.[61] It was
at once clear that Techimport considered CGG/CDF's answer as a
proposal and that the immediate task of the sessions was to conduct
technical negotiations. At the first meeting the Chinese indicated that
they were interested in a medium-size processing computer as well
as certain kinds of field equipment. Other points raised in subsequent
technical negotiations on August 8 and August 13 were the following:

The possibility to get a convolver or an array processor
in due time.
The balance of the possible configurations.
The possibility to easily extend the configuration in the
future.
The capacity of the proposed systems.
The easiness to adapt our software to the operating system
of each computer.
The technology of different computers.[62]

It is interesting to note that during the technical discussions Chinese specialists were convinced that IBM's computer technology was more advanced than that of CDC. Thus, the visit by the Chinese Electronic Society in October 1973 assumed all the more importance in light of the incipient technical negotiations between CGG/CDF and Techimport in which the Chinese were not knowledgeable about CDC.[63]

Such lack of knowledge about CDC was reemphasized during a discussion that a CDC official had in Washington, D.C., with the PRC commercial secretary on August 3, 1973. The CDC official reported that "although Mr. . . . had heard of IBM, he had not heard of CDC."[64] So CDC's negotiating problem in this instance was to persuade the Chinese technicians that CDC computer configurations could indeed compete with those of IBM.

During the negotiations the Chinese asked very detailed questions about the CDC computers to be involved in the transaction. Detailed answers to the questions covered sessions on August 17, 18, and 20. Following the meeting on August 20 the chief Chinese negotiator said that commercial negotiations could be started earlier than anticipated and that CGG/CDF would be advised when they would begin.

After this session the CGG/CDF negotiators concluded that it might be several months before negotiations might resume.

> According to our recent experience, confirmed by the talks we had in the hotel at Peking with a lot of people of many companies and nations having outstanding business with Techimport, it has to be foreseen that technical and commercial discussions about a major computer could last from 8 to 10 weeks.[65]

But despite the anticipated delays the negotiators concluded "that CDC and CGG have a fair chance" to secure the contract. At a meeting in Minneapolis on September 27, 1973, between CGG and CDC officials, the basic problem "of the need to convince the Chinese that CDC technology is and will continue to be state-of-the-art" was again highlighted.[66] Chinese computer specialists who were very familiar with integrated circuits were concerned about the technology of the two proposed CDC Cyber 172 computers to be included in the processing-center transaction. In order to address this problem it was agreed that during the visit of the Chinese Electronic Society in October 1973, the rationale for use of CDC technology would be covered.[67]

The CGG/CDF negotiators were correct. Negotiations were postponed until January 1974, while the Chinese made every effort to learn more about CDC's product. In fact, during January four Chinese geophysicists worked closely in Paris with CGG, and Cyber hardware and software presentations were made to them by CDF. Thus, in a

CDC "Summary of China Progress to Date" at the end of 1973, company officials were convinced that "responsible Chinese in the computer industry know Control Data, its products and capabilities."[68] This conviction was the result of no small CDC effort. During the period from September 21, 1973, through March 1974, no fewer than 18 meetings were held in various parts of the world between CDC and various Chinese organizations, Chinese officials, and influential U.S. persons.[69]

The meeting between CDC Canada officials and the Chinese in February 1974 at Peking is illuminating. During one of the many sessions devoted to briefing Chinese technical personnel on CDC Cyber equipment, the Chinese stated that "all decisions were political before financial."[70] [Emphasis added.] Thus, this was but another round in the "getting to know CDC" scenario.

As mentioned above, negotiations with the Chinese began again in January 1974. According to company "negotiating notes," there were four items of "concern":

Risk-of-loss clauses were to remain the same.
No concessions were to be made on benefits to on-site personnel. Also, the right to exchange them, if desired, was to be maintained.
No indirect damages were to be allowed.
Arbitration was acceptable and particularly in any country except China, France, Sweden, Switzerland. Moreover the law of the country should apply.

Payment terms were very explicit:

20 percent down
20 percent on preacceptance test; remainder on delivery;
(negotiable: we will accept 10 percent down)
50 percent total before delivery
90 percent on delivery, final 10 percent on completion
of acceptance[71]

Moreover, the negotiators were to quote "standard CDC prices for hardware to China." They were instructed specifically that "they may not discount." However, there is a 10 percent (of hardware price) "negotiating room" that includes the fee to CGG, and "other free things."

The notes indicated that the Chinese might bring up questions concerning deferred payment and payments for training. With regard to deferred payments the negotiators were instructed that it depended on financing. Deferred payments were acceptable if French government financing were available, otherwise no financing. On the question of training costs, CDC would supply a rental car and $12 per diem for living expenses for the Chinese while in Minneapolis. The total would come to $35 per day.

THE CHINESE NEED FOR THE CDC SYSTEM

The sale of the CDC Cyber 172s to the Chinese and the subsequent sale in 1978 must be qualified in the sense that the Chinese wanted the system very much. China in 1979 ranked about tenth in the world as an oil producer, and in its almost frenetic search for oil had accumulated a great deal of seismic data. Thus, it needed the processing capability that the two CDC Cyber 172s would provide. According to one CDC official, China's desire for the system "made the contractual negotiations somewhat easier than otherwise might have been the case."[72]

The Chinese were interested in developing their oil resources rapidly for at least two reasons. Internally, their plans to modernize the economy rapidly are constrained by shortages of fuel and power that in the past have resulted in high-cost, low-quality production. Also, China very much needs the foreign exchange that can be earned by the export of oil products to help pay for imports of heavy capital equipment, technology, and agricultural products that are integral to the modernization program. Despite this need for the CDC system, it was years before the final contract was signed and the systems delivered.

THE FINAL SIGNED CONTRACT

On August 14, 1974, some 18 months after receiving the Chinese proposal, a contract was signed between the China National Technical Import Corporation (Techimport) and CGG/CDF for the delivery of two Cyber 172 systems to the China National Oil and Gas Exploration and Development Corporation. The total value of the contract was approximately $6.8 million. At the time the contract was the largest contract signed between Techimport and a computer manufacturer.[73] It was a "turnkey" package for the large national seismic data processing center located in the Peking area. CGG/CDF, working as joint contractors, were to provide the following products and services:

Site planning, equipment, and engineering
Training of 12 Chinese engineers during 7.5 months
Two Cyber 172s and two system 17s or Raytheon

Complete set of spare parts
Complete CGG seismic product set and special electronic equipment

A complete listing of prices of these products and services is shown in Table 5.2. The purchase agreement essentially stipulated a 95 percent cash payment in U.S. dollars to CGG/CDF at the time of delivery, f.o.b. France, plus 5 percent after acceptance.

The equipment configuration of the first Cyber 172 consisted of the following:

Model	Type of Equipment
172-4	Central computer
7030-2	Extended-core storage 250K
Map II	Matrix algorithm processor
7054-1	Mass storage controller
4X844-21	Disk storage unit
2X7921-2	Magnetic tape controller
10X669-2	Magnetic tape transport
3447/405	Card reader
580-12/596-01	Line printer
415-30	Card punch controller

The second Cyber 172 consisted of the same equipment with some minor additions and subtractions in the peripheral equipment. *

The delivery of the Cyber equipment was planned for "not later than February 20, 1976." Chapter 12 of the contract addressed force majeure contingencies as follows:

> If either of the contract parties is prevented from performing his contractual obligations after signing the contract due to war, serious fire, flood, earthquake, or some other causes agreed upon between both parties as cases of force majeure, the time for performance of the contract shall be extended by a period equivalent to the effect of such causes. [74]

Of interest is that in the event of the force majeure instances mentioned, "the time for performance of the contract shall be extended"— the contract will not be revoked. After stipulating procedures to be followed in force majeure cases, the contract stated—quite fortuitously, as it turned out:

---

*For example, a Map II, 6 tape transports, was substituted for 10 units, and an additional 6671-3 was added.

TABLE 5.2

Prices of Goods and Services Sold to Techimport by CGG/CDF, 1974

| Goods/Services | List Price | | Discount Price (U.S. dollars) |
	French Francs	U.S. Dollars	
Cyber 172—4 seismic processing systems	22,708,955.00	4,682,258.76	4,260,855.00
System 17 seismic preprocessing system	2,396,960.00	494,218.56	499,739.00
Software of Cyber 170 and system 172	2,447,920.00	504,725.78	459,300.00
Interactive graphic system	426,000.00	87,835.05	79,930.00
Display equipments	1,409,825.00	290,685.57	264,524.00
Ancillary equipments	594,278.00	122,531.55	111,504.00
Site equipments	1,170,000.00	241,237.11	219,526.00
Consumables	1,371,550.00	282,793.81	257,342.00
Spare parts	2,872,013.81	592,167.82	538,873.00
Training and technical support	815,700.00	168,185.56	153,049.00
Total price of contract		7,466,639.57	
Total price after discount			6,844,642.00

Note: The conversion rate used in the contract was French francs 4.85 = U.S. $1.00.

Source: Control Data Corporation.

Should the effect of force majeure mentioned above last over 120 (one hundred and twenty) consecutive days, both parties shall settle a procedure of executing the contract through amicable consultations as soon as possible. [75]
[Emphasis added]

As it turned out, such "amicable consultations" were necessary because of difficulty in getting a U.S. export license.

EXPORT LICENSE NEGOTIATIONS

Although CGG/CDF signed a contract on August 14, 1974, more than two years passed before the U.S. government granted an export license. Chapter 4 has detailed some of CDC's efforts to present its case to the appropriate U.S. agencies. This section treats CDC's negotiations with the Chinese to ensure the proper maintenance and continuance of the contract.

As early as October 1973 company officials privately suggested that "there may be an export license problem."[76] Indeed, there was concern that the Chinese might refuse to sign a contract until the U.S. and French governments provided advance approval. The contract itself did not contain a "standard" statement for the imposition of force majeure due to CDC's inability to obtain an export license. Although CDC negotiators were informed of the omission at the last minute, they decided to submit this change in a separate memorandum of understanding rather than open up the final contract for further negotiations.[77] The Chinese accepted the memorandum but never indicated that they actually agreed to it. This became an important factor in CDC's later negotiations. The contract specifically called for a delivery of the systems no later than February 20, 1976, and penalties would be assessed unless force majeure was in effect.

Despite this concern, Techimport signed the contract on August 14, 1974, after sending CDC an "end use" statement in the form of a letter. The Chinese refused to fill out the official U.S. government form because they believed that signing official documents might constitute a de facto form of recognition that was not warranted until formal diplomatic relations were established.[78]

The letter from Techimport acknowledged the purchase of the Cyber 172-4 processing system as well as other peripheral equipment and described in some detail how the equipment would be used for "oil and gas exploration and seismic data processing as well as for other geophysic data and reservoir engineering."[79] The letter also stated that Techimport "shall invite the technicians from both CGG and CDF companies to China for the erection, calibration, and acceptance-test, etc. of the equipment." In an attempt to meet U.S. government end-use and verification requirements, the Chinese stated that "after the acceptance of the equipment, both CGG and CDF companies shall have the responsibility to dispatch, at the request of our side, technicians again to the site of installation for technical service."[80] The U.S. government end-use statement required far more in the way of certification than the Chinese acceded to in their letter. (The specifics of the U.S. end-use requirements are presented in detail in Chapter 4.)

Subsequent to the signing of the contract, CDC prepared an export license application and submitted it to the French government early in May 1975. An application for a reexport license was submitted to the U.S. government on May 29, 1975, at about the time the French government was approving the export license application and subsequently submitting it to the Coordinating Committee on Export Controls (COCOM, a multilateral organization of NATO referred to in Chapter 4). Of interest, in terms of overcoming obstacles in negotiations, are CDC's negotiations with the Chinese regarding the export license bind during the period April 15 to May 3, 1976. The negotiations took place about a week after the Tian An Men Square riots and Deng Xiaoping's fall from power, which appeared to presage the very rapid reversal of Deng's philosophy of reliance on Western products and exports. This occurrence may have made CDC's negotiations with the Chinese even more difficult.

In any case, the problem was to negotiate Chinese acceptance of U.S. government "safeguard" conditions for export license approval, such as having free access to the site for at least three years and submitting periodic reports to the U.S. government. CDC was convinced that the Chinese, as a matter of principle, would reject any conditions.[81] During the first meeting a CDC official described the most recent actions of the U.S. government.[82] The Chinese were informed that the U.S. government had stated its willingness to grant the export license subject to the conditions mentioned above. It was immediately apparent that the Chinese were going to reject any condition, even the most innocuous. Chinese negotiators maintained that the issue of safeguards was an internal problem between CDC and its government.

Interestingly, during a previous strategy meeting of the CDC team members it was decided that if the mention of special conditions elicited a negative response, CDC would take two courses of action. The first was not to present the actual written conditions nor the correspondence regarding them. The second was not to bring up the matter of a person living on-site for any period of time. The latter course was the one subsequently taken. However, some of the conditions were read almost verbatim, and the reaction was about what CDC anticipated—total rejection.

In response to both the U.S. position and the conditions as paraphrased by CDC, the chief negotiator for Techimport made the following comments:

> We cannot and will not do business with those who impose special conditions upon us in order to conduct that business. We wrote and gave you a statement on the use of these systems from our end user. This went far beyond the limitations of our usual business practice, but we did this in order to promote trade between our countries. At the time of our negotiations with CGG/CDF we were also negotiating with a firm from Canada, but we rejected the Canadian firm's offer because they involved the acceptance of certain conditions. Our position still stands. We have prepared a building, and it is ready to accept the equipment, and if the equipment is not delivered, we will have suffered a great loss. [83]

Moreover, the Chinese at this time changed their position on force majeure:

> We do consider the lack of an export license at this time as force majeure as we told you earlier, but we should point out to you that even accepting an export license as a condition for force majeure also went beyond the limitations of our normal business practice. Since force majeure has been in effect since February 20 and is to last for a period of 120 days (until June 20), we need to discuss how to implement the contract, as stated in the force majeure chapter. [84]

CDC's response was to propose an amendment to the contract that called for a technical assistance agreement. Under this agreement CDC would have a Western expert on-site for a period of three years to provide training with the actual equipment and technical assistance after acceptance of the equipment.

The initial response of the Chinese was a tentative rejection based on the then-prevalent philosophy of self-reliance. CDC's negotiating strategy then focused on holding separate meetings to distinguish between the technical aspects of the contract and those involving the "political" or export license conditions.

At the meeting devoted to the special conditions, CDC negotiators attempted to determine whether the early position of Techimport was also held by the top Chinese officials. During the first meeting there was a feeling among the CDC negotiators that possibly there was some room for acceptance of certain conditions. In order to test this belief, a seemingly minor, but significant, condition regarding the visitation requirement was proposed. The following paragraph was composed and submitted to the Chinese for consideration:

> Techimport would be pleased to have CGG or CDC representatives, coming to Peking during the conduct of normal business or for technical reasons, . . . visit the Seismic Data Processing Center for the furtherance of joint cooperation. [85]

At a subsequent meeting that day the Chinese made a counterproposal. Although it did not contain everything that was in the original proposal, it was apparent throughout the discussion that it could accomplish everything that was intended by the U.S. proposal:

> For the development of technical cooperation in seismic data processing in the future and according to the situation of new technology development in seismic data processing and the common desire of the Buyer and Seller, the Buyer and Seller will invite technical persons from the other party at their own expense to visit their Seismic Data Processing Centers for friendly visits and technical exchange. Specific times will be discussed later. [86]

The following day, however, the Chinese apparently reversed their position. The chief negotiator stated that discussion of technical services would be meaningful only after CDC obtained the export license. However, the Chinese did agree that since CDC needed time to select and prepare people who would conduct these technical services, and since there was explicit mention of technical services in the contract, further discussions of technical services might be warranted. CDC's focus then turned to the technical assistance agreement. And after many hours stretching into days, an agreement was negotiated. It stipulated that two CDC people were to be on-site for one year and one person for an additional year. Even though Techimport agreed to the contract amendment, it refused to sign until it had "a guarantee of the export license in writing." It did, however, agree to extend force majeure by 40 days, until July 31. A further round of discussions had been tentatively scheduled for sometime between the middle of June and the first of July.

By the middle of July, CDC still had not resolved its negotiations with U.S. government agencies. It was apparent to company officials that they had to visit China again, since force majeure was about to expire. During the last week in July, however, China suffered a catastrophic earthquake, so CDC used this "act of God" as an excuse to postpone the visit of the company's senior negotiator. [87] CDC's negotiator scheduled his return for mid-September, only to have it postponed again because of the death of Chairman Mao. Finally, on October 13, 1976, CDC officials arrived in Peking.

The Chinese were eager to hear the "positive news" regarding the export license. CDC begged off giving any information until the first official meeting the following day, at 3 P.M. [88] Prior to the meeting CDC scheduled a meeting with a U.S. official at the U.S. Liaison Office (USLO). It was hoped that by that time CDC would have U.S. government "guidance" as to whether an export license would be issued and the specific conditions for issuance. However, the last word the USLO had heard about the case was the cable it had received at the end of April.

At the first meeting the Chinese reiterated that they would refuse to accept any conditions in order to obtain U.S. approval of the necessary export license. CDC responded that the Chinese position made it difficult for the company to get an export license, but that it might still be possible. [89] CDC pointed out that this possibility would require the company to take the case to much higher levels within the U.S. government, and this it would try to do. However, CDC suggested that this action would take considerable time, and the company could not be certain of the outcome.

The Chinese thanked CDC for its presentation and for bringing them up to date. However, it was obvious that they had expected something far more positive. The chief negotiator stated that this situation had been pending for over one year, and that both sides had suffered great losses due to the lack of the export license. He then said that the Chinese could not delay any further "the business between us." Either CDC got the export license and proceeded with the contract, or the contract should be terminated immediately. He then asked CDC for its views on the next step.

CDC responded that since the news of approval or denial was due from the U.S. government momentarily, they should wait until they heard the final decision. CDC had already been told that whatever the decision, it would be final, with no further appeal. CDC suggested that if they heard that day, the two sides should plan to meet the next day at 10 A.M.; if not, they should wait until the following Monday to decide the next step.

Thus, after 20 days and many hours, CDC and the Chinese had a tentative contract that presumably met the requirements for a U.S. export license. Equally difficult "dual negotiations" with both the Chinese and the U.S. government were necessary to secure the final result. Ironically, in a CDC paper describing aspects of these negotiations, written in April 1979, the author noted that

Having finally received U.S. approval we then proceeded
to fulfill the contractual commitments by delivering the
system in September 1977, and having it accepted in
November 1977. We have since signed a contract for
twelve additional computer systems for oil exploration
(in December 1978), and hopefully will receive approval
of these systems without all the problems we encountered
before.[90]

As of June 1980, 18 months after the signing of a contract, CDC still
had not obtained an export license.[91]

FOLLOW-ONS

Cyber System Contracts

As noted above, in December 1978, CDC, with CDF/CGG as a
partner, signed contracts with the China National Oil and Gas Exploration and Development Corporation for Cyber Systems equipment valued
at $69.84 million. Table 5.3 summarizes these transactions. The
contract for the ten Cyber 172s, a Cyber 173, and a Cyber 175 was
signed December 22, 1978, with the China National Machinery Import
and Export Corporation, the end user being the China National Oil and
Gas Exploration and Development Corporation. Delivery of the systems was contracted for September 1, 1980.[92] A summary of the
contract chapters and annexes is shown in Table 5.4.

Although many contacts were made with the Chinese prior to
the actual negotiations, it was only in April 1978 that serious discussion got under way, with the visit by CDF management to Peking.[93]
A formal Chinese request for a proposal for three Cyber 173s for
seismic processing was received on May 10, 1978. At this time negotiations by the Chinese were already under way with Hitachi and
IBM.[94] The Chinese obviously were enamored with the prospect of
exploiting their offshore oil reserves, which one U.S. oil geologist
estimated as possibly totaling 30 billion barrels.[95]

The negotiations for these contracts, very similar to those for
the first contract, began in earnest on June 1, 1978, in Peking and
were conducted by CDF personnel. One of the principal questions of
the Machimpex negotiators concerned the possibility of the United
States granting an export license. In fact, the Chinese negotiator led
off by stating, "We do not propose Control Data equipment because
past experience has shown us that you have extreme difficulties in obtaining export licenses for it."[96] The CDC/CDF negotiator responded
by acknowledging that "licenses for the exportation of these first ma-

TABLE 5.3

1978 CDC China Business Closed with CDF/CGG as a Partner

Order Date	Customer Name	System Type
December 1978	Oil and Gas Corporation, Tsuoshien	Add-on equipment
December 1978	Oil and Gas Corporation, Urumchi	2 X Cyber 172s Map II
	Tsamkong	2 X Cyber 172s Map II
	Tientsin	2 X Cyber 172s Map II
	Peking	2 X Cyber 172s Map II
December 1978	Oil and Gas Corporation, Taching	Cyber 173 Map III
December 1978	Oil and Gas Corporation, Tsuoshien	Cyber 175 Map III
December 1978	Geology Corporation, Nanking	2 X Cyber 172s Map II

Source: Control Data Corporation.

chines were extremely difficult to obtain." He then countered saying that he would be "extremely surprised and disappointed" to discover that the Chinese penalize a company like CDC that "plays the role of a pioneer" in securing export licenses for such systems. The Chinese countered by asking if CDC was able to deliver this equipment rapidly to China. CDC responded affirmatively but did not ask for a precise explanation of what "rapidly" meant.

Following these sessions in Peking, CDC/CDF prepared a letter describing the Cyber equipment that could be negotiated and delivered rapidly. In an interoffice memorandum the CDC/CDF negotiators emphasized that the intent of the letter "was to put the accent on the rapid delivery of the Cyber equipment" while leaving the door open for the possibility of slightly more sophisticated equipment to be delivered on a medium- or long-term basis. The negotiators stressed, however, that considering the delivery requirements voiced by the Chinese, they had refused to undertake negotiations for the sale of this more advanced equipment.

TABLE 5.4

CDC Contract for Complete Equipment for a Large-Size Seismic Data Processing Center, 1978

Chapter/Annex	Contents
Contract Summary	
1	Subject of the contract
2	Price
3	Payment
4	Delivery and terms of delivery
5	Shipping documents
6	Packing and marking
7	Inspection
8	Erection, calibration, and acceptance test
9	Guarantees and claims
10	Penalty for delayed delivery
11	Dispatch of trainees and technical service
12	Force majeure
13	Taxes and duties
14	Arbitration
15	Effectiveness of the contract and miscellaneous
16	Legal addresses
Annexes	
1	Scope of supply and list of prices
2	Contents, time, and manner of delivery for technical documentation and drawings supplied by seller
3	Specimen of letter of guarantee issued by Banque Française du Commerce Extérieur, Paris
4	Stipulation of calibration and acceptance of "equipments"
5	Terms of seller's acceptance of trainees sent by buyer
6	Terms on service by seller's technical personnel
7	Terms on F.C.O.'s
8	Spare parts list

Source: Control Data Corporation.

During the next few months the "getting to know you" scenario described in detail earlier was played almost with abandon by the Chinese. On June 20, for example, CDF management was invited by the PRC ambassador to France for an evening of discussions. In July a Chinese delegation that included 12 potential computer users visited CDF in Paris. Prior to the visit to CDF, this same Chinese delegation had visited the United States to "tour" CDC and Univac facilities,[97] and to "further understand the products and capabilities" of Univac and CDC. While in the United States some members of the Chinese delegation commented on CDC's competition. Some members of the delegation were very impressed by the Japanese marketing skill, particularly with the Japanese management staff's ability to speak fluent Chinese, their use of technically competent people to give presentations, and the provision of complete and detailed technical information. Other CDC competitors were also singled out, particularly IBM. Some delegation members, however, did not believe that IBM would be very successful in China because of the company's orientation toward commercial machines. IBM's documentation work was averred "to be second to nobody."[98]

Continuing the "getting to know you" process, on September 15, 1978, the PRC ambassador to France again invited CDF management for a session with the Machimpex general manager, who was in Paris. In early November a Chinese Oil Ministry delegation visited CDF in Paris. This visit was followed, on November 23, by a Chinese invitation for CDF management to meet with the vice-minister of petroleum. A basic issue in these discussions was the equipment configuration. The Chinese, because of the immensity of the required exploration tasks, wanted the most powerful and sophisticated CDC computers and peripheral equipment available. CDC, aware of the export license problem, cautioned restraint. The issue was resolved and the $69.8 million contract was signed in Peking on December 22, 1978.

As of June 1980, however, the U.S. government still had not granted final approval for the transaction. CDC had been told "emphatically" at the very highest levels of U.S. government that the government wanted to provide special attention to China and that these systems should be approved and delivered promptly.[99] It was only a question of time. Ironically, in this instance it took CDC longer to negotiate with its own government concerning a commercial transaction than with the Chinese.

Other Ventures

CDC, like many other U.S. companies, is currently exploring a host of new ventures with the Chinese. It is much too soon to predic the outcomes in terms of benefits obtained by the parties to the ventures or the particular obstacles encountered in their commercial negotiations. In any venture with U.S. firms, the Chinese have stated that "mutual benefit, mutual cooperation and long-term relationship" must apply to any pending association. [100]

Concerning commercial proposals related to computer technology, China will want to export products as part of a system, but will agree not to sell original equipment outside China. In a striking departure from past policies, China will agree to deferred payment terms, but interest payments and other terms will have to be in accordance with the International Convention of Paris. [101]

In a January 1980 letter to CDC concerning the establishment of a joint venture, the Chinese reiterated many of the problems attendant on such an enterprise.

> Through the many talks, both sides are quite clear that
> two key problems should be solved first: 1) How the Joint
> Corporation should compensate for the dollar expenditure
> on your side with dollars . . . and, 2) what about profits? [102]

The Chinese proposed that the problem of dollar income be "solved" by the joint corporation's providing service in the United States through contracts to process and develop CDC software "for any other U.S. users." The dollar income of this business would be used "to compensate" for the necessary expenses in dollars. The Chinese suggested that it is "quite probable" that the joint venture "may lose in the first two years, balance in the third and make a little profit in the fourth and fifth years." In short, "if both sides trust and support each other, work hard together, it is possible to make a profit of ten percent after five years." [103]

The director of strategic studies and world wide product planning for General Motors has put the problem of negotiating venture arrangements with the Chinese in a wider perspective than just profit and loss. General Motors is negotiating an equity joint venture with the First Ministry of Machine Building covering the manufacture and sale of heavy-duty trucks to China. In addition to General Motors, three European companies and two other U.S. companies are negotiating with the First Ministry. This General Motors executive observed that discussion with Chinese officials regarding equity joint venture possibilities revealed a noticeable lack of communication between various ministries and government agencies as well as the presence of a high degree of competition and rivalry. This situation not only is at the center of bureaucracy; a similar condition exists between central and local authorities. This lack of cooperation and the overlapping of responsibilities complicate the joint venture negotiation process, since answers to critical questions may be different, depending on the source.[104]

CDC's approach to the China market is best summarized in one of the company's review memorandums written in April 1980:

> To assist China in its modernization and development plans, thereby securing long term markets and supply sources for CDC; large enough to get the attention of the power and policy centers in China and basic enough to be essential to their future; and a synergistic and total approach to specific product and geographical areas that link selling and buying in a cohesive package.[105]

In order to be successful in China, CDC suggests that a sustained, long-term effort of five to ten years may be required. In short, the substantial profits will go to the long distance runners—or, as the Chinese might say, "will go to the old friends."

NOTES

1. Hugh Donaghue, "Overview" (Washington, D.C.: Control Data, 1979), p. 1.

2. Basic questionnaire data.

3. One observer, emphasizing China's limited capacity to absorb new technology, noted that "China is still 85 percent rural, and it can't be converted overnight to an industrial society." "A China Connection for U.S. Companies," New York Times, February 26, 1978, p. 2.

4. Ibid.

5. Control Data Corporation, Annual Report 1979 (Minneapolis, Minn.: Control Data, 1979).

6. Donaghue, "Overview," p. 7. Also see R. K. Nelson, "China Briefing: Chinese Electronic Society Visit to CDC, October 23 and 24, 1973," Minneapolis, October 15, 1973, p. 18.

7. U.S., Central Intelligence Agency, The Computer Industry in the People's Republic of China (Washington, D.C.: National Foreign Assessment Center, 1973).

8. U.S., Congress, Office of Technology Assessment, Technology and East-West Trade (Washington, D.C.: Government Printing Office, 1979), p. 276.

9. Bohdan O. Szuprowicz, "Electronics in China," U.S.-China Business Review, May-June 1976, p. 34.

10. U.S., Congress, Office of Technology Assessment, Technology and East-West Trade, p. 276.

11. Nelson, "China Briefing," p. 18; "Computing in China: A Travel Report," Science 182 (October 12, 1972): 140.

12. U.S., Joint Publications Research, "Applications of Electronic Computers to Accounting," China Report—Economic Affairs no. 7 (Washington, D.C.: Foreign Broadcast Information Service, August 14, 1979).

13. Ibid.

14. "China's New Priorities for Technology Development," China Business Review, May-June 1978, p. 6.

15. Ibid.

16. "China 10 Years Behind in Computers, U.S. Professor Says," Electronic News, January 21, 1980, p. 1. Also see report of Japanese mission in 1979: John Hataye, "Find China Plants Years Behind West," Electronic News, July 30, 1979, p. 1.

17. Bohdan O. Szuprowicz and Maria R. Szuprowicz, Doing Business with the People's Republic of China, Industries and Markets (New York: John Wiley and Sons, 1979), p. 263. Also see Control Data Corporation, "Trip Report" (Minneapolis, January 2, 1980), p. 2; David C. Bowie, "The Electronics and Computer Establishment in the People's Republic of China" (Washington, D.C.: Trade Development Assistance Division, Bureau of East-West Trade, U.S. Department of Commerce, January 1980), p. 3.

18. Interview with Hugh Donaghue, March 1980.

19. Control Data Corporation, "Interoffice Memorandum on Mainland China" (Minneapolis, June 24, 1971), p. 1.

20. Ibid.

21. Control Data Corporation, "Minutes of China Task Force Meeting" (Minneapolis, September 21, 1973), p. 1.

22. Ibid.

23. Control Data Corporation, "Interoffice Memorandum—China Office" (Minneapolis, December 7, 1973), p. 1.

24. Ibid.

25. Henry Kissinger, White House Years (Boston: Little, Brown, 1979), p. 1053.

26. Control Data Corporation, "Marketing Plan for China" (Minneapolis, June 6, 1977), p. 5.

27. Ibid.

28. Ibid., p. 7.

29. Ibid.

30. Control Data Corporation, "Charter for Embryonic China Office" (Minneapolis, September 6, 1973).

31. Ibid.

32. Control Data Corporation, "Marketing Plan," p. 9.

33. Control Data Corporation, "CDC Contracts with the People's Republic of China to Date" (Minneapolis, September 6, 1973), p. 2.

34. Ibid.

35. Control Data Corporation, "Interoffice Memorandum on Mainland China," p. 1. Also see Control Data Corporation, "Interoffice Memorandum—Ministry of Science and Technology" (Minneapolis, September 2, 1971), p. 1.

36. Control Data Corporation, "Trading Companies" (Minneapolis, August 27, 1971), p. 2.

37. Control Data Corporation, "Trade—People's Republic of China" (Minneapolis, July 22, 1971), pp. 1-2.

38. Control Data Corporation, "Letter to Hugh F. Donaghue," April 18, 1973, p. 1.

39. Control Data Corporation, "Consultation and Sales Agreement between_____ and Control Data Corporation" (Minneapolis, October 1, 1971), p. 2.

40. Interview with Hugh Donaghue, February 1980.

41. Control Data Corporation, "Trip Report" (Minneapolis, April 16, 1973), p. 1.

42. Control Data Corporation, "Letter from Consultant" (Minneapolis, April 19, 1971).

43. Ibid.

44. Control Data Corporation, "Interoffice Memorandum" (Minneapolis, March 9, 1972), p. 2.

45. Alan H. Smith, "Standard Form Contracts," International and Comparative Law Quarterly 21 (January 1972): 137. The legal ramifications of dealing with China Resources appear to be quite nebulous, according to Smith. Of interest is that the consultant submitted a price list for CDC computers to China Resources in Hong Kong in September, and when he arrived in Peking in early October, the price list was not yet available at the Peking office. This indicates less than speedy communications between China Resources and Peking.

46. Control Data Corporation, "Letter from Consultant on China Trade" (Minneapolis, November 14, 1972), p. 1.

47. Control Data Corporation, "CDC Contracts," pp. 2-3.

48. Control Data Corporation, "Status Report" (Minneapolis, September 22, 1972), p. 1.

49. Ibid. CDC learned this in subsequent talks with China Resources personnel.

50. Control Data Corporation, "Letter to Chinese Foreign Trade Corporation" (Minneapolis, September 13, 1972).

51. Ibid.

52. Control Data Corporation, "Interoffice Memorandum" (Minneapolis, August 10, 1973), p. 1.

53. Interview with Hugh Donaghue, March 1980.

54. Control Data Corporation, "Fact Sheet on the Computer Visiting Group from the People's Republic of China" (Minneapolis, September 26, 1973), p. 1.

55. Control Data Corporation, "Minutes of Meeting" (Minneapolis, October 3, 1973), p. 2.

56. Control Data Corporation, "Letter to Computer Visiting Group of the Chinese Electronic Society" (Minneapolis, January 25, 1974), p. 1.

57. Control Data Corporation, "Letter to Control Data Corporation, Reference to Contract No. CF-7412" (Minneapolis, August 14, 1974), p. 1.

58. Ibid.

59. Control Data Corporation, "Interoffice Memorandum" (Minneapolis, May 19, 1973), p. 5.

60. Ibid.

61. Control Data Corporation, "Interoffice Memorandum" (Minneapolis, August 28, 1973), p. 2.

62. Ibid.

63. Control Data Corporation, "Trip Report to Washington, D.C." (Minneapolis, August 10, 1973), p. 1. Such lack of knowledge about CDC was rectified during the meeting.

64. Ibid.

65. Ibid.

66. Control Data Corporation, "Interoffice Memorandum—Minutes of Meeting of CGG" (Minneapolis, September 27, 1973), p. 2.

67. Ibid. During the September meeting with CDC, as an aside one of the CGG negotiators commented on the difference, based on his experience, between dealing with China and with the USSR. Specifically, the Chinese are more serious in their business discussions, and more honorable. Henry Kissinger, in The White House Years (Boston: Little, Brown, 1979), makes similar perceptive comments regarding the Soviet and Chinese approaches to negotiations:

> The Soviets offer their goodwill as a prize for success in negotiations. The Chinese use friendship as a halter in advance of negotiation; by admitting the interlocutor to at least the appearance of personal intimacy, a subtle restraint is placed on the claims he can put forward. . . . move from infallible dogma to unchangeable positions (however often they may modify them). Chinese, having been culturally preeminent in their part of the world for millennia, can even use self-criticism as a tool. The visitor is asked for advice—a gesture of humility eliciting sympathy and support. This pattern also serves to bring out the visitor's values and aims; he is thereby committed,

for the Chinese later can (and often do) refer to his own recommendations. The Soviets, with all their stormy and occasionally duplicitous behavior, leave an impression of extraordinary psychological insecurity. The Chinese stress, because they believe in it, the uniqueness of Chinese values. Hence they convey an aura of imperviousness to pressure; indeed, they preempt pressure by implying that issues of principle are beyond discussion.

In creating this relationship Chinese diplomats, at least in their encounters with us, proved meticulously reliable. They never stooped to petty maneuvers; they did not haggle; they reached their bottom line quickly, explained it reasonably, and defended it tenaciously. They stuck to the meaning as well as the spirit of their undertakings. As Chou was fond of saying: "Our word counts." (p. 1056).

68. Control Data Corporation, "Summary of China Progress to Date" (Minneapolis, December 31, 1973), p. 4.

69. Ibid., pp. 1-3.

70. Control Data Corporation, "Interoffice Memorandum—Trip Report to the People's Republic of China, January 17, 1974" (Minneapolis, March 7, 1974), p. 2.

71. Control Data Corporation, "Interoffice Memorandum—People's Republic of China-CGG Negotiation" (Minneapolis, February 20, 1974), p. 4.

72. Donaghue, "Overview," p. 2.

73. Control Data Corporation, "Seismic Contract with China" (Minneapolis, September 27, 1974), p. 1; "Interoffice Memorandum —Joint Contract with CGG in China" (Minneapolis, September 13, 1974), p. 4.

74. Control Data Corporation, "Interoffice Memorandum" (Minneapolis, September 17, 1978), p. 24. Also see Control Data Corporation, "Contract for Complete Equipment for Large Size Seismic Data Processing Centers, contract no. 78ME-45090F (1978)" (Minneapolis, December 22, 1978), p. 33. The language on force majeure in both contracts is the same.

75. Ibid.

76. Control Data Corporation, "Interoffice Memorandum— Minutes of China Task Force—Meeting No. 2—October 8, 1973" (Minneapolis, October 10, 1973), p. 1.

77. Donaghue, "Overview," p. 3.

78. Ibid., p. 2.

79. Chinese Foreign Trade Corporation, "Letter to Control Data Corporation" (Peking, August 14, 1974).

80. Ibid.

81. Donaghue, "Overview," p. 4.

82. Control Data Corporation, "Interoffice Memorandum" (Minneapolis, May 10, 1976), p. 3.

83. Ibid., pp. 4-5.

84. Ibid., p. 5.

85. Ibid., p. 7.

86. Ibid.

87. Donaghue, "Overview," p. 7.

88. Control Data Corporation, "China Trip Report" (Minneapolis, November 18, 1975), p. 1.

89. Ibid., p. 2.

90. Donaghue, "Overview," p. 9.

91. Interview with Hugh Donaghue, June 1980. CDC indicated that an export license for the 1978 sale was expected momentarily.

92. Control Data Corporation, "Contract for Complete Equipment for Large Size Seismic Data Processing Centers," p. 5. Portions of this contract are shown in Appendix A.

93. Control Data Corporation, "Presentation" (Minneapolis, August 30, 1979), p. 15.

94. Ibid., p. 32.

95. "The Scramble to Exploit China's Oil Reserves," Business Week, October 30, 1978, p. 155. According to A. A. Meyerhoff, a Tulsa, Oklahoma, geologist, these Chinese offshore oil reserves, if proved, could amount to all the proved reserves in the United States.

96. Control Data Corporation, "Trip Report" (Minneapolis, August 9, 1978), p. 1.

97. Control Data Corporation, "Interoffice Memorandum—The Visit of . . . July 1, 1978–July 14, 1978" (Minneapolis, July 24, 1978), p. 1. It is interesting that in May this delegation had been in Japan visiting with Fujitsu, Hitachi, and NEC.

98. Ibid.

99. Control Data Corporation, "Interoffice Memorandum" (Minneapolis, April 10, 1980), p. 1.

100. Control Data Corporation, "Interoffice Memorandum—People's Republic of China (PRC) Trip Report" (Minneapolis, August 20, 1979), p. 14.

101. Ibid.

102. Chinese Foreign Trade Corporation, "Letter to Control Data Corporation" (Peking, January 10, 1980), p. 1.

103. Ibid.

104. National Council for U.S.-China Trade, "Selling," Proceedings, p. 126.

105. Control Data Corporation, "Interoffice Memorandum" (Minneapolis, April 10, 1980), p. 2.

6

SUMMARY AND CONCLUSION

Whatever the outcome of the current U.S.-Chinese normalization of economic and political relations, the process has whetted the appetite of U.S. firms to develop China's market potential. In fact, Americans have long dreamed of entering the Chinese market. The "kerosene sellers" of yesterday perhaps have their counterparts in the soft drink salesmen of today. All are transfixed by the thought of millions of Chinese customers. Such optimism concerning the Chinese market must be tempered with the observation that the American salesman's dream of hundreds of millions of Chinese customers breaks down when one realizes that the millions of Chinese potential customers are not necessarily consumers with money to pay for foreign goods.

Of importance for U.S.-Chinese commercial negotiations is that tight control from the center in China has led to the development of a bureaucratic cast of mind that can contribute to a terrible slowness in negotiating commercial transactions. Reinforcing this terrible slowness are Chinese bureaucratic tendencies cultivated over centuries. Habits of caution, verbal obfuscation, and fear of written instructions are embedded in the lives of nearly all Chinese office-holders, and have little to do with whether an emperor or a minister is in charge. Such a bureaucratic cast of mind, not necessarily found in the Chinese foreign trade bureaucracy alone, may be expressed by Chinese personnel who do not respond to requests for decisions for months because of the necessity to consult with others in the system. Even more likely, this terrible slowness, endemic to the bureaucracy, may find expression in Chinese personnel seeking extra insurance for career maintenance and advancement by passing the decision making higher in the Chinese foreign trade bureaucracy.

The diminished importance of China's legal system, especially as it relates to commercial practices, heightens the importance of its trade bureaucracy. Particularly formidable is the difficulty for the U.S. business executive to make the first contacts with this trade bureaucracy. Perhaps one reason for this difficulty is the U.S. executive's perspective. The Chinese foreign trade bureaucracy is approached from a linear perspective, rather than from the total perspective of the Chinese classical landscape painter.

In classic Chinese painting the artist often deliberately avoided perspective as the Western painter understood it. The classic Western painter logically believed that, graphically, one could paint only what one saw from a narrowly defined point of view. The Chinese painter, in the words of one classical Chinese theorist, had to view "all landscapes from the angle of totality to behold the part, much as the manner in which we look at an artificial rookery in our gardens."[1] In conducting commercial negotiations, the U.S. business executive is well advised to do the same.

In this vein of "total perspective," Henry Kissinger observed the following:

> Every visit to China was like a carefully rehearsed play in which nothing was accidental and yet everything appeared spontaneous. . . . On my ten visits to China, it was as if we were engaged in one endless conversation with an organism that recalled everything, seemingly motivated by a single intelligence. This gave the encounters both an exhilarating and occasionally a slightly ominous quality. It engendered a combination of awe and sense of impotence at so much discipline and dedication—not unusual in the encounter of foreigners with Chinese culture.[2]

Although the U.S. executive negotiating a commercial transaction with the Chinese may not perceive, as Kissinger did, being "engaged in one endless conversation with an organism that recalled everything, seemingly motivated by a single intelligence," he may, like Kissinger at times, feel a combined sense of awe, frustration, and even impotence.

Also of importance in commercial negotiations with the Chinese is understanding the subtle Chinese art of kuan-hsi.* This term means relationship, but it has a semantic value that suggests mutual benefit. Kuan-hsi has incalculable importance when dealing with the bureaucracy in a country where people are uncomfortable in insisting on black-and-white rules or negotiating absolutely binding contractual legalisms. Friendship may be involved in kuan-hsi, but usually it is limited to a contractual relationship between two individuals for pro-

---

*This is the Wade-Giles transliteration. The Hanyu-Pinyin rendering of this term would be guanxi.

viding each access to certain goods and services for that which would otherwise have to be gotten from strangers. This may explain the Chinese penchant for dealing with "old friends," persons or business firms that have proven trustworthy in past relationships.

The procedural aspects of negotiations with the Chinese foreign trade system, involving both technical and commercial negotiations, often are a series of hindrances and impediments to be overcome by U.S. commercial negotiators. It is these hindrances and impediments in toto that can cause commercial negotiations to become deadlocked and delayed. Commercial negotiation with the Chinese foreign trade system is, in actuality, a two-stage procedure involving first technical clarification and then commercial negotiation to establish the terms and conditions of the transaction. In fact, technical clarification can take just as much time and be just as arduous as negotiation of the contractual terms and conditions.

The Chinese foreign trade system performs extensive regulatory and control functions while also serving as banker, manufacturer, and seller. The U.S. firm negotiating with a national Chinese foreign trade corporation, for example, may never learn the exact needs of Chinese producers, distributors, and consumers—and thus cannot adjust its negotiating strategy and tactics accordingly. In short, the Chinese foreign trade system is a formidable challenge to the U.S. firm negotiating a contract. In fact, it may constitute the most difficult impediment to the signing of a U.S.-Chinese commercial contract.

The Chinese tend to negotiate in very literal terms, primarily because of their complex bureaucratic structure that must review any commercial agreement. As a result, therefore, items that are taken for granted or given relatively cursory treatment in standard U.S. contracts are given careful, detailed treatment in U.S.-Chinese commercial negotiations. Such concern for detail makes the negotiations even more lengthy, arduous, and demanding.

There are at least five major impediments to be overcome in any U.S.-Chinese commercial negotiation: the dual character of the negotiation process, the time factor, the difficulty of establishing interpersonal relations, bargaining for concessions, and the difficulty of agreeing on final contractual provisions that cover such items as price, guarantees, delivery terms and date, and payment. As a result, negotiations with the Chinese foreign trade bureaucracy can easily take a year or longer. For example, Control Data Corporation's (CDC) negotiations for its first contract—which included the initial contacts, the "getting to know you" scenario, and the signing of the final contract—took more than two years.

No matter how successful negotiations with the Chinese government may be, the next step—the securing of an export license—can make or break the commercial transaction. Even if it were not difficult for the U.S. firm to obtain an export license, the time-consuming administrative procedures accentuate the impact that U.S. restrictions have on trade with China in general and the consummation of any commercial transcation with it in particular. Such export licensing procedures can, therefore, be viewed as an important hindrance and impediment to U.S. commercial negotiations.

In the highly competitive market that usually exists in selling to (or buying from) the Chinese, financial terms are often a key element in making a sale. The current difficulty in obtaining financing in U.S.-Chinese trade is a further major impediment to successful U.S.-Chinese commercial negotiations. In fact, there is evidence that U.S. restrictions on both government and private credit may have contributed to a diminution of U.S.-Chinese commercial transactions. Moreover, the problem of financing China's trade with the West will be a continuing one, since China will face the problem of how to obtain the hard currency required for its transactions.

Serious negotiations with the Chinese start, for the most part, with obtaining an invitation to China. Establishing contact with the appropriate end user of the U.S. company's product or service can be a major challenge, as the author's research has shown. In this effort at least six gambits may be pursued by the U.S. firm:

Letters with appropriate enclosures of technical literature directed to the relevant trade corporations and to the China Council for the Promotion of Foreign Trade in Peking
Direct approaches to members of the commercial section of the PRC's Embassy in Washington
Attendance at the Canton Fair
Representation on scientific or industrial delegations to China
Organizing a technical seminar
Engaging an experienced adviser or agent to assist, support, and coordinate the seller's approaches to China.

There appears, however, to be no tried-and-true gambit for making a first contact with the Chinese foreign trade bureaucracy.

Like commercial negotiations with the Soviet Union, negotiation of contracts with China is normally a two-stage procedure with technical clarification as the first stage. The negotiating logic for the Chinese is very simple: Why discuss price and other contract terms with the U.S. company before they know exactly what it proposes to sell? Thus, commercial negotiations to establish the terms and conditions of the transaction usually take place only after the Chinese have absorbed every possible technical detail, sometimes including design and research matters that a company may regard as proprietary.

Negotiations with the Chinese move slowly for several reasons. First, Chinese buyers will try to learn as much as possible about the technology related to a seller's product before the decision is made to purchase it. Second, the Chinese often request extremely detailed price breakdowns so that weak points in the seller's offer can be found, or substitutions of foreign or domestically made components can be proposed. Third, the Chinese negotiators may not have the authority to make quick decisions on important price aspects of negotiations. In short, it takes time and patience to enter the China market successfully, perhaps as long as five to ten years in the case of large sales or concluding joint ventures.

The experience of one U.S. firm's stiffest competitors for the China market is perhaps illustrative of the detailed preparation and follow-through necessary to conclude a large-scale commercial transaction or joint venture with the Chinese. This experience, depicted in the form of three flow charts showing the planning and conduct of technical exchange with China, is capsulized in Figures 6.1 through 6.3. As can be seen from these figures, the Japanese concentrate an enormous amount of detail in their technical exchanges with the Chinese. In many instances, according to the Japanese report, "the contacts developed in the course of these technical exchanges have led to the signing of sales contracts."[3]

American business persons who have had little previous contact with their Chinese counterparts tend to consider them an enigma. Most Chinese business practices are based on customs and traditions. They present a sharp contrast to the informality and pragmatic nature of U.S. business practice. In particular the Chinese place a premium on trust in relationships, and it takes a lot to gain their respect. Those who have long-standing relationships with the Chinese are known as "old friends," people who can be counted on personally and can be relied upon to recommend other trustworthy parties.

CDC's negotiations of sizable contracts for computer systems with the Chinese proved successful primarily because the Chinese needed the systems for their oil exploration efforts. In 1979 China ranked about tenth in the world as an oil producer, and in its search for oil had accumulated a great deal of seismic data. Therefore, it needed the processing capability that the two CDC Cyber 172s would provide. China's desire for this particular system, according to CDC, made the contractual negotiations somewhat easier than otherwise might have been the case.

Despite the efforts of CDC to establish contacts with Chinese end users and decision makers, perhaps the most important factor in securing substantive contact, and therefore substantive contractual negotiations, was the CDC decision to take a foreign partner. It was this "French connection" with a respected company that the Chinese

FIGURE 6.1

Technical Exchange with China: Flow Chart I, Planning Stage

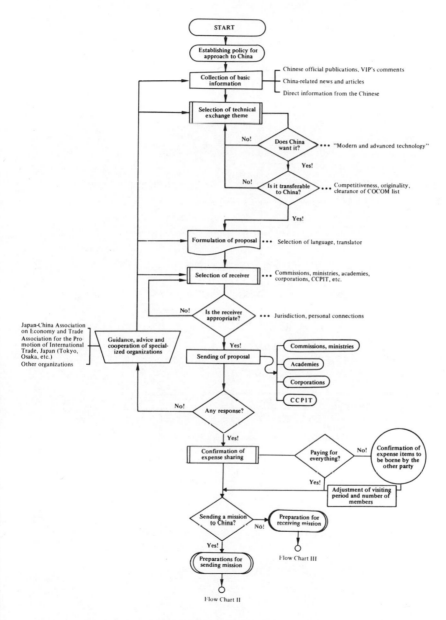

Source: Masaharu Hishida, "Japan's Experience in Technical Exchange with China," China Newsletter 24 (December 1979): 5.

FIGURE 6.2

Technical Exchange with China: Flow Chart II,
Sending a Mission to China

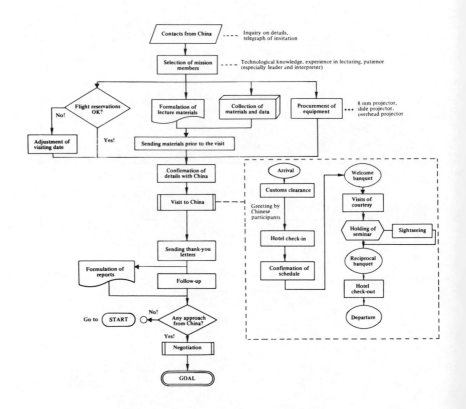

Source: Masaharu Hishida, "Japan's Experience in Technical Exchange with China," China Newsletter 24 (December 1979): 10.

FIGURE 6.3

Technical Exchange with China: Flow Chart III, Inviting a Chinese Mission

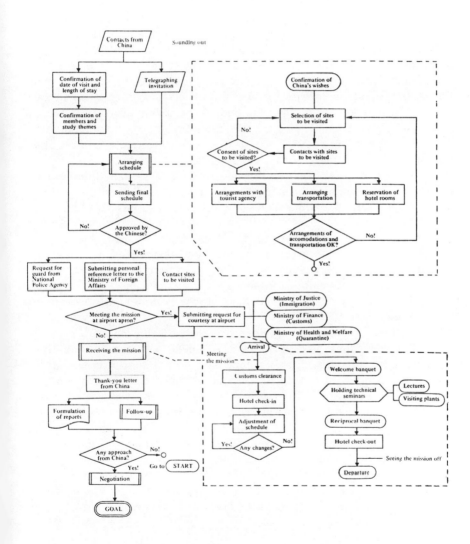

Source: Masaharu Hishida, "Japan's Experience in Technical Exchange with China," China Newsletter 24 (December 1979): 13.

considered an "old friend" that helped bring about the sale for CDC. Although CDC signed a contract in August 1974, it took more than two years for the U.S. government to grant an export license. The same lengthy "dual negotiations" with the U.S. government applied to CDC's second contract, signed in December 1978. As of June 1980 an export license had not been granted.

Although, as this study suggests, each negotiation is singular in its procedural aspects, there are nevertheless subtleties of dealing with the Chinese government and with U.S. officialdom that can make or break a U.S.-Chinese commercial negotiation. These subtleties are generally summarized as problems unique to U.S.-Chinese trade. For example, sales potential in a socialist economy depends, in general, on priorities set by the plan and not by market forces. It might be helpful, therefore, for U.S. government agencies to undertake a detailed study of the relationship of U.S.-Chinese trade to the Chinese economic plan and to publicize the results.

Another related problem for the U.S. firm is that Chinese commercial negotiations are conducted solely by a foreign trade system through specialized foreign trade organizations. Thus, for the U.S. firm, contact with product end users is normally limited and numerous official contacts must be arranged. Thus, the U.S. firm learns very quickly that if it wants to penetrate the Chinese market, it must work basically through one Chinese buyer for the whole China market. It might be helpful, therefore, for an agency such as the U.S. Department of Commerce to monitor U.S.-Chinese commercial negotiations to the extent possible, so as to aid U.S. firms, particularly the smaller ones, in competing for a share of the China market.

The procedural aspects of U.S.-Chinese commercial negotiations are unique for the U.S. firm, in that there are a host of unfamiliar issues confronting it in the areas of technical and commercial contract negotiation. Such difficulties and obstacles generally make negotiation lengthy, arduous, and demanding. Current information about these hindrances and impediments, disseminated in a timely fashion to U.S. firms interested in selling to the China market, might do much to foster increased U.S.-Chinese trade.

In the absence of such timely information, what is the U.S. business person to do? "Continue to negotiate, and if there are no perceptible routes to the conclusion of the negotiating chess game, invent them."

NOTES

1. Quoted in Michael Sullivan, The Arts of China, rev. ed. (Berkeley: University of California Press, 1979), p. 162. As a mat-

ter of fact, Chinese theorists distinguish three kinds of perspective in Chinese painting.

2. Henry Kissinger, White House Years (Boston: Little, Brown, 1979), p. 1056.

3. Masaharu Hishida, "Japan's Experience in Technical Exchange with China," China Newsletter 24 (December 1979): 3.

APPENDIXES

APPENDIX A
CONTRACT FOR COMPLETE EQUIPMENT FOR A
LARGE -SIZE SEISMIC DATA PROCESSING CENTER,
CONTRACT NO. 78MXE-45092F

BETWEEN THE SELLERS:

COMPAGNIE GÉNÉRALE DE GÉOPHYSIQUE

AND

CONTROL DATA FRANCE

AND THE BUYER:

CHINA NATIONAL MACHINERY IMPORT & EXPORT CORPORATION

SIGNED IN PEKING, CHINA

DECEMBER 22, 1978

CONTRACT SUMMARY

Chapter

1 Subject of the Contract

2 Price

3 Payment

4 Delivery and Terms of Delivery

5 Shipping Documents

6 Packing and Marking

7 Inspection

8 Erection, Calibration, and Acceptance Test

9 Guarantees and Claims

10 Penalty for Delayed Delivery

11 Dispatch of Trainees and Technical Service

12 Force Majeure

13 Taxes and Duties

14 Arbitration

15 Effectiveness of the Contract and Miscellaneous

16 Legal Addresses

ANNEXES

Annex

1 Scope of Supply and List of Prices

2 Contents, Time, and Manner of Delivery for the Technical Documentation and Drawings Supplied by the Seller

3 Specimen of Letter of Guarantee Issued by Banque Française du Commerce Extérieur, Paris

4 Stipulation of Calibration and Acceptance of the "Equipments"

5 Terms of the Seller's Acceptance of Trainees Sent by the Buyer

6 Terms of the Service of the Seller's Technical Personnel

7 Terms on FCOs

8 Spare Parts List

CONTRACT FOR COMPLETE EQUIPMENT FOR A LARGE-SIZE SEISMIC DATA PROCESSING CENTER, CONTRACT NO. 78MXE-45092F

DATE: December 22, 1978

China National Machinery Import and Export Corporation, Peking, China (the user is China National Oil and Gas Exploration and Development Corporation) (hereinafter referred to as the "Buyer"), on the one hand, and Compagnie Générale de Géophysique and Control Data France, both acting as joint contractor (hereinafter referred to as the "Seller"), on the other hand, agree to sign this Contract on the following terms and conditions:

Chapter 1

Subject of the Contract

1.1 The Buyer agrees to buy from the Seller and the Seller agrees to sell to the Buyer one complete Equipments for a large-size seismic data processing center. The scope of supply to be made by the Seller to the Buyer under the Contract is as follows:
   A. Equipments includes computer hardware, interactive graphic system, display equipments, ancillary equipments, site equipments, softwares, etc. (hereinafter referred to as the "Equipments").
   B. Spare Parts include spare parts, accessories, consumables, etc., used for the Equipments (hereinafter referred to as the "Spare Parts") set out in Annexes no. 1 and no. 8 to the Contract.
   C. Technical service, installation, and technical training. The detailed scope of supply, technical specification, performance, price, etc. are set forth in Annexes no. 1, 4, 5, 6, and 8 to the Contract.
1.2 The scope, copies, and time of delivery of the technical documentation . . .
1.3 Within 5 (five) years after acceptance test of the Equipments the Seller shall be obliged to supply to the Buyer all Spare Parts for Equipments on purchase terms mutually agreed upon.
   For CONTROL DATA Cyber System Equipments the Seller shall be obliged to supply the Buyer within 4 (four) years after the end of the guarantee period and at the Buyer's request with all the Spare Parts for the abovementioned equipment at a price mutually agreed upon at the time of purchase.

Chapter 2
Price

2.1 The total price for the Equipments, Spare Parts, FCO, technical training, installation, technical service, technical documentation, and drawings under the Contract is U.S. $12,207,591.60 (U.S. dollars twelve million, two hundred and seven thousand, five hundred and ninety-one and sixty cents). The individual prices are specified in Annex no. 1 to the Contract.

2.2 The above total Contract price shall be for delivery f.o.b. Marseilles port and Paris Airport, France, including the packing and loading charges and all other charges before the Equipment and Spare Parts are stowed on board the aircraft and or on board the carrying vessel assigned by the Buyer, and all charges for delivery of all technical documentation and drawings at Peking Airport, and the charges for technical service and technical training to be provided by the Seller.

2.3 The above total Contract price is firm and fixed except if stipulations of paragraph 4.13 (Chapter 4) and 10.3 (Chapter 10) hereafter are applied.

Chapter 3
Payment

3.1 All payments between the Seller and the Buyer under the Contract shall be made in U.S. dollars through the Bank of China, Peking, and Banque Française du Commerce Extérieur, Paris.

3.2 The first payment, covering 95% (ninety-five percent) of the total value of the Equipments and Spare Parts under the Contract and charges for technical service and training, namely, U.S. $11,620,997.91 (U.S. dollars eleven million, six hundred and twenty thousand, nine hundred and ninety-seven and ninety-one cents), shall be arranged as follows.

After the Buyer has received the following documents presented by the Seller:

A. One photostat copy of the export license issued by the relative authorities in France or other countries of export, or one photostat copy of a certificate issued by the same authorities, certifying that the export license is not required for exporting the Equipments and Spare Parts under the Contract.

B. Shipping advice and/or airlifting advice for the first shipment in triplicate, as specified in Chapter 4 to the Contract.

An irrevocable letter of credit with partial shipment allowed shall be issued by the Bank of China, Peking, 30 (thirty) days before the expected loading date in favor of the Seller for the value of the total Contract price, namely, U.S. $12,207,591.60 (U.S. dollars twelve million, two hundred and seven thousand, five hundred and ninety-one and sixty cents), which shall be valid until 60 (sixty) days after the last shipment has been made. The issuing bank shall effect the payment of 95% (ninety-five percent) of the total value of each shipment to the Seller not later than 30 (thirty) days after the said Bank has received the following documents and found them in order:

1) Full set (3/3) of negotiable and 3 (three) copies of non-negotiable clean on board ocean bill of lading made out to order and blank-endorsed, notifying "China National Foreign Trade Transportation Corporation at the port of destination," or 1 (one) original and 1 (one) copy clean-on-board airway bill indicating the stipulated air-way route under the Contract, marking (sic) "freight collected," with the China National Foreign Trade Transportation Corporation, Peking, as the consignee

2) 5 (five) copies of commercial invoice indicating the value to be collected

3) 3 (three) copies of quality certificate issued by the manufacturers

4) 5 (five) copies of detailed packing list

5) 1 (one) sight draft

6) 1 (one) original of air freight and insurance policy shall be submitted by the Seller separately if the Buyer asks the Seller to arrange the airlifting and insurance instead of the Buyer.

 Charges of training, namely, U.S. $106,285.80 (U.S. dollars one hundred and six thousand, two hundred and eighty-five and eighty cents), shall be paid by the Buyer along with the payment for the last shipment.

3.3 The second payment, covering 5% (five percent) of the total value of the Equipments and Spare Parts under the Contract, namely, U.S. $586,593.69 (U.S. dollars five hundred and eighty-six thousand, five hundred and ninety-three dollars and sixty-nine cents), shall be paid by the Buyer to the Seller after the erection, adjustment check, and acceptance test of the Equipments stipulated in subchapter 8.3 of the Contract . . . and not later than 15 (fifteen) days after the Buyer has received the following documents and found them in order:

A. One sight draft covering 5% (five percent) of the total value of the Equipments and Spare Parts under the Contract

B. An irrevocable letter of guarantee issued by the Seller's bank in favor of the Buyer (specimen as per Annex no. 3 to the Contract)

C. 5 (five) copies of commercial invoice indicating the value to be collected

D. Copy of the acceptance test certificate signed by both parties.

Should the Equipments not be accepted in time through the Buyer's fault, above said payment shall be paid 2 (two) months after the last shipment has been made.

3.4 For the FCO described in Annex no. 7, the payment of U.S. $25,000 (U.S. dollars twenty-five thousand) each year will be effected for CYBER 175 data processing center within four years after the expiration date of guarantee period.

Chapter 4
Delivery and Terms of Delivery

. . .

Chapter 10
Penalty for Delayed Delivery

10.1 If the Seller fails, through his own fault, to deliver any of the Equipments and Spare Parts in accordance with the delivery time stipulated in Chapter 4 of the Contract, with the exception of the reasons listed in Chapter 12 of the Contract, the Buyer shall collect penalties from the Seller commencing from the 31st day after the delivery time, as stipulated in the Contract, in the following ways:

For the 1st to 4th week of delay, the rate of the penalty for each week shall be 0.25% of the basic value.

For the 5th to the 8th week of delay, the rate of the penalty for each week shall be 0.5% of the basic value.

For the 9th week and above, the rate of penalty for each week shall be 1% of the basic value.

If the period of delayed delivery is less than one week, it shall be counted as one week for penalty calculation. However, the total penalty for delayed delivery shall not exceed 5% of the total Contract price. The payment of such penalty for delayed delivery made by the Seller shall not release the Seller from his obligation to delivery the Equipments of the referred processing center and Spare Parts on which the penalty for delayed delivery is collected.

If the delayed delivery period of the Equipments and Spare Parts exceeds 3 (three) months, the Buyer shall be entitled to terminate the Contract or part of it and the Seller shall refund the Buyer the payment for the Equipments and Spare Parts that has already been made by the Buyer, plus interest at the rate of 7.5% per annum, counting from the date when such payment is made until the date of refund from the Seller to the Buyer, as well as the banking charges. The expense paid by the Buyer for execution of the Contract (for instance, expense for signing and cancellation of the Contract, expense for transportation and erection of the Equipments and Spare Parts, all the payment made for training the technical personnel, etc.) shall also be reimbursed by the Seller to the Buyer.

10.2 In case the Equipments cannot be delivered at the time stipulated in Chapter 4 due to the late loading of the vessel and due to Buyer's faults, the Seller will not have to pay penalty.

10.3 In case the Seller is unable to deliver the Equipments on time due to circumstances beyond his control, the Seller will not have to pay penalty.

Chapter 11
Dispatch of Trainees and Technical Service

11.1 The Buyer shall have the right to send his trainees to the Seller's facilities (including factories, offices, laboratories, and so on) and the sites where such Equipments is operated in the Seller's country for training. The duration and content of training and the number of trainees are specified in Annex no. 5 to the Contract.

11.2 In order to ensure the smooth erection, calibration, and acceptance test of the Equipments under the Contract, the Seller shall send technical personnel to the Buyer's site of erection for technical service. The number, duration of work, responsibilities, and treatment conditions of the Seller's technical personnel are specified in Annex no. 6 to the Contract.

11.3 The Buyer will subscribe to the field change order distribution as specified in Annex no. 7.

Chapter 12
Force Majeure

12.1 If either of the Contract parties is prevented from performing his contractual obligation after signing the Contract due to war, serious fire, flood, earthquake, or some other cause agreed upon between both parties as a case of force majeure, the time for performance of the Contract shall be extended by a period equivalent to the delay.

12.2 The affected party shall notify the other party by cable within the shortest possible time of the occurrence of an above-mentioned case and send by registered airmail, within 14 (fourteen) days thereafter, a certificate from the authorities or departments concerned to the other party for his confirmation.

12.3 Should the effect of force majeure mentioned above last over 120 (one hundred and twenty) consecutive days, both parties shall settle on a procedure of executing the Contract through amicable consultations as soon as possible.

Chapter 13
Taxes and Duties

13.1 All taxes and/or duties of any kind whatsoever to be paid in connection with the performance of the Contract arising before the Equipments and Spare Parts are effectively loaded and stowed on board the carrying vessel or on board the aircraft assigned by the Buyer shall be borne by the Seller.

13.2 All taxes and/or duties of any kind whatsoever to be paid in connection with the performance of the Contract arising after the Equipments and Spare Parts are effectively loaded and stowed on board the carrying vessel or on board the aircraft assigned by the Buyer shall be borne by the Buyer.

Chapter 14
Arbitration

14.1 All disputes arising in connection with the Contract shall be settled through friendly negotiations between both parties. In case no agreement can be reached through such negotiations, the disputes shall be settled through arbitration.

14.2 An Arbitration Committee shall consist of one representative appointed by each party and a member of a third nationality agreed upon by both parties.

14.3 If the Buyer is the defendant, the arbitration shall take place in Peking.

If the Seller is the defendant, the arbitration shall take place in Paris.

14.4 The arbitration fee shall be borne by the losing party.

Chapter 15
Effectiveness of the Contract and Miscellaneous

15.1 The Contract is signed between the authorized representatives of both parties on December 22, 1978, in Peking and shall come into force immediately upon the signing.

15.2 The Contract is made out in 4 (four) originals in the English language, 2 (two) for each party.

15.3 Compagnie Générale de Géophysique, France, is the general representative of the Seller and shall undertake all the rights and obligations of the Seller in execution of the Contract.

15.4 Should any of the contents of the Contract be amended or supplemented, documents in written form shall be signed by the authorized representatives of both parties and shall form integral parts of the Contract.

15.5 Annexes no. 1 to no. 8 to the Contract shall form integral parts of the Contract.

15.6 All correspondence between both parties in connection with the execution of the Contract shall be written in the English language and in 2 (two) copies.

Chapter 16
Legal Addresses

16.1 The Buyer's legal address:
China National Machinery Import and Export Corporation
Er-Li-Kou, Hsi Chiao, Peking, China.
Cable: MACHIMPEX—PEKING. Telex: 22242 CMIEC CN

16.2 The Seller's legal address:
Compagnie Générale de Géophysique (CGG)
6 rue Galvani 91301 Massy France.
Cable: CGGEC MASSY. Telex: 692442F
Control Data France (CDF)
195 rue de Bercy
75582 Paris CEDEX 12
Cable: CONTROL DATA FRANCE
Telex: CODAT 67110F-PARIS

The Buyer	The Seller
China National Machinery Import and Export Corporation	Compagnie Générale de Géophysique Control Data France

APPENDIX B
PROTOCOL NO. 1 TO CONTRACT NO. 78MXE-45090F
FOR FOUR SEISMIC DATA PROCESSING CENTERS

China National Machinery Import and Export Corporation, Peking, China (hereinafter referred to as the Buyer), on the one hand, and Compagnie Générale de Géophysique and Control Data France (hereinafter referred to as the Seller), on the other hand, agree to sign the present protocol to contract No. MXE-45090F, signed in December 1978 in Peking, on the following terms and conditions.

1. The capacity of the processing centers will be increased by addition of the following equipment to the Cyber 172 computers:

Qty	Type	Description
8	10312-6	Cyber 172 memory increment adds 32,768 words, increasing memory from 65,536 to 98,304 words

2. Terms and conditions of contract No. MXE-45090F are applicable to this protocol except for the following:

    If the equipment under this protocol cannot be delivered together with the Cyber 172s, the acceptance test will be as described in paragraph 3 below.
    The add-on equipment will not be delivered and installed in more than one lot per processing center.
    During installation on the site, all the Cyber 172 computer systems will be fully available and will be given in good working condition to CDF installation team

3. Acceptance test (applicable only if the add-on equipment is delivered after the two Cyber 172 systems)
    Period A: 6.5 hours per machine. During this period only the S. M. M. test will be run.
    Period B: 90 minutes per machine loaded with all the CGG seismic software. During this period the jobs already run during the first acceptance test (Cyber 172) will be run again. The results show an increase of the seismic processing capability.

The Seller	The Buyer
Compagnie Générale de Géophysique	China National Machinery Impor
Control Data France	and Export Corporation

APPENDIX C
PROTOCOL NO. 2 TO CONTRACT NO. 78MXE-45090F
FOR FOUR SEISMIC DATA PROCESSING CENTERS

1.   The Buyer and the Seller agree to make all efforts to obtain
        an agreement from the competent authorities that can decrease
        or modify the length and/or the kind of the technical services
        over 3 (three) years, as described in the referred Contract,
        Annex 7, sec. 7.3.1.
2.   If success is obtained at any time, starting from the signature
        date of the contract, a new technical service will be decided,
        according to the agreement of the competent authorities.
3.   Up to the time that both parties can modify the technical ser-
        vice, the following will be applied:
3.1   Duration expenses.
        The duration of the technical service will be 36 (thirty-six)
        months, including 6 (six) months of vacation, distributed regu-
        larly on the three years. The total price, borne by the Buyer,
        will be 36 months - 6 months (vacation) = 30 months; 30 months
        x U.S. $10,262 = U.S. $307,860.
        This price includes all expenses except for local transporta-
        tion, which will be provided by the Buyer free of charge. In
        case the technical service is not performed in the Peking area,
        the Buyer will pay the technical personnel for all local trans-
        portation (at least one round trip per month to Peking).
        If the CDF technical service is replaced by CGG technical
        service, the latter will be charged at U.S. $14,000 per month,
        all expenses included.
3.2   Contents of CDF technical service.
3.2.1   The Seller's representative shall be the general representative
        of the Seller at the contract plant to give general technical in-
        structions and advice within the scope of the Contract, and to
        get in touch with the Buyer's general representative at the
        contract plant, to discuss and solve all technical and working
        problems.
3.2.2   The Seller's technical personnel shall give the Buyer overall
        technical instructions and necessary demonstrations, explain
        in detail the technical documents, drawings, data sheets, and
        performance of equipment, correct any faults and maintain
        and answer all the technical questions posed by the Buyer's
        technical personnel within the scope of the Contract.
3.2.3   All technical instructions given by the Seller's technical per-
        sonnel shall be correct. Any instructions in operation and
        maintenance that may result in damage to the contracted

Equipments should be put in writing by the Seller. In case of incorrect instructions given in writing, the Seller shall be liable for all direct expenses thus incurred, limited to the contracted Equipments. The Buyer shall be liable for all direct expenses incurred due to the Buyer's fault.

3.2.4 The Seller's technical personnel shall work 45 hours per week, including time of travel from hotel to installation site and return. Their working schedule shall be in accordance with the regulation of the contract plant. Sundays and the official holidays in the People's Republic of China shall be the holidays of the Seller's technical personnel.

During the vacation period the Seller will have the right to send visitors to the installation site at his own expense.

3.2.5 The Seller's technical personnel shall observe the laws and orders of the People's Republic of China and the rules and regulations of the contract plant. In case of any important reason, such as breach of the laws of the People's Republic of China and/or incompetence, the Buyer shall have the right to ask for replacement, and all the costs thus incurred shall be borne by the Seller.

3.2.6 The service fee for the Seller's technical personnel shall be paid from the date of their entering China to the date of their leaving China, both days included. The service fees shall be paid monthly by the Buyer through the Bank of China to the Seller within three (3) weeks after having received the invoices from the Seller and the time sheets signed by the general representatives of both parties and found them to be in order.

The actual work of the Seller's technical personnel shall be recorded daily on time sheets and in a log book, which shall be signed by the representatives of both parties and shall be taken as the basis for the payment of salary. Holidays and days off will be considered as worked days for the payment of the fee.

Both the time sheets and the log book shall be made in English and Chinese, in two (2) copies each, and shall be effective upon signature by both parties' representatives. One (1) copy of each shall be held by each party.

In case the Seller's technical personnel is absent from work on a normal working day, service fee shall be deducted for each absent day (with the exception of sickness certified by a doctor).

3.2.7 The Buyer shall provide the Seller's technical personnel, free of charge, with necessary office room and means of travel between the lodging and the workplace.

3.2.8 Whenever the Seller's technical personnel is unable to carry on the normal work due to sickness or other important reasons for more than two (2) weeks, the Buyer shall be entitled to demand that Seller send qualified technical personnel for replacement.

3.2.9 In case, at the request of the Buyer and with the agreement of the Seller, the Seller shall dispatch technical personnel to China for a short period to solve technical problems, the expenses shall be settled at that time.

The Buyer	The Seller
China National Machinery Import and Export Corporation	Compagnie Général de Géophysique Control Data France

APPENDIX D
"STANDARD" SALES CONTRACT

Contract No._____
Date_____

Sellers: China National Machinery Import and Export Corporation
Buyers: This Contract is made by and between the Buyers and the
Sellers; whereby the Buyers agree to buy and the Sellers agree to sell
the under-mentioned commodity according to the terms and conditions
stipulated below:

1. Commodity, Specification, Quantity, Unit Price and Total Value:
2. Total Value of Contract:
3. Packing:
4. Insurance:
5. Shipping Marks:
6. Port of Shipment:
7. Port of Destination:
8. Time of Shipment:
9. Terms of Payment:
10. Shipping Documents: The sellers shall present the following documents:
11. Claims: Should the quality, quantity, and/or specification of the goods be found not in conformity with the stipulations of the contract, the Sellers agree to examine any claim, which shall be supported by a report issued by a reputable surveyor approved by the Sellers. The Sellers are not responsible for claims arising out of incorrect installation or wrong operation. The Sellers are only responsible for claims against bad workmanship or faulty materials. Claims concerning quality shall be made within____months after the arrival of the goods at destination. Claims concerning quantity and/or specification shall be made within____days after the arrival of the goods at destination.
12. Force Majeure: The Sellers shall not be held responsible for late delivery or nondelivery of the goods due to Force Majeure. However, in such case, the Sellers shall submit to the Buyers a certificate issued by the China Council for the Promotion of International Trade or competent organizations as evidence thereof.
13. Arbitration: All disputes in connection with the execution of this Contract shall be settled through friendly negotiations.

Should an arbitration be necessary, either party shall appoint one arbitrator, and the arbitrators thus appointed shall nominate a third person as umpire, to form an arbitration committee. Arbitration shall take place at_____. The award of the Arbitration Committee shall be accepted as final by both parties. Arbitration fee, unless otherwise awarded, shall be borne by the losing party. The arbitrators and the umpire shall be confined to persons of Chinese or_____nationality.

In case the arbitration is to be held in Peking, the case in dispute shall then be submitted for arbitration to the Foreign Trade Arbitration Commission of the China Council for the Promotion of International Trade, Peking, in accordance with the "Provisional Rules of Procedure of the Foreign Trade Arbitration Commission of the China Council for the Promotion of International Trade." The decision of the Commission shall be accepted as final and binding upon both parties.

14. Other Conditions: Any alterations and additions to this Contract shall be valid only if made in writing and duly signed by both parties. Neither party is entitled to transfer its right and obligations under this Contract to a third party without a written consent thereto being obtained from the other party.

After the signing of this Contract all preceding negotiations and correspondence pertaining to the same shall become null and void.

15. Done and signed in_____on this_____day of_____196__.

16. Remarks:

The Sellers	The Buyers
China National Machinery Import and Export Corporation	
Address:	Address:
Cable Address: "MACHIMPEX"	Cable Address:

APPENDIX E
"STANDARD" PURCHASE CONTRACT

No._____

Peking. Date:_____

The Buyers: China National Machinery Import and Export Corporation
Erh-Li-kou, Hsi Chiao, Peking, China (Cable Address: "MACHIMPEX
Peking)
The Sellers:

This Contract is made by and between the Buyers and the Sellers;
whereby the Buyers agree to buy and the Sellers agree to sell the
under-mentioned commodity according to the terms and conditions
stipulated below:

1. Commodity, Specifications, Quantity, and Unit Price:
2. Total Value:
3. Country of Origin and Manufacturers:
4. Packing: To be packed in new strong wooden case(s) suitable
    for long-distance ocean transportation and well protected
    against dampness, moisture, shock, rust, and rough handling.
    The Sellers shall be liable for any damage to the commodity and
    expenses incurred on account of improper packing and for any
    rust damage attributable to inadequate or improper protective
    measures taken by the Sellers in regard to the packing.
5. Shipping Mark: On the surface of each package, the package
    number, measurements, gross weight, net weight, the lifting
    positions, such cautions as "Do Not Stack Upside Down," "Han-
    dle with Care," "Keep Away from Moisture," and the following
    shipping marks shall be stenciled legibly in fadeless paint:
6. Time of Shipment:
7. Port of Shipment:
8. Port of Destination:
9. Insurance: To be covered by the Buyers after shipment.
10. Payment: for/by (1) In case of payment by L/C: The Buyers,
    upon receipt from the Sellers of the delivery advice specified in
    clause 12(1) hereof, shall, 15-20 days prior to the date of de-
    livery, open an irrevocable Letter of Credit with the Bank of
    China, Peking, in favor of the Sellers, for an amount equivalen
    to the total value of the shipment. The Credit shall be payable
    against the presentation of the draft drawn on the opening bank
    together with the shipping documents specified in clause 11
    hereof. The Letter of Credit shall be valid until the 15th day
    after the shipment. (2) In case of payment by collection: After

174

delivery is made, the Sellers shall send through the Sellers' bank the draft drawn on the Buyers together with the shipping documents specified in clause 11 hereof, to the Buyers through the Buyers' bank, the Bank of China, Peking, for collection.
(3) In case of payment by M/T or T/T: Payment to be effected by the buyers not later than seven days after receipt of the shipping documents specified under clause 11 hereof.

11. Documents: (1) The Sellers shall present the following documents to the paying bank for negotiation (or collection):

  a) One full set of clean-on-board ocean bills of lading marked "Freight to Collect" and made out to order, blank-endorsed, and notifying the China National Foreign Trade Transportation Corporation at the port of destination.

  b) Five copies of invoice, indicating contract number and shipping mark (in case of more than one shipping mark, the invoice shall be issued separately).

  c) Two copies of packing list with indication of shipping weight, number, and date of corresponding invoice.

  d) Two copies of certificate of quality and quantity issued by the manufacturers as specified in item (1) of clause 16 hereof.

  e) Certified copy of cable to the Buyers advising of shipment immediately after the shipment has been made, as specified in clause 13 hereof.

  (2) The Sellers shall, within 10 days after the shipment is effected, send by airmail another two sets of one copy of the above-mentioned documents with the exception of item (e) of this clause; one set to the Buyers and the other set to the China National Foreign Trade Transportation Corporation at the port of destination.

12. Terms of shipment: (1) The Sellers shall,____days before the date of shipment stipulated in clause 6 hereof, advise the Buyers by cable/letter of the contract number, commodity, quantity, value, number of packages, gross weight and measurement, and date of readiness at the port of shipment in order for the Buyers to book shipping space. Should any package reach or exceed 20 tons in weight, 10 meters in length, 3.4 meters in width, or 3 meters in height, the Sellers shall provide the Buyers with 5 copies of drawing delineating the shape of the external packing, with indication of the detailed measurement and weight, 50 days before dispatch of the goods in order to enable the Buyers to arrange transportation. (2) Booking of shipping space shall be attended to by the Buyers' shipping agents, China National Chartering Corporation, Peking, China (Cable address: Zhongzu Peking), with whom the Buyers are requested to keep in close contact on the matter of shipment. (3) China National

Chartering Corporation, Peking, China, or their port agents, shall send the Sellers, 10 days before the estimated date of arrival of the vessel at the port of shipment, a preliminary notice indicating the name of vessel, estimated date of loading, and contract number in order for the Sellers to arrange shipment. When it becomes necessary to change the carrying vessel or in the event of her arrival having to be advanced or delayed, the Buyers or the shipping agents shall advise the Sellers in time. Should the vessel fail to arrive at the port of loading within 30 days after the arrival date advised by the Buyers, the Buyers shall bear the storage and insurance expenses incurred from the 31st day. (4) The Sellers shall be liable for any dead freight or demurrage, should it happen that they have failed to have the commodity ready for loading after the carrying vessel has arrived at the port of shipment on time. (5) The Sellers shall bear all expenses and risks (involved in the handling) of the commodity before it passes over the vessel's rail and is released from the tackle, whereas after it has passed over the vessel's rail and has been released from the tackle, all expenses (involved in the handling) of the commodity shall be for the Buyers' account.

13. Shipping Advice: The Sellers, immediately upon the completion of the loading of the commodity, shall notify the Buyers by cable of the contract number, name of commodity, quantity, gross weight, invoiced value, name of carrying vessel, and date of sailing. If any package is of weight above 9 metric tons, width over 3,400 mm. or height on both sides over 2,350 mm., the Sellers shall advise the Buyers of the weight and measurements of each such package. In case the Buyers fail to arrange insurance in due time, owing to the Sellers not having thus cabled in time, all losses shall be borne by the Sellers.

14. Technical Documents: (1) One complete set of the following technical documents, written in English, shall be packed and dispatched together with each consignment.
    a) Foundation drawings.
    b) Wiring instructions, diagrams of electrical connections, and/or pneumatic/hydraulic connections.
    c) Manufacturing drawings of easily worn parts and instructions
    d) Spare parts catalogs.
    e) Certificate of quality as stipulated in item 1 of clause 16 hereof.
    f) Erection, operation, service, and repair instruction books.

15. Guarantee of Quality: The Sellers shall guarantee that the commodity is made of the best materials, with first-class workmanship, brand new, unused, and complies in all respects with

the quality, specifications, and performance as stipulated in
this Contract. The Sellers shall also guarantee that the goods,
when correctly mounted and properly operated and maintained,
will give satisfactory performance for a period of____months,
counting from the date on which the commodity arrives at the
port of destination.

16. Inspection and Claims: (1) The manufacturers shall, before
making delivery, make a precise and comprehensive inspection
of the goods as regards the quality, specifications, performance,
and quantity/weight, and issue certificates certifying that the
goods are in conformity with the stipulations of this Contract.
The certificate shall form an integral part of the documents to
be presented to the paying bank for negotiation (or collection)
of payment, but shall not be considered as final in respect of
quality, specifications, performance, and quantity/weight.
Particulars and results of the test carried out by the manufacturers must be shown in a statement to be attached to the said
quality certificates. (2) After arrival of the goods at the port
of destination, the Buyers shall apply to the China Commodity
Inspection Bureau (hereinafter called the Bureau) for a preliminary inspection in respect of the quality, specifications, and
quantity/weight of the goods, and a survey report shall be issued therefor by the Bureau. If any discrepancies are found by
the Bureau regarding the specifications or the quantity or both,
except when the responsibilities lie with the insurance company
or shipping company, the Buyers shall, within____days after
arrival of the goods at the port of destination, have the right to
reject the goods or to claim against the Sellers. (3) Should the
quality and specifications of the goods be not in conformity with
the Contract, or should the goods prove defective within the
guarantee period stipulated in clause 15 hereof for any reason,
including latent defect or the use of unsuitable materials, the
Buyers shall arrange for a survey to be carried out by the Bureau, and have the right to claim against the Sellers on the
strength of the survey report issued therefor by the Bureau.
(4) The claims mentioned above shall be regarded as being accepted if the Sellers fail to reply within 30 days after receipt of
the Buyers' claim.

17. Settlement of Claims: In case the Sellers are liable for the discrepancies and a claim is made by the Buyers within the time
limit of inspection and quality guarantee period, as stipulated
in clauses 15 and 16 of this Contract, the Sellers shall settle
the claim upon the agreement of the Buyers in one or a combination of the following ways: (1) Agree to the rejection of the
goods and refund to the Buyers the value of the goods so rejected

in the same currency as contracted herein, and to bear all direct losses and expenses in connection therewith, including interest accrued, banking charges, freight, insurance premium, inspection charges, storage, stevedore charges, and all other necessary expenses required for the custody and protection of the rejected goods. (2) Devaluate the goods according to the degree of inferiority, extent of damage, and amount of losses suffered by the Buyers. (3) Replace with new parts that conform to the specifications, quality, and performance as stipulated in this Contract, and bear all the expenses incurred and direct losses sustained by the Buyers. The Sellers shall, at the same time, guarantee the quality of the parts thus replaced for a further period as specified in clause 15 of this Contract.

18. Force Majeure: The Sellers shall not be held responsible for the delay in shipment or nondelivery of the goods due to force majeure, which might occur during the process of manufacturing or in the course of loading or transit. The Sellers shall advise the Buyers immediately of such occurrence and within fourteen days thereafter, the Sellers shall send by airmail to the Buyers for their acceptance a certificate issued by the competent government authorities where the accident occurs as evidence thereof. Under such circumstances the Sellers, however, are still under obligation to take all necessary measures to hasten the delivery of the goods. In case the accident lasts for more than ten weeks, the Buyers shall have the right to cancel the Contract.

19. Late Delivery and Penalty: Should the Sellers fail to make delivery on time as stipulated in the Contract, with exception of force majeure causes specified in clause 18 of this Contract, the Buyers shall agree to postpone the delivery on condition that the Sellers agree to pay a penalty that shall be deducted by the paying bank from the payment under negotiation (or collection). The penalty is charged at a rate of 0.5% for every seven days, periods less than seven days counting as seven days. The total penalty, however, shall not exceed 5% of the total value of the goods involved in the late delivery. In case the Sellers fail to make delivery ten weeks later than the time of shipment stipulated in this Contract, the Buyers shall have the right to cancel the contract and the Sellers, in spite of the cancellation, shall still pay the aforesaid penalty to the Buyers without delay.

20. Arbitration: All disputes in connection with this Contract or the execution thereof shall be settled through friendly negotiations. In case no settlement can be reached through negotiations the case . . . (it should be referred to arbitration in a third country agreed upon by both parties) should then be submitted

for arbitration to the Arbitration Commission of the China Council for the Promotion of International Trade in accordance with the Provisional Rules of Procedure promulgated by the said Arbitration Commission. The arbitration shall take place in Peking and the decision of the Arbitration Commission shall be final and binding upon both parties; neither party shall seek recourse to a law court or other authorities to appeal for revision of the decision. Arbitration fee shall be borne by the losing party.

Supplementary Condition:

This Contract is made in two original copies, one copy to be held by each party in witness thereof.

The Buyers: The Sellers:
China National Machinery Import
  and Export Corporation

BIBLIOGRAPHY

BOOKS

Allen, George C., and Audrey G. Donnithorne. Western Enterprise in Far Eastern Economic Development. New York: Macmillan, 1954.

American Management Association. Trade with China. Washington, D.C.: American Management Association, 1972.

Arnold, Julean Herbert. China through the American Window. Shanghai: American Chamber of Commerce, 1932.

Barnett, A. Doak. China after Mao. Princeton, N.J.: Princeton University Press, 1967.

_____. Communist China in Perspective. New York: Frederick A. Praeger, 1962.

_____. Communist Economic Strategy: The Rise of Mainland China. Washington, D.C.: National Planning Association, 1959.

_____. Uncertain Passage. Washington, D.C.: Brookings Institution, 1974.

Barnett, A. Doak, and Edwin O. Reischauer. The United States and China: The Next Decade. New York: Praeger, 1970.

Bartos, Otomar J. Process and Outcome of Negotiations. New York: Columbia University Press, 1974.

Behrman, Jack H., and Harvey W. Wallender. Transfers of Manufacturing Technology within Multinational Enterprises. Cambridge, Mass.: Ballenger, 1976.

Berliner, Joseph S. The Innovation Decision in Soviet Industry. Cambridge, Mass.: MIT Press, 1976.

Blair, Patricia. Development in the PRC: A Selected Bibliography. Washington, D.C.: Overseas Development Council, 1977.

Boarman, Patrick, ed. Trade with China. Los Angeles: Center for International Business, 1973.

Boarman, Patrick M., and Jayson Mugar. Trade with China: Assessments by Leading Businessmen and Scholars. New York: Praeger, 1974.

British Overseas Trade Board. The People's Republic of China. Hong Kong: British Overseas Trade Board, 1975.

Burke, William. The China Trade. San Francisco: Federal Reserve, 1972.

Business International. Doing Business with the People's Republic of China. New York: Business International, 1973.

_____. Selling the Mainland China Market, Management Monographs, no. 51. New York: Business International, 1971.

Cahill, Harry K. China Trade and U.S. Tariffs. New York: Praeger, 1973.

Campbell, Charles S., Jr. Special Business Interests and the Open Door Policy. New Haven, Conn.: Yale University Press, 1968.

Chaojin, Liu, and Wang Linsheng. China's Foreign Trade: Its Policy and Practice. San Francisco: CTPS-USA, June 1980.

Cheng, Yu-kwei. Foreign Trade and Industrial Development of China: An Historical and Integrated Analysis through 1948. Washington, D.C.: University Press, 1956.

Chow, Shi-san. Handbook of Business Training, with Special Reference to Systems Used in China. Shanghai: Commercial Press, 1917.

Cohen, Jerome. "Chinese Law and Sino-American Trade." In China Trade Prospects and United States Policy, edited by Alexander Eckstein. New York: Praeger, 1971.

Coldiron, Aaron L. "The Boeing Experience in China: A Brief Overview." Appendix 8 to Doing Business with China: Legal, Financial, and Negotiating Aspects, by Law and Business, Inc. New York: Harcourt Brace Jovanovich, 1979.

COMTEC Data, Inc. A Directory of Computer Organizations and Corporations: People's Republic of China. Minneapolis: COMTEC, March 1980.

Control Data Corporation. Annual Report 1979. Minneapolis: Control Data Corporation, 1979.

Crossman, Carl L. The China Trade. Princeton, N.J.: Pyne Press, 1972.

Crow, Carl. 400 Million Chinese Customers. New York: Harcourt Brace, 1973.

Dashkevich, Z. V., and A. A. Zhemchug. Osnovnyye vedenia o vneshne torgovle Kitaya. Moscow: Mysl', 1965. This work is an abridged translation of a 1958 handbook edited by the Ministry of Foreign Trade of China.

Davies, John Paton, Jr. Dragon by the Tail. New York: W. W. Norton, 1972.

Dawson, Owen L. Communist China's Agriculture. New York: Praeger, 1970.

De Pauw, John. Soviet-American Trade Negotiations. New York: Praeger, 1979.

Domes, Jurgen. The Internal Politics of China, 1949-1972. New York: Praeger, 1973.

Donnithorne, Audrey G. China's Economic System. London: George Allen and Unwin, 1967.

Dulles, Foster Rhea. The Old China Trade. New York: AMS Press, 1930.

Eckstein, Alexander. China's Economic Revolution. Cambridge, Mass.: Cambridge University Press, 1977.

_____. Communist China's Economic Growth and Foreign Trade: Implications for U.S. Policy. New York: McGraw-Hill, 1966.

Eckstein, Alexander, ed. China Trade Prospects and U.S. Policy. New York: Praeger, 1971.

Eckstein, Alexander, et al. The National Income of Communist China. New York: Free Press of Glencoe, 1961.

Eckstein, Alexander, Walter Galenson, and Ta-chung Liu. Economic Trends in Communist China. Washington, D. C.: Social Science Research Council, 1965.

Fairbank, John King. Trade and Diplomacy on the China Coast: The Opening of the Treaty Ports, 1842-1854. Rev. ed. Stanford, Calif.: Stanford University Press, 1969.

Feonova, L. A., et al. Organizatsiia i tekhnika vneshney torgavli SSSR [Organization and technique of Soviet foreign trade]. Moscow: I. M. O., 1974.

Gordon, Leonard H. D., and Frank J. Shulman. Doctoral Dissertations on China: A Bibliography of Studies in Western Languages, 1945-1970. Seattle: University of Washington Press, 1972.

Greaves, Fielding. Ancient Dragon: China in Perspective. San Rafael, Calif.: Scribe Press, 1979.

Greenbie, Sydney. Gold of Ophir: The China Trade in the Making of America. Wilmington, Del.: Scholarly Resources, 1972.

Guaranty Trust Company of New York. Trading with China: Methods Found Successful in Dealing with the Chinese. New York: Guaranty Trust, 1919.

Handbook on People's China. Peking: Foreign Languages Press, 1957.

Hao, Yen-ping. The Comprador in Nineteenth Century China. Cambridge, Mass.: Harvard University Press, 1970.

Hauge, Gabriel. The China Trade. New York: Manufacturers Hanover Trust, 1974.

Hersh, Marc. Trade with China. New York: Pan American World Airways, 1972.

Hersh, Marc, and Michael Lent. Trade with China. New York: Pan American World Airways, 1971.

Hewes, Agnes. Two Oceans to Canton: The Story of the Old China Trade. New York: A. A. Knopf, 1944.

Ho, Ping-ti. China in Crisis: China's Heritage and the Communist Political System. Chicago: University of Chicago Press, 1968.

Holtzman, Howard M. Legal Aspects of Doing Business with China. New York: Practising Law Institute, 1976.

Holtzman, Howard M., and Walter Sterling Surrey. A New Look at Legal Aspects of Doing Business with China: Developments a Year after Recognition. New York: Practising Law Institute, 1979.

Holzman, Franklyn D. International Trade under Communism. New York: Basic Books, 1976.

Hsiao, Gene. The Foreign Trade of China: Policy, Law, and Practice. Berkeley: University of California Press, 1977.

Hsu, Francis L. K. Americans and Chinese. New York: Natural History Press, 1970.

_____. "Chinese Kinship and Chinese Behavior." In China in Crisis. Chicago: University of Chicago Press, 1968.

_____. Kinship and Culture. Chicago: Alpine, 1971.

_____. Psychological Anthropology. Cambridge, Mass: Harvard University Press, 1972.

Japan Air Lines. Executive Business Guide to China. Tokyo: Japan Air Lines, 1980.

Japan External Trade Organization. How to Approach the China Market. Tokyo: Press International, 1972.

Jernigan, T. R. China's Business Methods and Policy. Shanghai: Kelly and Walsh, 1904.

Kaplan, Fredric, Julian M. Sobin, and Stephen Andors. Encyclopedia of China Today. Fair Lawn, N.J.: Eurasia Press, 1979.

Karrass, Chester L. The Negotiating Game. New York: Thomas Y. Crowell, 1970.

Kihl, Eric. "Market Overview of Activities in China." In China: Proceedings of China-Telcom '79. Brookline, Mass.: Information Gatekeepers, 1979.

Kirby, E. S., ed. Contemporary China. Vol. 3, 1958-59. Hong Kong: University Press, 1960.

Kissinger, Henry. White House Years. Boston: Little, Brown, 1979.

Klein, Donald W. "The Foreign Trade Apparatus." In Law and Politics in China's Foreign Trade, edited by Victor H. Li. Seattle: University of Washington Press, 1977.

Lall, Arthur S. How Communist China Negotiates. New York: Columbia University Press, 1968.

Lardy, Nicholas R. China's Economic Readjustment: Recovery of Paralysis. New Haven, Conn.: Yale University, March 1980.

Law and Business, Inc. Doing Business with China: Legal, Financial, and Negotiating Aspects. New York: Harcourt Brace Jovanovich, 1979.

Lee, Luke T. China and International Agreements. Durham, N.C.: Rules of Law Press, 1969.

Lew, Julian D. M., Clifford A. Ralhkopf, Jr., and Robert Starr. Selected Bibliography on East-West Trade and Investment. Dobbs Ferry, N.Y.: Oceana, 1976.

Lewin, Pauline. The Foreign Trade of Communist China: Its Impact on the Free World. New York: Frederick A. Praeger, 1964.

Li, Choh-ming. Economic Development of Communist China: An Appraisal of the First Five Years of Industrialization. Los Angeles: University of California Press, 1959.

_____. The Statistical System of Communist China. Los Angeles: University of California Press, 1962.

Li, Fu-chun. Report on the First Five-Year Plan for the Development of the National Economy of the People's Republic of China for 1953-1957. Peking: Foreign Language Press, 1955.

Li, Victor, ed. Law and Politics in China's Foreign Trade. Seattle: University of Washington Press, 1977.

Liu, Chao-chin. China's Foreign Trade and Its Management. Hong Kong: Economic Information Agency of the PRC, 1978.

MacDougal, Colina. Trading with China. New York: McGraw-Hill, 1980.

Mah, Feng-hwa. Foreign Trade of Mainland China. Chicago: Aldine, 1971.

Metcalf, John E. China Trade Guide. New York: First National City Bank, 1972.

Mobius, J. Mark, and Gerhard F. Simmel. Trading with China. Hong Kong: Interasia Publications, 1972.

Modern China Studies International Bulletin. London: University of London, 1970.

Namba, Toshio, and George F. Leslie, Jr., trans. Handbook of Trade with China. Tokyo: Tokyo-Chugoku Bo'chi Jiten, 1974.

National Council for U.S.-China Trade. The Chinese Export Commodities Fair. Washington, D.C.: National Council for U.S.-China Trade, 1973.

_____. Selling Technology to China: A Workbook for the Conference on Selling Technology to China. Washington, D.C.: National Council for U.S.-China Trade, December 1979.

_____. Selling Technology to China: Proceedings of the Conference on Selling Technology to China. Washington, D.C.: National Council for U.S.-China Trade, December 1979.

Nau, Henry R. Technology and U.S. Foreign Policy. New York: Praeger, 1976.

Neilan, Edward, and Charles R. Smith. The Future of the China Market: Prospects for Sino-American Trade. Washington, D.C.: American Enterprise Institute for Public Policy Research, 1974.

Nierenberg, Gerald I. Fundamentals of Negotiating. New York: Hawthorne Books, 1973.

Nove, A., and D. Donnelly. Trade with Communist Countries. London: Hutchinson, 1960.

Oksenberg, Michael C. A Bibliography of Secondary English Language Literature on Contemporary Chinese Politics. New York: Columbia University Press, 1970.

Overseas Assignment Directory Service. Business with China. White Plains, N.Y.: Knowledge Industry, 1979.

Pao, Ta-kung. Trade with China. Hong Kong: British Overseas Trade Board, 1957.

Pisar, Samuel. Coexistence and Commerce: Guidelines for Transactions between East and West. New York: McGraw-Hill, 1970.

Pozdniakov, V. S. Sovetskoye gosudarstvo i vneshniaia torgovliya: Pravovye voprosy [The Soviet state and foreign trade: legal questions]. Moscow: Mezhdunarodnye Otnosheniia, 1976.

Pratt, Keith. Visitors to China. London: St. Martin's Press, 1968.

_____. Visitors to China: Eyewitness Accounts of Chinese History. New York: Praeger, 1970.

Richman, Barry. Industrial Society in Communist China. New York: Random House, 1969.

Rostow, W. W. The Prospects for Communist China. New York: MIT and John Wiley & Sons, 1954.

Schelling, T. C. The Strategy of Conflict. Cambridge, Mass.: Harvard University Press, 1960.

Schultz, Jeffrey. China's Foreign Trade Corporations . . . Organizations and Personnel. Washington, D.C.: National Council for U.S.-China Trade, April 1979.

Schurmann, Franz. Ideology and Organization in Communist China. Berkeley: University of California Press, 1966.

Snow, E. The Other Side of the River. London: Victor Gollancz, 1963.

Sobin, Julian M. Bilateral Breakthrough: Discovering the New People's Republic of China. New York: Praeger, 1974.

Stahnke, Arthur A. China's Trade with the West: A Political and Economic Analysis. New York: Praeger, 1972.

Stover, Leon E. The Cultural Ecology of Chinese Civilization. New York: Pica Press, 1974.

Sullivan, Michael. The Arts of China. Rev. ed. Berkeley: University of California Press, 1979.

Szczepanik, E. F., ed. Symposium on Economic and Social Problems of the Far East. London: Oxford University Press, 1964.

Szuprowicz, Bohdan O., and Maria R. Szuprowicz. Doing Business with the People's Republic of China: Industries and Markets. New York: John Wiley & Sons, 1979.

Ten Great Years: Statistics of the Economic and Cultural Achievements of the People's Republic of China. Peking: Foreign Languages Press, 1960.

Theroux, Eugene A. "China's Standard Form Contracts and Related Legal Issues in U.S.-China Trade." In Standard Form Contract of the People's Republic of China. Special report no. 13. Washington, D.C.: National Council for U.S.-China Trade, June 1975.

Whitson, William W. Doing Business with China: American Trade Opportunities in the 1970's. New York: Praeger, 1974.

Wu, Yuan-li. An Economic Survey of Communist China. New York: Bookman Associates, 1956.

Young, Kenneth T. Negotiating with the Chinese Communists—The United States Experience, 1953-1967. New York: McGraw-Hill, 1968.

Zartman, I. William. The Negotiation Process: Theories and Application. Beverly Hills, Calif.: Sage, 1978.

NEWSPAPERS AND PERIODICALS

Aaron, Bob. "Business Pace Quickens, Problems Remain." Washington Report, March 3, 1980.

Abboud, A. Robert. "China: Market and Source of Truly Staggering Potential." Financier, August 1979.

"Aging of Leadership Is Worrying Peking." New York Times, November 26, 1979.

"Alas! The Chinese Market." Asiamail, vol. 3 (August 1979).

Alford, William P. "Law and Chinese Foreign Trade." Problems of Communism, vol. 28 (September-December 1979).

"America Shops Canton Trade Fair." Washington Post, April 17, 1979.

Arenson, Kathy. "Bank Links with China Upgraded." New York Times, January 24, 1979.

"Asarco Sells Chinese $6 Million in Copper." New York Times, March 14, 1979.

Atlas, Terry. "Capitalistic Look at Chinese Bank." Chicago Tribune, April 15, 1979.

Babcock, William A. "China's Hunger for Know-How." Christian Science Monitor, November 7, 1978.

"Bank of China Given Its Own Identity Abroad." Christian Science Monitor, March 11, 1980.

"Bank of China Planning to Set Up Office Here." Journal of Commerce, July 16, 1979.

Barnett, Robert W. "China and Taiwan: The Economic Issues." Foreign Affairs, April 1972.

Bayar, Charles. "China's Frozen Assets in the U.S., Their Present Status and Future Disposition." U.S.-China Business Review, September-October 1975.

"Bell Helicopter Lifts Off." China Business Review, November-December 1979.

Berney, Karen A. "Dual-Use Technology Sales." China Business Review, July-August 1980.

_____. "U.S. Frees More Support Equipment for Sale to China." China Business Review, March-April 1980.

"Bethlehem Steel Gets Chinese Mining Job Topping $100 Million for Iron-Ore Work." Wall Street Journal, December 5, 1978.

"Big Loans for a Big Spender." Economist, February 17, 1979.

Boone, William. "The Foreign Trade of China." China Quarterly, Autumn 1975.

Bourne, Eric. "China Offers Oil for Technology." Christian Science Monitor, September 6, 1978.

"Browsing for Goods from the Land of Mao." New York Times, May 27, 1973.

Brunner, James A., and George Taoka. "Marketing Opportunities and Negotiating in the People's Republic of China." Baylor Business Studies, Fall-Winter 1977. Perceptions of American businessmen who attended the 1975 Canton Fair.

Buxbaum, David C. "American Trade with the People's Republic of China: Some Preliminary Perspectives." Columbia Journal of Transnational Law, vol. 12 (1973).

_____. "Trade Agreement Facilitates Joint Ventures." Legal Times of Washington, vol. 2 (August 6, 1979).

Campbell, Charles Soutter. "Special Business Interest and the Open Door Policy." Far Eastern Quarterly, November 1941.

"Canton Fair Last of Kind?" Journal of Commerce, May 19, 1980.

"Canton's Autumn Trade Rite." Business China, October 17, 1979.

"Carter Blocks Sale of Computer." Washington Post, June 13, 1977.

Casey, William R. "China Trade Will Grow, but Quantum Jumps Are a Pipe Dream." Dun's Review, vol. 114 (October 1979).

"Cashing in on the China Trade." Dun's Review, November 1978.

"CDC Gets the Green Light: Export Controls." U.S.-China Business Review, November-December 1976.

Charkin, Wallace. "The China Trade: An Unfulfilled Promise." Columbia Journal of World Business, vol. 8 (Spring 1973).

"Chase Signs Agreement with China." Journal of Commerce, April 2, 1979.

"China." China, Hong Kong, North Korea (Economist Intelligence Unit), 3d Quarter 1978.

"China." China, Hong Kong, North Korea (Economist Intelligence Unit), 2d Quarter 1978.

"China." China, Hong Kong, North Korea (Economist Intelligence Unit), 2d Quarter 1977.

"China." Economic Review, annual supplement 1976.

"China." Economist, December 31, 1977.

"China: An Awesome Effort to Industrialize." Business Week, May 29, 1978.

"China Apparently Turning to American Know-How." Washington Post, November 11, 1978.

"China Buy Signals New Markets." Aviation Week and Space Technology, September 18, 1972.

"China Cites New Policy on Growth." New York Times, May 7, 1979.

"A China Connection for U.S. Companies." New York Times, February 26, 1978.

"China Goes West for Steel Mill." Business Week, March 26, 1966.

"China in the 1980's." Economist, December 29, 1979.

"China Is Establishing Two Key Commissions for Joint Ventures." Wall Street Journal, August 1, 1979.

"China Links Imports to Export Sales." Christian Science Monitor, July 26, 1979.

"China Marks New Policy with Joint Venture Law to Encourage Investments." Business America, vol. 2 (August 27, 1979).

"China May Issue Bonds to Overseas Buyers." Wall Street Journal, December 13, 1979.

"China Most Favored Nation Status." Congressional Quarterly Weekly, vol. 37 (December 15, 1979).

"China Nears Approval of Joint Ventures Including Hotel Backed by U.S. Investors." Wall Street Journal, December 13, 1979.

"China: Over 900 Million Customers." Economist, October 14, 1978.

"China Partly Opens the Door to U.S. Business." Fortune, vol. 80 (August 1972).

"China Reassessing Its Liberalization Drive." New York Times, April 23, 1979.

"China Recognizes Form 629: Permits Monitoring of Sensitive Equipment." China Business Review, July-August 1979.

"China Releases Figures Indicating Budget Deficit." New York Times, June 22, 1979.

"China Reveres but Revises the Teaching of Chairman Mao." Washington Post, September 12, 1978.

"China Seems to Eye Global Tourist Traffic with Its Purchase of 10 Boeing Transports." Wall Street Journal, September 13, 1972.

"China Seen Facing Bar to Growth." New York Times, January 29, 1979.

"China 10 Years Behind in Computers, U.S. Professor Says." Electronic News, January 21, 1980.

"China: The Trade Wall Is Coming Down but Not as Fast as Expected." Banking Journal, July 1979.

"The China Trade: A Note of Caution." Forbes, vol. 123 (February 5, 1979).

"China Trade: A Special Report." London Times, March 21, 1973.

"China Trade Means Wealth but It Won't Come Easily." Chicago Tribune, September 20, 1979.

"China Trade to Mushroom, Blumenthal Says." Washington Post, December 21, 1978.

"China's Borrowing Signals Commitment to Imports in Modernizing Economy." Business China, May 30, 1979.

"China's Foreign Trade Structure." U.S.-China Business Review, September-October 1976.

"China's Good Credit Entices Foreign Bankers." Christian Science Monitor, March 28, 1979.

"China's Great Leap Sideways." Economist, November 5, 1977.

"China's Modernization Said to Cause 1978 Deficit." New York Times, June 15, 1979.

"China's New Priorities for Technology Development." China Business Review, May-June 1978.

"China's Oil: Peking Turns to West for Its Technology." Washington Post, August 18, 1978.

"China's Shopping Spree." Time, December 24, 1972.

"China's Slow Turn toward a Free-Market System." Business Week, May 19, 1980.

"China's State Economic Commission." China Business Review, July-August 1979.

"Chinese Law: At the Crossroads." China Quarterly, January-March 1973.

"A Chinese Millionaire Leads Peking's Search for Foreign Investors." Wall Street Journal, November 14, 1979.

"The Chinese Morsel." New York Times, January 21, 1980.

"Chinese Shortage of Capital Called Big." New York Times, January 23, 1979.

"Chinese Shuffle Trade Policies to Accommodate U.S." Washington Post, December 24, 1978.

"Chinese Trade Pact Is Sent to Congress." New York Times, October 24, 1979.

Chou, C. Y. "How to Sell to the People's Republic of China." Journal of Commerce, August 31, 1979.

Chou, S. H. "The Pattern of China's Trade." Current History, vol. 77 (September 1978).

Chung, Chu-e. "An Acute Struggle to Smash the Capitalist Road." Chinese Economic Studies, Fall 1971.

Clarke, William W. "China's Steel, The Key Link." U.S.-China Business Review, July-August 1975.

"Coca-Cola Scores Its Own Breakthrough, Signing Agreement to Sell Coke in China." Wall Street Journal, December 20, 1978.

"Coca-Cola's Back in China Just in Time for New Year's Party." Los Angeles Times, January 24, 1979.

Cohen, Jerome A. "Chinese Law and Sino-American Trade." Harvard Law School Studies in Chinese Law, vol. 15 (1971).

"Coke Adds Life in China Too: Agreement Called 'First Step.'" Atlanta Constitution, December 20, 1978.

"Computing in China: A Travel Report." Science, vol. 182 (October 12, 1973).

"Confusion and Changes Mark Opening of Semi-Annual Canton Fair." Business China, April 25, 1979.

"Contracts in China Revisited." China Quarterly, vol. 28 (1966).

"Control Data Sales to Soviets and China Clear White House." Wall Street Journal, November 1, 1976.

Cookson, David. "In Negotiating with the Chinese There's No Magic Formula." China Business Review, March-April 1977.

"Counsel from an Old China Hand." Fortune, March 26, 1979.

"The Customer Is Suddenly Right." Economist, September 9, 1978.

Davidson, Frederick S. "U.S. Control of Exports to the PRC." Contemporary China, Fall 1979.

de Keijzer, Arne. "Business Catches China Fever." Saturday Review, vol. 6 (March 17, 1979).

Dellin, John. "China Poised for Economic Leap." Christian Science Monitor, November 29, 1978.

Demaree, Allant. "The Old China Hands Who Know How to Live with the New Asia." Fortune, vol. 84 (November 1971).

Denny, David L. "Recent Developments in the International Financial Policies of the People's Republic of China." Stanford Journal of International Studies, vol. 10 (Spring 1975).

Denny, David L., and Daniel Stein. "Recent Developments in Trade between the U.S. and the P.R.C.: A Legal Economic Perspective." Law and Contemporary Problems, vol. 38 (Summer-Autumn 1973).

Denny, David L., and Frederic M. Suris. "China's Foreign Financial Liabilities." U.S.-China Business Review, January-February 1975.

Dingle, J. "Technical Selling in China." Quoted in Stanley Lubman, "Trade between United States and the People's Republic of China: Practice, Policy and Law." Law and Policy in International Business, vol. 8 (1976).

Dohmen, Holger. "China's Foreign Trade Policy." Intereconomics, July 1976.

"Doing Business with China." Aviation Week and Space Technology, October 6, 1975.

"Doing Business with China." Wall Street Journal, August 31, 1979.

"Doing Business with Peking." New York Times, May 30, 1979.

Donnithorne, Audrey. "China as a Trading Nation." China Survey, vol. 10 (February 7, 1972).

"Dramatic Developments in China Portend Vast Opportunities in 1979." Business China, December 27, 1978.

Dreyer, H. Peter. "China Dickering over Pacts Takes Time." Journal of Commerce, May 9, 1979.

_____. "Innumerable Deals Arranged in Canton." Journal of Commerce, May 9, 1979.

Eckstein, Alexander. "China's Trade Policy and Sino-American Relations." Foreign Affairs, vol. 57 (October 1975).

Egan, Jack. "U.S. Banks Scrambling for China Loan Business." Washington Post, November 17, 1978.

"End-User Corporations Emerge in China." Asian Wall Street Journal, June 25, 1979.

"Energy: A Bottleneck in China's Industrial Drive." Business Week, May 19, 1980.

"Entering the China Market." Business America, vol. 2 (February 26, 1979).

"Excerpts from a Speech Mondale Made in Peking." New York Times, August 28, 1979.

"Export Control: U.S. Frees More Support Equipment to the PRC." China Business Review, March-April 1980.

"Export Trade with China." China Business Review, January-February 1979.

"Exporting to China: Two Examples of Timing." U.S.-China Business Review, July-August 1974.

"Faster Process Ahead for China Sales?" China Business Review, July-August 1979.

Field, Robert Michael. "A Slowdown in Chinese Industry." China Quarterly, December 1979.

"First Clues Point to China's View of Coming Joint Ventures." Business China, January 24, 1979.

Fisher, Ann. "U.S. Firms, Trademarks and China." U.S.-China Business Review, May-June 1974.

"Foreign Partners in Ventures with China Offered Package of Incentives, Protection." Wall Street Journal, July 9, 1979.

"Foreign Trade Statistics." Chinese Economic Studies, Summer 1970.

Forger, Gary. "Selling to China." Plastic World, October 1978.

"Forget about the Rabbit Routine." Forbes, vol. 109 (January 15, 1972.)

Francis, David. "To Start Oil Flowing to United States China Picks a Friend." Christian Science Monitor, November 24, 1978.

Freud, Andreas. "French Get Trade Pact with China." New York Times, December 5, 1978.

"A Friend in Need." Economist, August 19, 1978.

Fry, Richard. "China's Financing Prospects." Banker, vol. 124 (December 1974).

"FTC Branches and End Users May Now Sign Contracts Directly." China Business Review, November-December 1978.

Garner, Harvey. "Computing in China, 1978." Computer, March 1979.

Gayle, Andrew M. "Law and Lawyers in China." American Bar Association Journal, vol. 64 (March 1978).

"The Geologic of China's Oil." Economist, March 3, 1979.

"Geometrics, Reaching Chinese End Users." U.S.-China Business Review, September-October 1975.

"Getting a Hotel Room in China: You're Nothing without a Unit." New York Times, October 31, 1979.

Gibson, W. David. "China's Door Is Open but It Takes Time to Get In." Chemical Week, January 24, 1979.

Goldring, Mary. "Tea at the Bank of China." Euromoney, March 1979.

Green, Stephanie R. "Chinese Technicians in the United States." China Business Review, November-December 1977.

Grossman, Bernard. "International Economic Relations of the People's Republic of China." Asian Studies, September 1970.

Grzybowski, Kazimierz. "Control of U.S. Trade with China: An Overview." Law and Contemporary Problems, Summer-Autumn 1973.

"A Guide to Barter in the China Trade." China Business Review, September-October 1979.

"Guide to Negotiating Contracts with China: Pay Attention to Risks." Business China, November 7, 1979.

Haley, P. Edward, and Harold W. Rood. "China's Major Trading Partner, Japan, Dependent." Stanford Journal of International Studies, vol. 10 (Spring 1975).

"Halter Marine Purchases Chinese Marine Diesel Engine." U.S.-China Business Review, November-December 1976.

Hataye, John. "Find China Plants Years behind West." Electronic News, July 30, 1979.

Henderson, Jay F., Nicholas H. Ludlow, and Eugene A. Theroux. "China and the Trade Act of 1974." U.S.-China Business Review, January-February 1975.

Hishida, Masaharu. "Japan's Experience in Technical Exchange with China." China Newsletter, vol. 24 (December 1979).

Hoffmann, Charles. "The Maoist Economic Model." Economic Issues, vol. 5 (September 1971).

"How Boeing Sold 707's to Peking." New York Times, September 18, 1972.

"How Chase Group Scored Peking Victory in Race for Huge Trade Center Contract." Wall Street Journal, April 10, 1979.

"How China Prepares to Buy from Abroad." U.S.-China Business Review, vol. 3 (July-August 1976).

"How China Prepares to Import: Foreign Quotations." China Business Review, January-February 1977.

"How China Views Claims and Arbitration in Foreign Trade." U.S.-China Business Review, September-October 1975.

"How China Views Importing: Preparatory Work Prior to Trade."
U.S.-China Business Review, January-February 1976.

"How China Views Terms for Delivery of Goods in Foreign Trade."
U.S.-China Business Review, November-December 1975.

"How China Views Trademarks in Foreign Trade." U.S.-China Business Review, May-June 1975.

"How Kaiser Engineers Found a Formula in China." China Business Review, November-December 1979.

"How Much Can China Export?" Economist, March 3, 1979.

"How Peking Shops for Machine Tools." U.S.-China Business Review, vol. 3 (July-August 1976).

"How RCA Got Offer to Build a TV Plant in China." Christian Science Monitor, October 25, 1978.

"How Rolligon Sold Petroleum Equipment to the PRC." China Business Review, November-December 1977.

"How to Dicker with the Chinese." Time, February 19, 1979.

"How to Open a Bank Account in China." U.S.-China Business Review, May-June 1974.

"How to Start Trading with China." Plastics World, October 1978.

"How to Succeed in Business with China? U.S. Firms Find Friendship Is the Key." Asian Wall Street Journal, April 9, 1980.

"How Wabco Sold to China." U.S.-China Business Review, July-August 1975.

Hsia, Tao-tai, and Kathryn A. Haun. "Laws of the People's Republic of China on Industrial and Intellectual Property." Law and Contemporary Problems, vol. 38 (Summer-Autumn 1973).

Hsiao, Gene T. "Communist China's Foreign Trade Contracts and Means of Settling Disputes." Vanderbilt Law Review, vol. 20 (March 1967).

_____. "Communist China's Foreign Trade Organizations." Vanderbilt Law Review, vol. 20 (March 1967).

_____. "Communist China's Trade Treaties and Agreements (1949–1964)." Vanderbilt Law Review, vol. 21 (October 1968).

_____. "The Organization of China's Foreign Trade." U.S.-China Business Review, May–June 1974.

"IBM Gets Computer Order from China: Approvals Are Needed in Landmark Sale." Wall Street Journal, May 26, 1978.

Immel, Richard. "Sino-U.S. Thaw Means an Increase in Business for California Lawyer." Wall Street Journal, February 14, 1979.

"Impasse in China's Bid for Joint Ventures Is Attributed to Gaps in Its Legal Structure." Wall Street Journal, February 29, 1980.

"Improving the Chinese Side." China Business Review, January–February 1978.

"In Search of Roots." East-West Markets, July 24, 1978.

"Initial Approaches of U.S. Companies Selling to China." U.S.-China Business Review, July–August 1975.

"The Institution of Contracts in the Chinese People's Republic." China Quarterly, vol. 14 (April–June 1963).

"Japan Firm to Assemble Its Computers in China." Wall Street Journal, February 6, 1980.

"Japan Would Like to Help, but . . . ." New York Times, April 29, 1979.

"Joint Venture Law in China Analyzed." Journal of Commerce, July 23, 1979.

"Julian, Come Back." Petroleum News Southeast Asia, December 1978.

"Kaiser Engineers Win in China." Business Week, October 16, 1978.

Katz, Robert N. "The Canton Trade Fair 1976, Implications for U.S.-China Trade." California Management Review, vol. 19 (Fall 1976).

" 'Keep Your Cool,' U.S. Firms Doing Work in China Told." Wall
Street Journal, March 28, 1979.

Kraar, Louis. "China: Trying the Market Way." Fortune, December 31, 1979.

_____. "China's Narrow Door to the West." Fortune, March 26,
1979.

_____. "I Have Seen China—And They Work." Fortune, vol. 86 (Au-
gust 1972).

Kramer, Barry. "China's Decision to Open Up Its Economy to Outsiders Is Starting to Produce Gains." Wall Street Journal,
January 14, 1980.

_____. "In a Policy About-Face, China Seeks Help from Foreigners
in Search for Inland Oil." Wall Street Journal, February 22,
1980.

Kulkarni, V. G. "Chinese on Spree in West." Christian Science
Monitor, August 18, 1978.

Landeau, Jean-François. "Do the Chinese Have an International Marketing Strategy?" U.S.-China Business Review, vol. 2 (May-
June 1975).

Lee, Luke T., and John B. McCobb, Jr. "United States Trade Em-
bargo on China, 1949-1970: Legal Status and Future Prospects."
New York University Journal of International Law and Politics,
Spring 1971.

Lee, Luke T., and Whalen W. Lai. "The Chinese Conception of Law:
Confucian, Legalist and Buddhist." Hastings Law Journal,
vol. 29 (July 1978).

Lewis, Christopher. "A Downward Trend in Canton's Appeal." Far
Eastern Economic Review, vol. 84 (June 10, 1974).

_____. "An End to the Bargain Price Days." Far Eastern Economic
Review, vol. 86 (October 4, 1974).

Lewis, David. "Japan and the West, Sharing the China Market."
New Leader, June 4, 1974.

Leys, Simon. "China's Opening Door Policy." New York Times, January 3, 1979.

Li, Victor H. "Legal Aspects of Trade with Communist China." Columbia Journal of Transnational Law, vol. 3 (1964).

_____. "Ups and Downs of Trading with China." Columbia Journal of Transnational Law, vol. 13 (1975).

Lieberthal, Kenneth. "China: The Politics behind the New Economics." Fortune, December 31, 1979.

"Likely Meaning, Outcome of China's Suspension of Contracts, Slower Buying." Business China, March 7, 1979.

Liu, Melinda. "Rock-Bottom Terms Are a Must for Foreigners." Far Eastern Economic Review, September 21, 1979.

Livezey, Emile. "China Trade: The Thread That Linked the World." Christian Science Monitor, April 3, 1979.

Lubman, Stanley. "The Canton Fair Still Plays a Big Role." Boston Sunday Globe, October 28, 1979.

_____. "On Understanding Chinese Law and Legal Institutions." American Bar Association Journal, vol. 62 (May 1976).

_____. "Trade between the United States and the People's Republic of China: Practice, Policy and Law." Law and Policy in International Business, vol. 8 (1976).

_____. "What to Expect at the Canton Fair." Wall Street Journal, April 28, 1972.

McClenahen, John S., and William H. Miller. "Tackling the China Challenge." Industry Week, vol. 201 (May 28, 1979).

McCobb, J. B., Jr. "Foreign Trade Arbitration in the People's Republic of China." New York University Journal of International Law and Politics, vol. 5 (Summer 1972).

"Making a Decision on 'Purchase of Foreign Technology.'" China Business Review, May-June 1978.

"Man of the Year." Time, January 1, 1979.

Markus, S. "Marcus Polo at China Trade Fair: Adventures of a
Dallas Executive in Canton." New York Times, June 4, 1972.

Matthews, Jay. "China Planning Sharp Slowdown in Modernization."
Washington Post, May 3, 1979.

Middleton, Drew. "Military Gains for China Seen in U.S. Ties."
New York Times, December 18, 1978.

Ministry of Foreign Trade. Foreign Trade Practice. Rev. ed.
Shanghai: Institute of Foreign Trade, 1972. As translated in
U.S.-China Business Review, January-February 1976.

"Money and Credit in China." Chinese Economic Monthly, August
1924.

"More Dealing with Chinese." New York Times, January 7, 1978.

Moritz, Frederick A. "China: Canton Fair Improves Its Appeal to
Buyers." Christian Science Monitor, March 28, 1979.

Nambeil, Ira. "Trade Missions to China Not the Best Way to Go."
Journal of Commerce, May 2, 1974.

National Council for U.S.-China Trade. "New Reference Tells How
to Sell Technology to China." China Trade News, December
17, 1979. A news release.

"Negotiating the Sale of Mining Equipment in Peking." U.S.-China
Business Review, November-December 1974.

"Negotiating with the Chinese?" Worldwide Projects, December
1978-January 1979.

Nehemkis, Peter, and Hans Schoolhammer. "International Business
Transactions with the Soviet Union and Mainland China: Prospects and Hazards." Business Lawyer, November 1972.

"New Acting Head of Chinese Government." New York Times, April
25, 1980.

"New Opportunities Emerge as China Reshuffles Priorities." Business China, April 4, 1979.

"Nine New Guidelines Tell How China May Buy Technology in Future." Business China, July 3, 1979.

"Nixon's Boeing Move." Far Eastern Economic Review, July 15, 1972.

"Obstacles Seen to U.S.-China Trade." Journal of Commerce, May 18, 1979.

"Oiling the Doors." Economist, August 19, 1978.

Oksenberg, Michael. "Communications within the Chinese Bureaucracy." China in the Seventies, vol. 87 (1973).

"Opening a Traveler's Letter of Credit with the Bank of China." U.S.-China Business Review, May-June 1975.

"Over 100,000 Visitors Converge on Canton as Trade Fair Begins." Wall Street Journal, April 20, 1979.

Palay, Marc. "Legal Aspects of China's Foreign Trade Practices and Procedures." Journal of International Law and Economics, vol. 12 (1977).

"Patience Prescribed in Selling to China." New York Times, May 16, 1979.

Pattison, Joseph E. "A Transactional Guide to China Trade." Practical Lawyer, vol. 25 (October 15, 1979).

"Payment Pact Set, U.S. and China Near a Trade Agreement." New York Times, May 11, 1979.

"Peking Invests in Overseas Banking." Christian Science Monitor, July 25, 1979.

"Peking Issues Rules to Lure Investment." New York Times, July 9, 1979.

"Peking OKs U.S. Computer Show." Electronic News, June 11, 1973.

Perkins, Dwight H. "To Where a China Market?" Foreign Policy, vol. 5 (Winter 1971/72).

"Pfizer Will Sell Scanners to China." New York Times, March 14, 1979.

Phillips, Christopher. "Breakthroughs in U.S.-China Business Relations." Columbia Journal of World Business, December 1973.

"The PRC's Agencies in Hong Kong." U.S.-China Business Review, September-October 1975.

"The PRC's Investment Control and Import-Export Commissions." China Business Review, March-April 1980.

"Product Advertising Offers Foreign Firms New Access to China Market." Business China, March 7, 1979.

Randt, Clark T., Jr. "Trademark Law in the PRC: Case Fables with Morals for Western Traders." U.S.-China Business Review, May-June 1975.

"Rapid Withdrawal from Vietnam Is Key to PRC Business Outlook." Business China, February 21, 1979.

Redick, Charles F. "Recent Changes in United States Trade Regulations Affecting the People's Republic of China: A Market Recontrolled." Virginia Journal of International Law, vol. 13 (1972).

Reghizzi, Gabriele. "Legal Aspects of Trade with China: The Italian Experience." Harvard International Law Journal, vol. 9 (Winter 1968).

"Remarks by Yuan Bachua, Vice Minister, S.E.C., in June 1979 to National Council for U.S.-China Trade's Board of Directors' Delegation to China." China Business Review, July-August 1979.

"Roadblocks to China Trade." Journal of Commerce, August 13, 1979.

"Rong Yiren: The Man to See about Joint Ventures." China Business Review, September-October 1979.

Rosenbaum, Michael. "Joint Venture Law in China Will Allow Removal of Profits." Journal of Commerce, October 29, 1979.

Rosenbloom, Joseph. "China's Boston Man." Boston Sunday Globe, December 10, 1978.

Ross-Skinner, Jean. "Can We Do Business with China?" Dun's Review, June 1971.

"Scaled Down Scope of China Imports in Study." New York Times, March 9, 1979.

Schneider, Hans. "The China Hand's China Hand." U.S.-China Business Review, September-October 1974.

"The Scramble to Exploit China's Oil Reserves." Business Week, October 30, 1978.

"The Scrutable Logic of Dining Out in Peking." New York Times, December 19, 1979.

"Selling a System, How International Harvester Found Need in China." China Business Review, March-April 1978.

Sheng, Richard. "Outsiders' Perception of the Chinese." Columbia Journal of World Business, Summer 1979.

Silk, Leonard. "How Japan Sees Chinese Market." New York Times, May 18, 1979.

"Sino-U.S. Thaw Means an Increase in Business for California Lawyer." Wall Street Journal, February 14, 1979.

Smith, Alan H. "Standard Form Contracts in the International Commercial Transactions with the People's Republic of China." International and Comparative Law Quarterly, vol. 21 (January 1972).

Snow, Lois Wheeler. "China's Foreign Trade and Aid." Journal of World Trade Law, March-April 1977.

Sobin, Julian. "The Coming Leap Forward in China Trade." Nation's Business, July 1977.

_____. "Good Health, the First Chinese Mark Registered in the U.S." U.S.-China Business Review, November-December 1975.

_____. "Pilgrimage to the Canton Fair." Columbia Journal of World Business, November-December 1972.

"Soviet and American Negotiators Similar in Style Despite Contrasts." New York Times, August 27, 1979.

"Soviets Seek to Improve Ties to China." Washington Post, April 8, 1980.

"Spares Take a Little Longer, How Rolligon Sold Petroleum Equip-
    ment to the PRC." China Business Review, November–Decem-
    ber 1977.

Speedhar, L. "Modernization of China's Armed Forces: The Eco-
    nomic Factors." Institute for Defense Studies and Analyses
    Journal, vol. 10 (January–March 1978).

Stark, Steven R. "An Analysis of the Foreign Trade Practices of the
    People's Republic of China, Including Comments on the Cana-
    dian Experience." University of British Columbia Law Review,
    vol. 5 (1970).

Starr, R. "Developing Trade with China." Virginia Journal of Inter-
    national Law, vol. 13 (Fall 1972).

"A Starting Point for Deals with China." Business Week, March 31,
    1973.

"Steel and Jasmine Tea." Fortune, vol. 73 (June 1966).

Stevens, William K. "U.S. to Get Low–Sulfur Chinese Oil." New
    York Times, November 22, 1978.

Stout, Richard. "Global Events Tend to Strengthen U.S.–China Ties."
    Christian Science Monitor, January 8, 1980.

Strauss, Paul. "Special Skills Needed to Deal with Chinese." Jour-
    nal of Commerce, May 14, 1978.

Sun, Y. T. "Cosmopolitan Shanghai." Coca-Cola Overseas, March
    1949.

Surrey, Walter S., and Stephen M. Soble. "Chinese Removing Joint
    Venture Investment Barriers." Legal Times of Washington,
    vol. 2 (October 22, 1979).

Sutherland, Daniel, and John Cooley. "U.S. Technology for Sale to
    China." Christian Science Monitor, December 28, 1979.

Szuprowicz, Bohdan O. "CDC's China Sale Soon Focusing Western
    Attention." Computerworld, November 6, 1976.

_____. "China's Computer Industry." Datamation, vol. 21 (June
    1975).

_____. "Chinese Developing Homegrown Computer Industry." Computerworld, July 28, 1971.

_____. "Computers in Mao's China." New Scientist, vol. 65 (March 15, 1975).

_____. "Electronics in China." U.S.-China Business Review, May-June 1976.

_____. "The Sino-Comecon Connection." Contemporary China, vol. 2 (Fall 1978).

"The Taiwan-Peking Game, like Chinese Chess, Is Subtle." New York Times, January 11, 1979.

"Techniques and Tools for Dealing with China: A BI Checklist." Business International, March 30, 1979.

Theroux, Eugene A. "Legal Resources for Trade with China." U.S.-China Business Review, January-February 1976.

"Things in China Go Better with Coke." Atlanta Journal, December 19, 1978.

"Third Country Banks in the U.S. through Which Trade with China Can Be Transacted." U.S.-China Business Review, January-February 1974.

Timberlake, Percy. "China as a Trading Nation." World Development, vol. 3 (July-August 1975).

Torbert, Preston M. "The American Lawyer's Role in Trade with China." American Bar Association Journal, vol. 63 (August 1977).

"Trade: A Guide to Barter in the China Trade." China Business Review, September-October 1979.

"Trade with China." Law and Contemporary Problems, vol. 68 (Summer-Autumn 1973).

"Trading with China." Christian Science Monitor, November 12, 1978.

"Transactions with the Soviet Union and Mainland China." Business Lawyer, November 1972.

Tsuchiya, Masaya. "Recent Developments in Sino-Japanese Trade." Law and Contemporary Problems, vol. 38 (Summer-Autumn 1973).

Tsurumi, Yoshi. "Your Check List for an Approach to China." Columbia Journal of World Business, Summer 1979.

Tuthill, Mary. "China: Open for Business?" Nation's Business, vol. 67 (February 1979).

"Two Most Favored Nations?" Economist, March 10, 1979.

"The Uncontrollable Stateless Money." Far Eastern Economic Review, September 21, 1979.

"United States Study Sees Trade Increase with Pragmatic Post-Mao China." New York Times, August 11, 1977.

"An Unticd, Cautious Borrower Be." Economist, April 7, 1979.

"An Unusual Deal Is Set by China." New York Times, December 8, 1979.

"Unwritten Code of Chinese Commercial Law." Chinese Economic Monthly, vol. 2 (June 1925).

"U.S. Agrees to Sell China a Computer with Defense Uses." New York Times, October 29, 1976.

"U.S.-China Trade and the Law." China Trade Report, vol. 17 (May 1979).

"U.S.-China Trade Pact Is Initiated." New York Times, May 15, 1979.

"U.S. Companies Still Have a Good Chance to Help Rebuild China." Business Week, May 19, 1980.

U.S. Firms Are Given Key to China Trade: It's Called Friendship." Wall Street Journal, April 4, 1980.

"U.S. Technicians in China: The Pullman Kellogg Story." U.S.-China Business Review, September-October 1976.

"U.S. Willing to Sell China Copters, Transport Planes." Washington Post, March 19, 1980.

"USDA and FDA Regulations and China." U.S.-China Business Review, March-April 1974.

Van Slambrouck, Paul. "Trading with China: As Awkward as Chopsticks." Christian Science Monitor, September 12, 1978.

Vanik, Charles A. "Prospects for Approving a Trade Agreement and Granting Most Favored Nation Status to the People's Republic of China." Case Western Reserve Journal of International Law, vol. 11 (Spring 1979).

Wain, Barry. "A Hard Bargainer." Far Eastern Economic Review, vol. 77 (September 30, 1972).

"Walter Surrey's Remarks to Deng Xiaoping." China Business Review, July-August 1979.

Wang, Kenneth. "Foreign Trade Policy and Apparatus of the People's Republic of China." Law and Contemporary Problems, vol. 38 (Summer-Autumn 1973).

Wang, Yao-ting. "China's Foreign Trade." Peking Review, vol. 17 (October 11, 1974).

Weiss, Udo. "China's Aid to and Trade with the Developing Countries of the Third World." Asian Quarterly, vol. 3 (1974).

_____. "China's Aid to and Trade with the Developing Countries of the Third World." Asian Quarterly, vol. 4 (1974).

_____. "Imperial China's Tributary Trade and the Foreign Trade Policy of the People's Republic of China: A Comparison of Attitudes." Asian Quarterly, 1976.

"Why China May Be Next." Forbes, vol. 110 (December 1, 1972).

"Why Peking Whets European Appetities." Business Week, January 10, 1970.

"Wide Variety of U.S. Firms Now in Search for China Connection." Business America, March 26, 1979.

Wilson, Dick. "The Bank of China's Expanding Role in International France." U.S.-China Business Review, November-December 1974.

_____. "How Banks Work in China." Banker, vol. 130 (January 1980).

Winder, Sally. "Exclusive from the PRC." China Business Review, November–December 1977.

Witkin, Richard. "3-Jet Order from China." New York Times, December 20, 1978.

Wolfgang, Ernst. "The Foreign Trade Policy of the Mao Tse-tung Clique." Chinese Economic Studies, Fall 1969.

Wong, William. "Chinese-Americans Help U.S. Employers Bridge the Language Gap in China Trade." Wall Street Journal, July 3, 1979.

Wrightman, Alistair. "Dispute Settlement, Japan's Experience with Imports from China." China Business Review, March–April 1978.

_____. "Financing China's Steel Imports from Japan." U.S.-China Business Review, September–October 1975.

_____. "How Japan Finances Trade with China." U.S.-China Business Review, March–April 1975.

Yu, George T. "The Great China Trade Fever." Illinois Business Review, vol. 36 (March 1979).

PUBLIC DOCUMENTS

Presidential Papers. "Agreement on Trade Relations between the United States of America and the People's Republic of China." Proclamation 4697, October 23, 1979. Federal Register, vol. 44, no. 207 (1979).

U.S., Central Intelligence Agency. China: International Trade, 1976-77. Research paper. Washington, D.C.: National Foreign Assessment Center, November 1977.

_____. China: Post-Mao Search for Civilian Industrial Technology. Research paper. Washington, D.C.: National Foreign Assessment Center, February 1979.

_____. China's Economy. Research paper. Washington, D.C.: National Foreign Assessment Center, November 1977.

_____. The Computer Industry in the People's Republic of China. Washington, D.C.: National Foreign Assessment Center, 1973.

_____. Directory of Officials of the People's Republic of China. Washington, D.C.: National Foreign Assessment Center, November 1978.

_____. People's Republic of China: Atlas. Washington, D.C.: Government Printing Office, 1971.

_____. People's Republic of China: International Trade Handbook. Washington, D.C.: Central Intelligence Agency, October 1976.

U.S., Code. 63 Statute 7 (1949), as amended 50, app. secs. 2021-32 (1964).

U.S., Comptroller General. Administration of U.S. Export Licensing Should Be Consolidated to Be More Responsive to Industry. ID 78-60. Washington, D.C.: General Accounting Office, October 1978.

_____. Export Controls: Need to Clarify Policy and Simplify Administration. ID 79-16. Washington, D.C.: General Accounting Office, March 1, 1979.

U.S., Congress, House. Concurrent Resolution 204, 96th Cong., 20th sess., January 24, 1980.

_____. "Export Administration Act Amendments of 1979." Congressional Record, March 1, 1979.

_____. "Export Administration Act of 1979." Public Law 96-72. Congressional Record, September 29, 1979.

U.S., Congress, House. Special Study Mission to South Korea, Japan, and the People's Republic of China, March 31-April 12, 1980, 96th Cong., 2d sess., September 1980.

U.S., Congress, House, Committee on Commerce and International Relations, Subcommittee on International Trade and Commerce. Export Licensing of Advanced Technology: A Review, 94th Cong., 2d sess., 1976.

U.S., Congress, House, Committee on International Relations. Export Licensing: COCOM List Review Proposals of the United States, 95th Cong., 2d sess., June 14 and 26, 1978.

U.S., Congress, House, Subcommittee on Domestic and International Scientific Planning, Analysis, and Cooperation of the Committee on Science and Technology. Testimony by Rauer Meyer, director of the Office of Export Administration, U.S. Department of Commerce. Washington, D.C.: Government Printing Office, October 4, 1978.

_____. Science and Technology in the People's Republic of China: Background Study No. 1, 94th Cong., 2d sess., September 1976.

U.S., Congress, Joint Economic Committee. China: A Reassessment of the Economy, 94th Cong., 1st sess., July 10, 1975.

_____. Chinese Economy Post-Mao. Vol. 1, Policy and Performance. Washington, D.C.: Government Printing Office, November 9, 1978.

_____. Economic Profile of Mainland China. New York: Praeger, 1968.

_____. Mainland China in the World Economy, 90th Cong., 1st sess., April 1967.

_____. People's Republic of China: An Economic Assessment. Washington, D.C.: Government Printing Office, 1972.

U.S., Congress, Office of Technology Assessment. Technology and East-West Trade. Washington, D.C.: Government Printing Office, 1979.

U.S., Congress, Senate. "The China Trade," by K. H. J. Clarke. Congressional Record, December 20, 1973.

_____. United States Relations with the People's Republic of China. Washington, D.C.: Government Printing Office, 1971.

U.S., Congress, Senate, Committee on Foreign Relations. China and the United States, Today and Yesterday. Washington, D.C.: Government Printing Office, 1972.

U.S., Department of Commerce. "Basic Data on the Economy of the People's Republic of China." Overseas Business Reports, September 1972.

_____. "China's Foreign Trade Policy: A Current Appraisal." Overseas Business Reports, October 1974.

_____. Doing Business with China. Washington, D.C.: Department of Commerce, March 1979.

_____. Highlights of Exports and Imports. FT-990 Series. Washington, D.C.: Government Printing Office, 1970-80.

_____. "Trading with the People's Republic of China," by George Driscoll and Susan S. Medgyesi-Mitschang. Overseas Business Reports, August 1971.

_____. "Trading with the People's Republic of China 1-2." Overseas Business Reports, March 1973.

U.S., Department of Commerce, Bureau of East-West Trade, Domestic and International Business Administration. The Chinese Economy and Foreign Trade Perspective—1976. Washington, D.C.: Department of Commerce, June 1977.

U.S., Department of Commerce, Industry and Trade Administration. Prospects for PRC Hard Currency Trade through 1985, Prepared by Gary R. Teske, Hedija H. Kravalis, and Allen Lenz. Washington, D.C.: Department of Commerce, February 8, 1979.

U.S., Department of Commerce, Industry and Trade Administration, Office of East-West Country Affairs. China's Economy and Foreign Trade, 1978-79. Washington, D.C.: Department of Commerce, September 1979.

U.S., Department of State. Munitions Control Newsletter, March 1980.

U.S., Department of the Army. China: An Analytical Survey of Literature. Washington, D.C.: Department of the Army, January 1978.

U.S., Export-Import Bank. Eximbank and the World of Exports. Statement of condition, fiscal year 1973. Washington, D.C.: Government Printing Office, 1974.

U.S., General Accounting Office. Administration of U.S. Export Licensing Should Be Consolidated to Be More Responsive to Industry," by the Comptroller General of the United States. Washington, D.C.: General Accounting Office, October 31, 1978.

_____. Export Controls: Need to Clarify Policy and Simplify Administration," by the Comptroller General of the United States. Washington, D.C.: General Accounting Office, March 1, 1979.

U.S., International Trade Commission. Implications for U.S. Trade of Granting Most-Favored-Nation Treatment to the People's Republic of China. Publication 816. Washington, D.C.: International Trade Commission, May 1977.

_____. International Technology Transfer: A Review of Related Legal Issues. Washington, D.C.: International Trade Commission, January 1979.

U.S., Joint Publications Research. "Applications of Electronic Computers to Accounting." China Report—Economic Affairs, no. 7. Washington, D.C.: Foreign Broadcast Information Service, August 14, 1979.

_____. "Foreign Trade: Recent Japan-China Trade Explored," November 1979.

_____. "How to Improve the Economic Effectiveness of Imported Technology and Equipment," by Wang Furang. China Report—Economic Affairs, no. 7. Washington, D.C.: Foreign Broadcast Information Service, August 14, 1979.

_____. No. 73845.

_____. "On Reform of the Foreign Trade Management System," by Zhou Renhuan and Li Younglin. China Report—Economic Affairs, no. 38. Washington, D.C.: Foreign Broadcast Information Service, January 21, 1980.

_____. "The System of Foreign Trade Must Be Reformed," by Zhang Chongwen. China Report—Economic Affairs, no. 49. Washington, D.C.: Foreign Broadcast Information Service, March 21, 1980.

_____. "A Talk Based on Giving Greater Decision-Making Power to Enterprise in Sichuan—A Tentative Discussion of Problems in

Reforming the Economic Management System," by Xiong Fu. Hongqi (Beijing) 16 (August 16, 1980): 21. Translated in PRC Daily Report, September 11, 1980, p. L49.

_____. "The United States Is a Paradise of Democracy," by Jie Jun. JPRS no. 73987. Washington, D.C.: Foreign Broadcast Information Service, August 23, 1979.

U.S., Library of Congress. Export Trading Associations and Companies, by Raymond Ahearn. Issue Brief no. 1B80044. Washington, D.C.: Library of Congress, April 4, 1980.

U.S., Office of the Special Representative for Trade Negotiations. "Most Favored Nation Status for China." Federal Register, January 30, 1980.

"U.S.-China Agreement, Shanghai Communiqué." Los Angeles: U.S.-China People's Friendship Association, May 1975.

UNPUBLISHED MATERIALS

Bowie, David C. "The Electronics and Computer Establishment in the People's Republic of China." Washington, D.C.: Trade Development Assistance Division, Bureau of East West Trade, U.S. Department of Commerce, January 1980.

Brunner, James A. "Frequency Distributions: U.S.-People's Republic of China Trade Survey." Toledo, Ohio: Department of Marketing, University of Toledo, 1975.

Buryn, Walter M. "The Pullman Kellogg Experience." Keynote address, National Council for U.S.-China Trade. Washington, D.C., December 5, 1979.

Campbell, Charles Soutter. "American Business Interests and the Open Door in China." Master's thesis, Yale University, 1938.

Carr, William Keith. "A History of the Development of Anthropology in China." Master's thesis, Columbia University, 1958.

Chinese Foreign Trade Corporation. "Letter to Control Data Corporation." Peking, January 10, 1980.

_____. "Letter to Control Data Corporation." Peking, December 9, 1978.

_____. "Letter to Control Data Corporation." Peking, August 14, 1974.

Cohen, Jerome A., and Jack T. Huang. "China's Joint Venture Law." Paper given at Business International Chief Executive Officers Roundtable, Lake Buena Vista, Fla., January 6-9, 1980.

Control Data Corporation. "CDC Contracts with the People's Republic of China to Date." Minneapolis, September 6, 1973.

_____. "Charter for Embryonic China Office." Minneapolis, September 6, 1973.

_____. "China Task Force—Meeting No. 1—September 24, 1973." Minneapolis, September 6, 1973.

_____. "China Trip Report." Minneapolis, November 18, 1975.

_____. "Chinese Manners." Minneapolis, November 1977.

_____. "Concepts for Consideration . . . in PRC." Background paper, Minneapolis, February 8, 1974.

_____. "Consultation and Sales Agreement between _____ and Control Data Corporation." Minneapolis, October 1971.

_____. "Contract for Complete Equipment for a Large Size Seismic Data Processing Center." Contract no. 78ME-45090F. Minneapolis, December 22, 1978.

_____. "Control Data Export License Application for Dual CDC Cyber 172s Seismic Data Processing Center." Minneapolis, May 29, 1975.

_____. "Fact Sheet on the Computer Visiting Group from the People's Republic of China." Minneapolis, September 26, 1973.

_____. "Interoffice Memorandum." Minneapolis, April 10, 1980.

_____. "Interoffice Memorandum." Minneapolis, April 10, 1979.

_____. "Interoffice Memorandum." Minneapolis, March 26, 1979.

_____. "Interoffice Memorandum." Minneapolis, September 17, 1978.

_____. "Interoffice Memorandum." Minneapolis, May 10, 1976.

_____. "Interoffice Memorandum." Minneapolis, October 15, 1975.

_____. "Interoffice Memorandum." Minneapolis, February 24, 1975.

_____. "Interoffice Memorandum." Minneapolis, April 2, 1974.

_____. "Interoffice Memorandum." Minneapolis, August 28, 1973.

_____. "Interoffice Memorandum." Minneapolis, August 10, 1973.

_____. "Interoffice Memorandum." Minneapolis, May 19, 1973.

_____. "Interoffice Memorandum." Minneapolis, March 29, 1972.

_____. "Interoffice Memorandum—April Export License Status and Forecast." Minneapolis, May 25, 1978.

_____. "Interoffice Memorandum—China Office." Minneapolis, December 7, 1973.

_____. "Interoffice Memorandum—China Task Force Agenda." Minneapolis, March 8, 1974.

_____. "Interoffice Memorandum—China Task Force Meeting No. 3—December 27, 1973." Minneapolis, December 10, 1973.

_____. "Interoffice Memorandum—China Visit." Minneapolis, April 23, 1973.

_____. "Interoffice Memorandum—Chinese Academy of Sciences." Minneapolis, April 10, 1979.

_____. "Interoffice Memorandum—Export License . . ." Minneapolis, February 8, 1974.

_____. "Interoffice Memorandum—Future Sales to People's Republic of China." Minneapolis, November 8, 1977.

_____. "Interoffice Memorandum—Joint Contract with CGG in China." Minneapolis, September 13, 1974.

_____. "Interoffice Memorandum—Joint Venture Data Center." Minneapolis, January 9, 1980.

_____. "Interoffice Memorandum—Meeting with CCPIT—August 27, 1979." Minneapolis, September 11, 1979.

_____. "Interoffice Memorandum—Ministry of Science and Technology." Minneapolis, September 2, 1971.

_____. "Interoffice Memorandum—Minutes of China Task Force—Meeting No. 2—October 8, 1973." Minneapolis, October 10, 1973.

_____. "Interoffice Memorandum—Minutes of Meeting of CGG." Minneapolis, September 27, 1973.

_____. "Interoffice Memorandum—Minutes of PRC Strategy Meeting January 26, 1977." Minneapolis, February 1, 1977.

_____. "Interoffice Memorandum—Monthly Report to December 15, 1979—P. R. China." Minneapolis, December 11, 1979.

_____. "Interoffice Memorandum on Mainland China." Minneapolis, June 24, 1971.

_____. "Interoffice Memorandum—Opportunities in China." Minneapolis, July 17, 1977.

_____. "Interoffice Memorandum—People's Republic of China." Minneapolis, August 9, 1978.

_____. "Interoffice Memorandum—People's Republic of China." Minneapolis, September 29, 1971.

_____. "Interoffice Memorandum—People's Republic of China—CGG Negotiations." Minneapolis, February 20, 1974.

_____. "Interoffice Memorandum—People's Republic of China—Marketing Office." Minneapolis, January 22, 1974.

_____. "Interoffice Memorandum—People's Republic of China (PRC) Trip Report." Minneapolis, August 20, 1979.

_____. "Interoffice Memorandum—PRC Delegations." Minneapolis, September 4, 1979.

_____. "Interoffice Memorandum—PRC Export License." Minneapolis, December 10, 1976.

_____. "Interoffice Memorandum—PRC License Application." Minneapolis, April 25, 1975.

_____. "Interoffice Memorandum—PRC Proposal Guidelines." Minneapolis, July 20, 1978.

_____. "Interoffice Memorandum—(PRC Trip Report—August 1979)." Minneapolis, August 27, 1979.

_____. "Interoffice Memorandum—Results of Fourth Ministry Visit." Minneapolis, December 28, 1979.

_____. "Interoffice Memorandum to the Executive Committee." Minneapolis, November 4, 1974.

_____. "Interoffice Memorandum—Trip Report—July 24, 1979." Minneapolis, August 16, 1979.

_____. "Interoffice Memorandum—Trip Report—May 4th." Minneapolis, May 14, 1976.

_____. "Interoffice Memorandum—Trip Report to the People's Republic of China, January 17, 1974." Minneapolis, March 7, 1974.

_____. "Interoffice Memorandum—Trip to People's Republic of China." Minneapolis, May 4, 1976.

_____. "Interoffice Memorandum—Trip to PRC." Minneapolis, September 11, 1979.

_____. "Interoffice Memorandum—The Visit of . . . July 1, 1978–July 14, 1978." Minneapolis, July 24, 1978.

_____. "Interoffice Memorandum—Visit with Gov. Anderson, December 20, 1973." Minneapolis, December 27, 1973.

_____. "Letter from Consultant." Minneapolis, April 19, 1971.

_____. "Letter from Consultant on China Trade." Minneapolis, November 14, 1972.

_____. "Letter to China National Technical Import Corporation." Minneapolis, October 7, 1976.

_____. "Letter to Chinese Foreign Trade Corporation." Minneapolis, December 21, 1978.

_____. "Letter to Chinese Foreign Trade Corporation." Minneapolis, June 13, 1975.

_____. "Letter to Chinese Foreign Trade Corporation." Minneapolis, January 29, 1975.

_____. "Letter to Chinese Foreign Trade Corporation." Minneapolis, January 25, 1974.

_____. "Letter to Chinese Foreign Trade Corporation." Minneapolis, September 13, 1972.

_____. "Letter to Computer Visiting Group of the Chinese Electronic Society." Minneapolis, January 25, 1974.

_____. "Letter to Control Data Corporation, Reference to Contract No. CF-7412." Minneapolis, August 14, 1974.

_____. "Letter to Hugh F. Donaghue." Minneapolis, April 18, 1973.

_____. "Letter to U.S. Department of Commerce." Minneapolis, May 23, 1979.

_____. "Letter to U.S. Department of Commerce." Minneapolis, October 18, 1976.

_____. "Marketing Plan for China." Minneapolis, June 6, 1977.

_____. "Minutes of China Task Force Meeting." Minneapolis, September 21, 1973.

_____. "Minutes of Meeting." Minneapolis, October 3, 1973.

_____. "Presentation." Minneapolis, August 30, 1979.

_____. "PRC Trip Report." Minneapolis, July 9, 1979.

_____. "PRC Trip Report." Minneapolis, April 5, 1979.

_____. "Seismic Contract with China." Minneapolis, December 27, 1974.

_____. "Status Report." Minneapolis, September 26, 1972.

_____. "Summary of China Progress to Date." Minneapolis, December 31, 1973.

_____. "Technical Service and Cooperation Frame Agreement." Minneapolis, May 3, 1976.

_____. "Trade—People's Republic of China." Minneapolis, July 22, 1971.

_____. "Trading Companies." Minneapolis, August 27, 1971.

_____. "Trip Report." Minneapolis, January 2, 1980.

_____. "Trip Report." Minneapolis, July 24, 1979.

_____. "Trip Report." Minneapolis, March 26, 1979.

_____. "Trip Report." Minneapolis, August 9, 1978.

_____. "Trip Report." Minneapolis, November 4, 1974.

_____. "Trip Report." Minneapolis, April 16, 1973.

_____. "Trip Report from PRC (CGG-China Contract)." Minneapolis, May 19, 1976.

_____. "Trip Report on Visit to Hong Kong." Minneapolis, May 11, 1972.

_____. "Trip Report—Peking, October 12-November 2, 1976." Minneapolis, December 13, 1976.

_____. "Trip Report to Washington, D.C." Minneapolis, August 10, 1973.

_____. "Trip Reports." Five meetings with PRC organizations. Minneapolis, September 11, 1979.

Cookson, David. "The People's Republic of China." Digest of remarks at a seminar, Executive House, Chicago, August 17, 1972.

Donaghue, Hugh. "Overview." Unpublished paper. Washington, D.C.: Control Data Corporation, April 1979.

Fishbourne, Benjamin P., III. "Drafting and Negotiating Contracts in China." Paper given at China Telecom Conference, Washington, D.C., June 21, 1979.

Haight, James. "Current Legal Aspects of Doing Business with Sino-
Soviet Nations." Paper presented to American Bar Association,
San Francisco, August 15, 1972.

Memorex Corporation. "Memorandum for . . . Telecommunications
and Electronics Committee, National Council for U.S.-China
Trade." McLean, Va., July 17, 1979.

Ministry of Trade. "How to Sell to China." Unpublished notes for
British exporters, London, November 1974.

Morton, Clinton G. "The Art of Negotiating." Paper for U.S. Army
War College, Carlisle, Pa., 1956.

National Council for U.S.-China Trade. "Results of the National
Council Delegation's Meeting in Peking." Text of the statement
released at a press conference in Hong Kong, November 16,
1973.

Nelson, R. K. "China Briefing: Chinese Electronic Society Visit to
CDC, October 23 and 24, 1973." Minneapolis, October 15,
1973.

_____. "Control Data's China Activities, from August 1973 to Present."
Presentation to International Development Committee, Minneapolis, November 18, 1973.

People's Republic of China, National Affairs Bureau. "Second Part
of Zhao Ziying's Speech on Economic Reform." Peking, April
22, 1980.

Schroeder, James V. "Some Legal Considerations in Joint Venture
and Countertrade Arrangements in U.S.-China Trade." Address
before the American Management Association Meeting on Barter
Principles in the People's Republic of China," Chicago, February 27, 1980.

"Selling to the People's Republic of China." Business International
Executive Seminar, Hong Kong, March 23, 1971.

Sobin, Julian M. The China Trader. Washington, D.C.: Mass Communications, 1978.

_____. "The U.S.-China-Japan Trade Web." Address at the Changing
Asian Market Conference, Washington, D.C., September 23,
1975.

Tung, Rosalie. "Summary of Findings of U.S.-China Trade Negotiations Study." Graduate School of Management, University of Oregon, February 1980.

U.S., Department of Commerce. "Authorization to Dispose of Commodities or Technical Data Previously Exported." Export license for Control Data Corporation, Washington, D.C., May 28, 1975.

_____. "Letter to Control Data Corporation." Washington, D.C., April 30, 1979.

_____. "Letter to Control Data Corporation." Washington, D.C., October 20, 1976.

_____. "Letter to Control Data Corporation." Washington, D.C., June 18, 1974.

U.S., Department of Health, Education and Welfare. "Introducing Metalinguistic Instructional Material into Language and Area Studies Programs: A Syllabus . . . for American-Chinese Intercultural Training," by William K. Carr. Washington, D.C.: Department of Health, Education and Welfare, April 1974.

U.S., Liaison Office. "Letter to Control Data Corporation." Peking, October 23, 1976.

Wald, Michael H. "Negotiating International Franchising Agreements with the People's Republic of China." Washington, D.C., 1979.

Wilhelm, Neil C. "A Report on My Visit to the People's Republic of China." Control Data Corporation files, Minneapolis, December 1978.

Zhang, Jingfu. "Presentation at the First National Bank of Chicago." Chicago, July 16, 1979.

PERSONAL INTERVIEWS AND CORRESPONDENCE

Alper, William. Lawyer. Washington, D.C., May 1980.

Austin, Barry. Boeing Company, Seattle, June 1979.

Carr, William. Consultant. Washington, D.C., August 1979.

Chan, Chou. Lawyer. Washington, D. C. , May 1980.

Clarke, William. Bureau of East-West Trade, Washington, D. C. ,
September 1979.

Donaghue, Hugh P. Vice-President of Control Data Corporation, Ar-
lington, Va. , May, October, and December 1979; February,
March, April, May, and June 1980.

Emerson, John Philip. Bureau of Economic Analysis, U. S. Department of Commerce, Washington, D. C. , November 1979 and
April 1980.

Holliday, George. Economist. Library of Congress, Washington,
D. C. , August 1979.

Holstine, Jon. Asia Pacific Subcommittee, House Foreign Affairs
Committee, Washington, D. C. , June 1980.

Kolaric, William. Bureau of East-West Trade, Washington, D. C. ,
August 1979.

LaDue, Frank. President, McCracken Concrete Pipe Machinery Company, Sioux City, Iowa, January 1980.

Lubman, Stanley. Lawyer. San Francisco, August 1979.

Ludlow, Nicholas. National Council for U. S.-China Trade, Washington, D. C. , August 1979.

Moulder, Virginia. Special Projects Coordinator, Coca-Cola Company, Atlanta, November 1979.

Olmer, Lionel H. Director of International Programs, Motorola,
Washington, D. C. , June 1979.

Poon, Judy. President, CTPS-USA (SF), San Francisco, February
1980.

Rehm, John B. Lawyer. Washington, D. C. , June 1979.

Sobin, Julian M. Chairman, Sobin Chemicals, Boston, November
1979.

Stollenwerk, James H. Vice-President, Rexnord, Milwaukee, May 1980.

Uretsky, Myron. Director, Management Decision Laboratory, New York University, Washington, D.C., May 1980.

INDEX

Academy of Sciences, Chinese, 114 n, 119
Agriculture Department, U.S., 91
Atlantic Richfield, 20 n
Australia, products of, 37

Bank of China, 24, 34, 39-40, 78
bargaining (see negotiations)
BESM-1, 112 n
Boeing, 55, 59, 60, 63, 67, 68, 70, 77, 79
British Aircraft, 63
Burroughs, 114

Canada: and first contacts, 120; products of, 37; technology of, 38
Canton Export Commodities Fair, 55, 57-58
Carter, Jimmy, 4, 90
Caterpillar, 59-60
CDC STAR, 114
centralization: disadvantages of, 20; trends against, 17
Chase Pacific Trade Advisors, 53 n
Chen Jie, 2
China (see People's Republic of China)
China Council for the Promotion of Foreign Trade, 55, 151
China Council for the Promotion of International Trade (CCPIT), 13, 23-24
China International Trust and Investment Corporation (CITIC), 36
China National Light Industrial Products, 43

China National Machinery Import and Export Corporation (Machimpex), 55, 60, 63, 121, 122, 137
China National Oil and Gas Exploration and Development Corporation, 129, 137
China National Technical Import Corporation (Techimport), 58, 103, 125, 127, 129, 132
China Petroleum Corporation, 20 n
China Resources Company, 121-22, 124
China Silk Corporation, 31
China Vegetable Oil Corporation, 31
Chinese Economic Monthly, 65
Chinese Electronic Society, 124, 127
Chinese People's Insurance Company, 36
Chinese Technology Import Corporation, 19
Chou En-lai, 109, 121
Chung Kuo, 1 n
CIA, 110
Civil Aviation Administration, Chinese, 55
Clark Equipment Company, 63, 70
Coca-Cola Company, 69
Code for Uniform Customs, 38
Columbus, Christopher, 1
Commerce Department, U.S., 53, 55, 62, 69, 78, 91, 92, 94-102, 119, 156; Commodity Control List, 90, 92; Export Information Service, 97; Office of Export Administration, 88, 95, 97, 100;

ABOUT THE AUTHOR

JOHN W. DE PAUW is a Commodity Analyst with the U.S. International Trade Commission, Washington, D.C., and has extensive experience in international trade of minerals and metals. Prior to his position Dr. De Pauw served with the Department of Commerce as an expert in Soviet economic affairs.

Dr. De Pauw wrote <u>Soviet–American Trade Negotiations</u>, which was published by Praeger in March 1979. In addition, he has contributed articles to such professional journals as <u>Slavic Review</u> and <u>Monthly Labor Review</u>. He has also coauthored a paper for the Joint Economic Committee of Congress, "Population Policy and Demographic Trends in the Soviet Union."

Dr. De Pauw received his formal training in political science, Soviet affairs, and international relations. He earned his B.A. at Swarthmore College and his master's degree in Soviet studies at American University. His doctoral degree in international studies is also from American University.

DISCARD